THE LY

A Family

Nineteε

BETTY ASKWITH

1975

CHATTO & WINDUS

LONDON

Published by
Chatto & Windus Ltd.
40–42 William IV Street
London W.C.2

*

Clark, Irwin and Co., Ltd.
Toronto

ISBN 0 7011 2109 2

© Betty Askwith 1975

Printed in Great Britain
by Ebenezer Baylis & Son Ltd.
The Trinity Press, Worcester, and London

CONTENTS

ILLUSTRATIONS

ACKNOWLEDGEMENTS

My first thanks are due to Her Majesty the Queen for her gracious permission in allowing me to quote from the Royal Archives and to reproduce a picture and a photograph from the Royal Collections.

I am enormously indebted to Viscount Cobham who not only gave me access to the relevant Hagley Papers but allowed me to take them away to work on them. Without this great generosity the book could never have been written.

I am also most grateful to the Hon. Richard and Mrs. Lyttelton who so greatly encouraged me at the very beginning and who lent me many of the Glynne family papers. I should like to thank Earl Spencer for allowing me to look through and quote from the Althorp Papers, Sir William Gladstone for sparing a whole afternoon to show me over Hawarden and for lending me a copy of *Glynnese*, Mr. T. G. Talbot for allowing me to quote from his family papers, the Earl of Harewood for permitting the publication of Lord Lyttelton's letters to Lady Canning and the Duke of Devonshire and the Chatsworth Trustees for allowing me to use Lady Frederick Cavendish's unpublished Diaries.

My thanks are also due to the staffs of the Royal Archives, of the Kent County Archives and of the Flintshire County Archives for giving me facilities to work on their premises and for their help and kindness; also to the National Portrait Gallery, the Courtauld Institute and the Department of Prints and Drawings of the British Museum for assisting me with illustrations.

I am grateful to Miss Jane Bailey, to Mrs. Virginia Surtees, to Doctor G. Kitson Clark and to Mr. T. S. Wragg for their help, and I should like to thank Anne Cubitt for her great assistance in connexion with the educational side of the 4th Lord Lyttelton's activities.

Finally, to Sir John Betjeman and Messrs. John Murray (Publishers) for permission to quote from the poem, "Hymn", on p. 133.

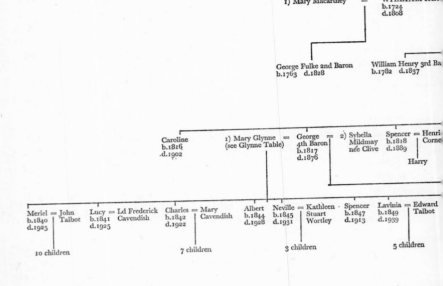

1) Mary Macartney = WILLIAM HEN‥
b.1724
d.1808

George Fulke 2nd Baron   William Henry 3rd Ba‥
b.1763   d.1828   b.1782   d.1837

Caroline   1) Mary Glynne = George = 2) Sybella   Spencer = Henri‥
b.1816   (see Glynne Table)   4th Baron   Mildmay   b.1818   Corne‥
.d.1902   b.1817   née Clive   d.1889
                          d.1876   Harry

Meriel = John   Lucy = Ld Frederick   Charles = Mary   Albert   Neville = Kathleen   Spencer   Lavinia = Edward
b.1840 | Talbot   b.1841 | Cavendish   b.1842 | Cavendish   b.1844   b.1845 | Stuart   b.1847   b.1849 | Talbot
d.1925   d.1925   d.1922   d.1928   d.1931 | Wortley   d.1913   d.1939

10 children   7 children   3 children   5 children

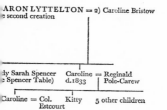

ARON LYTTELTON == 2) Caroline Bristow
e second creation

dy Sarah Spencer   Caroline == Reginald
e Spencer Table)   d.1833   Pole-Carew

Caroline == Col.   Kitty   5 other children
       Estcourt

liam Henry == 1) Emily   Lavinia == Henry Glynne
ly)   Pepys   b.1821   (see Glynne Table)
820   2) Constance   d.1850
884   Yorke

== Kathleen   Robert == 1) Edith   Edward == Caroline   Alfred == 1) Laura Tennant   Sarah == John   Sybil == Lionel   Hester == Cy
   Clive   (Bob)   Santley   b.1855   West   b.1857   b.1870   Bailey   b.1873   Cust   b.1874   Ali
               b.1854 2) Olive   d.1942   d.1913 2) Edith Balfour   d.1942   b.1873   d.1958
               d.1939   Clarke

children   2 children   4 children   3 children   1 child   6 children

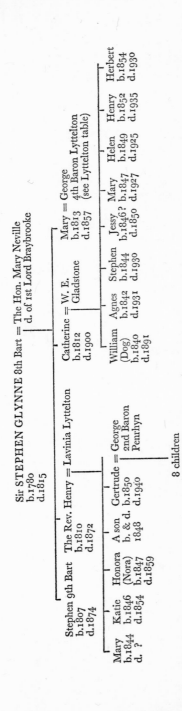

GEORGE 2nd EARL SPENCER = Lady Lavinia Bingham
b.1758 d.1834   d. of 1st Earl Lucan

John 3rd Earl = Esther Acklom
(Viscount Althorp)
b.1782
d.1845

Sarah = William Henry
3rd Ld Lyttelton
(see Lyttelton Table)
b.1787
d.1870

Robert
(Bob)
b.1791
d.1830

1) Elizabeth Poyntz = Frederick (Fritz) = 2) Adelaide Seymour
4th Earl
b.1798
d.1857

3 children   2 children

George
(Hodgekin)
Father Ignatius
b.1799
d.1864

Georgiana = Ld George Quin
(Nigs)
b.1794
d.1823

3 children

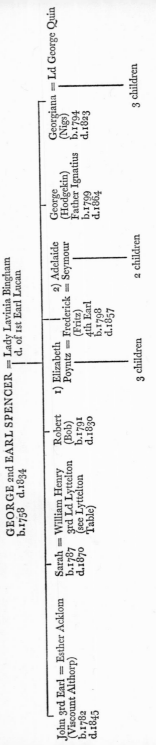

Sir STEPHEN GLYNNE 8th Bart = The Hon. Mary Neville
b.1780   d. of 1st Lord Braybrooke
d.1815

Stephen 9th Bart
b.1807
d.1874

The Rev. Henry = Lavinia Lyttelton
b.1810
d.1872

Catherine = W. E. Gladstone
b.1812
d.1900

Mary = George
4th Baron Lyttelton
(see Lyttelton table)
b.1813
d.1857

Mary
b.1844
d. ?

Katie
b.1846
d.1854

Honora
(Nora)
b.1847
d.1859

A son
b. & d.
1848

Gertrude = George 2nd Baron Penrhyn
b.1850
d.1940

8 children

William
(Dog)
b.1840
d.1891

Agnes
b.1842
d.1931

Stephen
b.1844
d.1930

Jessy
b.1846?
d.1850

Mary
b.1847
d.1927

Helen
b.1849
d.1925

Henry
b.1852
d.1935

Herbert
b.1854
d.1930

T HIS is a family chronicle, whose scene is set during the first three-quarters of the nineteenth century. The Lytteltons of that time moved in the most important circles, both political and social, and they contributed a great deal to the ethos of the period. It has been said that during the nineteenth century it was impossible to find a committee concerned with good works which did not include a Lyttelton; and it has also been said that when several of the family were gathered together an outsider was tempted to raise his hand and exclaim: "Please, I'm here too"; but in spite of their clannishness and their sometimes aggressive piety, they were a likeable family. Although they were members of the established ruling class they were never conventional figures. Their standards of conduct and propriety were extremely high, but they cared not a jot what the rest of the world thought of them. In a conforming age they exhibited an engaging eccentricity.

The years 1800–1875 form an exceedingly interesting period in English social history. During those years there occurred one of the most remarkable changes in the English aristocracy which with extraordinary unanimity executed a surprising right turn in belief and in behaviour. It was not, as it is so often described, a Victorian phenomenon. It began when Victoria and Albert were both in their respective nurseries. In the early 1800s the younger generation among the aristocracy and the upper middle classes of England turned away from being on the whole tolerant, free-thinking, free-living and free-loving, and became respectable, religious, and enclosed in an almost claustrophobic family atmosphere. As Lord Saltire in Henry Kingsley's *Ravenshoe* put it: "In his day it was the custom to talk with considerable freedom on sacred subjects, and he himself had been rather notorious for that kind of thing; but look at him now, he conformed with the times and went to church. Everyone went to church now."

Already throughout the Regency and the two succeeding

1

reigns, although the surface of society was dominated by the older generation, the new growth was pushing up as green bracken fronds push upwards through the surface of last year's leaves.

What caused the change? It is very hard to pin down the exact genesis of a Zeitgeist. Something must of course have been due to the inevitable revolt in feeling of one generation against another, more marked at some periods than at others. Something also must be laid at the door of the Evangelical Movement, which had such an influence on the working classes and, in the opinion of many, prevented revolution in England. But Evangelicalism was essentially a middle-class movement and the aristocracy were not prone to take their tone from the class immediately below theirs. More can, I think, be ascribed to the French Revolution. For this was to the upper classes a clear indication of where loose morals and free-thinking led. They looked and they did not like what they saw. The trial of Queen Caroline augmented this unease. For the first time the "lower orders" made their opinion felt about the morals and mores of their betters. "I get a good deal from Boo" [her maid] wrote Lady Caroline Stuart Wortley [the mother of that Mrs. Talbot whom we shall encounter frequently during the Lyttelton history] on the subject of the Queen's trial, "about the feelings of servants and tradesmen and the universal refrain is 'well if she is so bad, the King is as bad himself, & therefore she is cruelly used'."

A new climate of opinion became perceptible. The succession of a well brought-up young queen and a morally spotless consort favoured it. By the early forties the pious revolution was in full swing.

Lady Sarah Spencer, who became the 3rd Lady Lyttelton, was a typical product of this new set of values. Her family was one of the greatest among the Whig aristocracy, whose way of life was liberated enough. Sarah's two aunts, the Duchess of Devonshire and Lady Bessborough, had numerous lovers and both bore illegitimate children. Her maternal uncle, Lord Lucan, eloped with someone else's wife whom he subsequently married but then deserted. Her uncle by marriage, the Duke of Devonshire, brought up his two bastards in the Cavendish nursery together with his legitimate children. Such were the morals of the generation immediately preceding Sarah's. Yet she herself, her brothers and sister and all her cousins, legitimate and illegitimate (with the exception of Caroline Lamb who would have been a sport in any family in any generation) became moral, respectable, monogamous church-going persons.

We can follow the development of Sarah's character and of her opinions during her early twenties because, between the years of 1808 and 1813, she wrote a great number of long diary letters to her younger brother Bob who was a midshipman at sea.

Sandwiched between charming descriptions of home life and racy glimpses of Regency society we find many illustrations of the new current of feeling; as for instance, when describing the home that her father had built at Ryde, she dwells fondly on "the remembrance of my own room upstairs for in it we prayed together".

It was to Bob that she expressed her great disgust at the conduct of her uncle by marriage, the Duke of Devonshire, who had recently become a widower and planned to remarry.

"A marriage is said to have taken place which . . . is a dead secret, only told in whispers by everybody to everybody as yet. But, my Bob, you are so far, so very far away from us all, that before it reaches you it will have been publickly declared; besides, you know it already, I dare say. It is not an interesting *union de deux jeunes coeurs*, I must say, but rather the crowning of a perseverance in vice and artfulness, which is I fancy unheard of; Clifford of course knows it, as it is no other than the long-expected wedding of his venerable parents."

The Duke of Devonshire's second marriage to his mistress, Lady Elizabeth Foster, by whom he already had two grown-up children,* seems to us a very logical end to a long liaison but it immensely shocked Sarah. In another letter she apostrophises the Duke as: "His Grace who ought to be known as His Disgrace", and in 1838, a year after the accession of Queen Victoria, she is still harping on the same theme. "Are you not mistaken in thinking 'our morals deteriorated?' " she wrote to her friend Lady Pembroke. "Are they more than they were in the days of Lady Melbourne . . . and all that was *fostered* [I meant no pun] by Devonshire House of fifty years ago?"

---

* Caroline St. Jules and Augustus Clifford. Clifford was Bob's shipmate and intimate friend.

Sarah was convinced that in her life-time morals and manners had immensely improved. In the same letter she writes of the "monstrous irreligion" professed by the free-thinkers of her young days and nearly thirty years later, commenting on a life of Miss Berry, she describes the then state of society as being one of "universal worthlessness".

Many of us today feel that the eighteenth century provided a more sympathetic atmosphere, one in which we should have felt more at home, than the immediately succeeding period. The Victorians, although nearer to us in time seem infinitely further from us in spirit. They were, or appeared to be, so happy, so undoubting, so secure. We feel for them a measure of fascination, repulsion, and — is it just possible? — envy.

The Victorians had many sorrows and some black moments, but on the whole they felt themselves to be anchored in a way we find it hard to comprehend. Lucy Lyttelton, Sarah's granddaughter, expressed this sense of invulnerability when she stood on the tower at Chichester Cathedral and looked at the "delightful and intensely English" view. "Somehow," she wrote in her diary, "this sort of sight always gives me a strong sense of the healthiness and peace of England, with her church and her home life deep-rooted in the hearts of her people; and all notions of disestablishment or revolution seem a perverse dream."

For about fifty years the educated classes of England (this happy certainty did not extend to the rest of Europe) believed that they had the answers to everything, in the heavens above, the earth beneath and the waters under the earth. It was an age of certainty and of faith only paralleled by the great cathedral-building epoch of the Middle Ages.

It was a certainty underpinned by religion and as we watch the Lyttelton family through three generations we shall see the observances of this religion become more and more important till the church, its dues and its services, becomes almost more prominent than the lessons she is supposed to teach.

In the early years of the century, however, piety had not taken quite so strong a hold. Sarah was able to enjoy her father's account of a shooting party at Lord Robert Spencer's where he met the latter's mistress, her "ill-fated husband, a poor old twaddle", Charles Fox's widow who had been a well-known courtesan and his natural daughter by somebody else.

Her grand-daughter, who edited her letters, thought it necessary to comment: "It is difficult to realize that it is the account given by a most punctilious and respectable father to his daughter, a girl of twenty-two who passes it on to her brother of seventeen." Sarah herself, however, simply remarked cheerfully: "There's a set of people for you!"

Sarah's own home life was a happy one, although as we shall see it had its drawbacks, and a good deal can be attributed to her own sweet contented nature. "Such a home as mine is," she wrote, "wherever it is planted, makes everything *riant*." Just occasionally a sigh escapes at the limitations imposed on her by her condition. "I wish it were the fashion," she writes to Bob with gentle mockery, "for young ladies to go and travel in the Mediterranean, why shouldn't it? I am sure most of the young gentlemen who do, are much more helpless than any girl, and I am convinced we should manage quite as well, and perhaps, *n'en déplaise pas à vos hautes puissances* ye lords of the creation, we might derive something more of knowledge and advantage from the journey than is common to the said young gentlemen."

Nor was she so oblivious and unaware of the war raging around the isolated little island of England as the characters in Jane Austen's novels. She lived in a wider sphere and politics were the daily stuff of life to all the great Whig families. "Politics, politics, and more politics," she writes in 1810, "that's all one hears of in these parts at present." But of course her greatest interest lay in the running naval combat that our fleet was keeping up through the dark years in the Mediterranean and the Atlantic. There was a naval action at Las Rosas in Spain in 1809 in which Bob Spencer, a midshipman of eighteen, was involved. "You have been actually engaged, you have boarded a ship & in this glorious action, and in all the noble exploits that precede it, the Tigre [his ship] has been first, foremost & most noted . . . you My own dearest Bob have been in the thickest of it all, and not one of you hurt, and you quite well and safe after it! . . . Here I sit with those blessed letters of yours all round me, every line of which I have read about 50 times, all those dear precious details of your service I have deeply printed in my heart for ever I am sure."

The war was not the only danger in those days. There were also plenty of home troubles — Sarah describes the Burdett riots: "the look of the mob, sulky, black & determined; their continued loud shouts; the horrid sight of the heavy horse guards riding in amongst them & over them; vainly trying to disperse them; the eager anxious frightened faces of every creature one saw in the streets at the increase of the tumult & noise."

In spite, however, of war and riots life at home seems to have proceeded evenly and peacefully. It revolved round the three great houses, Althorp, the family seat in Northamptonshire; Wimbledon Park, in what was then the country; and Spencer House, looking across the Green Park to Piccadilly. Under the aegis of the head steward, "the great Venables", the family passed from one to the other and Sarah's letters help us to reconstruct the life that the Spencers led in them.

This is particularly so at Althorp because though Wimbledon Park* has been pulled down and Spencer House turned into offices, Althorp, buried deep in its green leafy park, still looks much as it did when Henry Holland encased the original red-brick Elizabethan mansion in rather forbidding greyish-white tiles. This was done in 1789 when Sarah was two years old. She never therefore saw the exterior of the old house but she was familiar with the black and white marble-paved entrance hall, with its large pictures of grooms and horses, and hunts chasing away across the Pytchley countryside, painted by John Wootton. She also knew the great oak staircase with the galleries which Holland had added enclosing the big inner hall; the picture gallery, whose oak panelling Holland had covered in green paper, and the chapel with its screened family pew. It is, however, hard to guess exactly what rooms the family used and what they looked like since inevitably various owners have rearranged the furniture, added to its beauties from other Spencer properties, pulled down or replaced partitions, and so on. We can imagine diminutive Signor Ocheda, the Italian librarian, whom Lady Spencer described as having "a dark and lurid countenance" pacing between the bookshelves, while a turkey pie, "tendant les bras aux passans [*sic*]", was rather oddly set out in the long library, but we don't know exactly where "the Refuge", the room that the family used, was situated. One would like to think of it as being the small square

---

* It stood on what are now the Wimbledon tennis courts, and the lake, designed by Capability Brown, still exists.

room facing south which Holland decorated so charmingly in Pompeian bas reliefs, but this was Lavinia Spencer's dressing-room and cannot have been used as a general sitting-room. The Refuge must have been a small drawing-room, possibly the smaller portion of the Marlborough Room before the partition was removed in 1911. It was hung with an "india paper" and there "Mammy" sat reading in the mornings; there Sarah's younger sister Georgiana, always known as Gin or Nig or Niggin, practised her ten string harp; there Althorp dropped in after hunting and there the ladies of the family indulged in "prawn lunches" (where did they get the prawns one wonders?).

They were nearly always at Althorp during the winter and the descriptions abound of relatives arriving in calèche or coach peering out of the befogged windows after having been held up for hours on the snow-bound roads; of hunters coming in splashed and muddy, Althorp having put his shoulder out for the fifteenth time; of frozen toes and frost-bitten fingers. For the cold of these large country houses must have been intense. "Can you read me?" Sarah writes from Althorp in 1810. "If you can't My Dear it is because of the cold. I am now admiring the beautiful mixture of blue and crimson tints which colour my hands and fingers, and really can hardly hold my pen, or use my nose and chin, they are so frozen up and shrivelled."

London may have been a little warmer than Northamptonshire but it had its own drawbacks. Over and over again in the letters we read of black fog pressing against the panes, of it being impossible to write without candles at eleven o'clock in the morning. It was perhaps owing to the discomforts of the great houses that the aristocracy had what seems rather a curious delight in rushing off to the seaside and cramming themselves into uncomfortable lodgings. Sarah describes the house they took at Ryde in the Isle of Wight as being "surrounded by pigsties, butchers' shops, ill-covered sewers, drunken sailors, noisy children, red brick houses, and dusty roads". Her bedroom looked out over the butcher's yard where the pigs were killed, an unpleasant prospect owing to the smell and the squealing. Nevertheless the whole family were so delighted with Ryde that after several years of furnished lodgings Lord Spencer finally built his own house there.

Lord and Lady Spencer were happily married; there are charming little vignettes in the letters of the "old pipple" together, cleaning Lord Spencer's gun, or travelling to Bath without their numerous family. But if she was a loving wife Lady Spencer was not an ideal mother.

She was very fond of her children but she wanted them to be as beautiful, as witty and as intelligent as she was herself. If they did not come up to her standards she lashed them with her quick temper and her merciless tongue. The eldest son, Lord Althorp, suffered the most from this unkindness. In early youth he had been his mother's darling; yet fifteen years later her husband's niece, Harriet Cavendish, would describe her as laughing "at poor Lord Althorp without mercy", and having "no compassion on him when he gets bewildered, which often happens to him in the course of conversation".

When he sat down to play patience she would say his hands were too dirty to touch the cards; once when he offered to read aloud the immediate response was: "And who, my dear Jack, would understand you if you did?"

Such treatment was not calculated to encourage a shy, clumsy young man. His latent abilities (and also his great affection for his lovely teasing mother) were shown when she suddenly remarked to him after his first term at Cambridge: "Jack, we expect you to take honours." He immediately gave up his hunting, sold his horses and worked so hard that he obtained a First Class. A feat rare enough in a young nobleman in those days. This devotion to duty and strength of mind were later shown when he went into public life and became the rock and stay of the Whig Cabinet which brought in the Reform Bill. His heart, however, remained at Althorp with the Pytchley. He was always on the road between London and Northampton and he is said to have loathed London so much that he refused to keep his pistols in his bedroom there in case he should be tempted to commit suicide.

He was not the only member of the family who suffered from his mother's uncertain temper and violence of expression. Sarah too was subject to the same sort of repression. "She has the strongest feelings," wrote her first cousin Harriet Cavendish, "but she has been taught to check and controul [sic] them as if they were crimes." Harriet also expatiates on the improvement wrought in Sarah by living with people "whose tongues are not invariably two-edged swords", a phrase which implies a very fair description of Lady Spencer.

Sarah had, however, her own consolations. She was a sort of surrogate mother to the rest of the family and she expended her talent for loving on her brothers and sisters. It was she who wrote regularly to the absent brother at sea; she who coached the little boys* in their holiday tasks; she who sat over the fire with Althorp when he came in from hunting "all bespattered in mud, and in a red jacket that bears many a mark of hard service", and listened to him while he told her the details of the day's run and the "several leaps, tumbles and feats of each man, horse and hound".

Outside her immediate family Sarah's chief young companions were her various cousins. The relation she was fondest of was probably her mother's sister Lady Anne Bingham. She is always writing that she longs to have a "good gossip with Nanette". At one time her greatest friend was Harriet Cavendish, but after Harriet's marriage to Lord Granville, who had once been the devoted lover of Lady Bessborough, aunt to both Harriet and Sarah, the friendship seems to have languished and died.

Other cousins who came to stay at Ryde were the newly-married Duncannons, who only remembered to provide transport for their horse and their wine, blithely ignoring such necessities as coal, candles, basins and towels, thus incurring the displeasure of the Spencers' house steward "the great Venables". "I expect he will hardly take off his hat to them when they arrive" wrote Sarah gaily. And another newly-married couple were Duncannon's sister, Caroline, and her husband William Lamb. Sarah reports them as being the Spencers' constant companions on sailing parties and Harriet Cavendish describes Caroline as being: "One minute on a Pillion, the next in a boat, but the wand to effect these changes always in Columbine's hand — Lady Spencer exclaiming — 'William Lamb is an angel, nothing like the school of adversity!'"

---

* These were Fritz, who became the 4th Earl, and George, known in the family as Hodge or Hodgekin, who after a spell in the family living became a Roman Catholic priest, Father Ignatius. His father was kind about it and continued his allowance; his mother went into mourning. Sarah always remained fond of him though she was rather embarrassed when he came to call on her at Buckingham Palace in his Roman clerical garb and she felt he paid insufficient attention to personal hygiene. After his visits she had to open the window.

In none of Sarah's extant letters is there any criticism of Caroline Lamb. The Spencers frequently had her mentally-retarded child, Augustus, to stay and in one of Sarah's letters there is a charming friendly glimpse of Caroline reading with her cousin and being taught "country dances on the pianoforte".

Unfortunately most of the correspondence with Bob Spencer during 1812 has been destroyed so we know nothing of Sarah's reactions to the Byron affair. They would surely have been disapproving. She must have disapproved even more strongly of Caroline's earlier liaison with Sir Godfrey Webster (Lady Holland's son by her first marriage) since she was already violently prejudiced against this obviously insensitive young man. I quote her diatribe at length partly because hitherto it has not been published and partly because it exemplifies so well Sarah's pungent, uninhibited style when she is writing to her brother.

"By the by," she writes in June 1809, "do you know My Bob, that a thing has happened here in poor old England, which almost makes me fear that I shall live to see the time when we shall all paint our faces blue & yellow, wear rings thro' our noses, & dance round a bonfire where a few prisoners of war are roasting for our supper; when we shall hang up human bones for ornaments to our rooms, & in short be complete savages, as bad as any in Robinson Crusoe — What will you say when I tell you this thing? A young officer in our army, ay an officer, a man of rank & fortune, a man who was educated at Harrow & Cambridge, a schoolfellow of yours & Althorp's, *Sir Godfrey Webster* went with one of the expeditions to Spain (trembling all the way I am sure, he *must* be a coward) to fight the French. Well in some battle he somehow or other fell in with a french trumpeter, dead or alive; he says alive, I say dead, because If he had been alive tho' he had no arms, I am sure Sir Godfrey would never have ventured to go up to him and do what he did, cut off his head. When he had done this, what do you think happened next? Perhaps you think he did what you would have done, what any brave man would have done after having performed the duty of a soldier, (tho' why a soldier is to kill an *unarmed* enemy I don't see very well) that he felt something like pain at having had such a duty to perform, and then that he passed on leaving the wretched corpse & head to themselves — Not a bit of all this — He took the nasty head, and says he to himself 'this fellow has a fine round skull of his own, and a good set of teeth — I'll carry the skull away with me, and see what can be done with it' — He did carry it home, and having properly prepared it, took it aboard his transport and brought it to England, his barbarous thoughts running all the time on the best way of *having it set.* Yes Bob, he has *had it set* — He has employed Wirgman the jeweller (whom I shall abhor for ever after having done it) to set, to mount with gold, the trumpeter's skull in the shape of *a drinking cup*, with all the teeth left in, and the top taken out, to pour in the wine he means to drink out of this skull of a fellow creature whom he has killed — He gave 100 guineas for the mounting of this thing, and then it was to be seen at Wirgman's shop till t'other day; it is now sent home — All London has been made sick by it. There is no name of horror & disgust which has not been showered upon the amiable youth; till at last they say he is rather ashamed of himself pretty innocent, and won't show it to anybody."

Sarah cast an amused if slightly disapproving eye on all the London beaux, particularly on her male cousins, whom she plainly contrasted with her brothers much to the former's disadvantage. She records with amused disapproval how Hartington, the Duke of Devonshire's son and heir, spent all his time learning cotillions, instructed by the principal dancer of the Opera, Monsieur Des Hayes, and how while sitting in the Spencers' box Hartington received a nod and a smile from the dancer just about to go on the stage *"en turban bleu celeste and argent, petit jupon de gauze d'argent,* and flesh coloured shoulders and knees". The young gentleman was deeply offended in his ducal dignity and drew back blushing indignantly and saying to Lady Spencer in "his deliberate Cavendish way 'Aunt don't you think he was very impertinent'." Sarah's disapproval was more for the undesirable intimacy induced by the cotillion system than for Hartington's *de haut en bas* attitude and she does not seem to have been at all shocked by another occasion when Hartington and another first cousin, Willy Ponsonby, Caroline Lamb's brother, appeared at a masquerade in drag, "as two tall young ladies dressed in the latest fashion, with diamonds, spotted muslin, and silver turbans and feathers." "I would have given anything to have seen them," she writes, "I hear they were capital figures."

In general, however, she has no good word for Willy Ponsonby. She tells Bob that he is "now going to *promener ses ennuis* in Spain" (the Mediterranean fleet which included Bob's ship was stationed at Gibraltar) "which is now considered in no other light than as a good lounge, by *young* gentlemen, who can't get up in time for the barouche club, & eat too much to be pedestrians, or boxers, & therefore of course can find nothing to do at all in the wide world, but sleep, yawn, stuff and whisper."

We cannot leave Sarah's girlhood without commenting on some of the peculiar words which she frequently uses in her letters. In the eighteenth century most of the aristocratic families had a "little language" of their own. "Gulchy" was a Hervey word meaning affecting, tearful, emotional. The Stuart Wortleys described any disappointment or ill-fortune as "monkey", from the French *manqué*. Sarah Spencer writes of modeure, sisteure, brodeure, a pronunciation probably adopted from one of the numerous foreigners who surrounded the Spencer family; Signor Ocheda the librarian or Mademoiselle Müller, Gin's Swiss governess. Her favourite word is "ziti" which roughly corresponds to darling. It was originally used for children, since she writes to Bob that she supposes he is now too old (at the age of sixteen) to be called one any longer, and the small fry are frequently referred to as the "zits". In time, however, the term came to be applied to almost anyone. Grandmother Lucan for instance is frequently apostrophized "the old ziti" though I do not think Grandmother Spencer is ever so described. Another word for the young, applied exclusively to them is "lects" or "lectolds". "Ziti" may just possibly come from a childish pronunciation of little — liti — ziti, and "leetolds" or "lectolds" is said to have started as "little olds".

In most cases the daughters of the big houses took their vocabulary with them and introduced it to their new families as Sarah Spencer did to the Lytteltons; until, in its turn, the Spencer "little language" was superseded by that of a daughter-in-law and every Lyttelton began to speak Glynnese.

By the end of 1812 Sarah Spencer may have become resigned to remaining unmarried. She was now twenty-five and, as we know from Lydia Bennett, that was considered a great age at the beginning of the nineteenth century. All Sarah's contemporary cousins were married and already rearing their families. The younger generation, her sister Gin and her cousin Liz Bingham, seven years junior to herself, were coming out and dancing "very merrily".

It is never easy being the plain daughter of a strikingly beautiful mother — the best anyone ever said of Sarah's looks was to call her "pleasing" — and we do not know if she had many suitors. The only one we hear of is Sir Watkin Williams Wynn, a young gentleman of very ancient family and great sporting proclivities — Sir Watkin Wynn's hounds still flourish in North Wales — and all we know about him is his withdrawal from the scene. "I have now to announce," she writes to Bob in 1812, "that *affair* to use the fashionable phrase, is entirely for ever and for aye over — gone! past! — fled!! — I have to humble myself further by the unfeminine confession that it is not *this* time over in consequence of a refusal on my part, but in consequence of my quondam swain having thought better of it — He . . . returned to town, evidently resolved upon preserving an independence, he has grown too much accustomed to take leave of it with a good grace — He is a man of an honourable mind, and has behaved on this occasion perfectly right, and heaven knows I thank him from the bottom of my heart; for I never in my life I think felt happier than I have felt since I have been secure (as secure as human thing can be) of a quiet and unbroken *avenir* in this world."

But if the security implied the unmarried state it was not to last long. Lady Hood, the wife of Admiral Sir Samuel Hood, was one of the Spencers' intimate circle. This circle consisted mostly of relations, distinguished men of science and the upper echelons of the navy. The conversation was doubtless stimulating and the moral tone higher than that of most London drawing-rooms but it was not a very good setting for matrimony. It was doubtless reprehensible that all the Devonshire House girls married men who had been in love with their mother or their aunt; nevertheless the fact remained that scores of young eligibles flitted round Devonshire House while Spencer House attracted ineligible blue-stockings. Lady Hood, however, a great personal friend of Sarah's, redressed the balance. She was intimate with the Honourable William Lyttelton, who had recently been refused by a young lady, and she told him that Sarah Spencer was the girl for him. He must have had great confidence in her judgement for he immediately proposed himself for a visit to the Spencers at Ryde.

He had of course some slight acquaintance with the family for he was a Whig and a great friend of Lord Althorp's, but Sarah seems to have had only the most superficial knowledge of him. In "a London ball-room" she writes, "he is the most extraordinary mixture of brilliant wit, childish nonsense, frivolous small-talk, and a universal sort of scrambling information, which seems all to come out, whether he will or not from an incessant flow of wild spirits. What such a being can be like at a place like Ryde ... is so beyond me that I am really curious about it ... At any rate, I am glad to grow really acquainted with a London *beau*, it is a gratification I never had before. I ought to finish Mr. Lyttelton's picture, to tell you that he dances out of time, and is remarkably handsome — the two most striking properties of his one hears mentioned in this thinking town."

That Mr. Lyttelton was remarkably handsome is certainly borne out by his portraits; his dancing out of time and his brilliant wit we must take on trust. The only two examples we have of the latter are recorded in Mrs. Spencer Stanhope's letters to her son, which quote: "a bon mot of your friend Mr. Lyttelton". The occasion was a ball given by Charles Fox after his marriage. As he had married Mrs. Armistead* the respectable ladies in London society were not anxious to meet her. "There goes all the world," said Mr. Lyttelton, "but little of his wife." Mrs. Stanhope in a subsequent letter wrote:

---

* Mrs. Armistead was a courtesan who had been Fox's mistress for many years.

"Have you heard the latest story of your friend Lyttelton? It appears that at some large party he was seated at the card table next to Mrs. Beaumont" (A rich but ill-bred neighbour of the Stanhopes) "who expressed herself very dissatisfied with the smallness of the stakes. "In the great houses which I frequent," she explained grandly to Lyttelton, "we constantly play for *paper*." "Madam," said Lyttelton in a solemn whisper, "in the little houses which I frequent, we play for notepaper." Neither of these jokes seems likely to set the Thames on fire, but then even the bon mots of such an established wit as Sydney Smith often sound flat enough today. One must suppose it was not so much what Mr. Lyttelton said as the way he said it.

An interesting opinion of his character and abilities is given in a letter from Bishop Coplestone written in 1847. "He (the 3rd Lord Lyttelton) disappointed in public life the expectation raised by an extraordinary display of talents at the University. His conversation was more brilliant than that of any man I had then met with — but it wanted polish and tact, and discretion. In the latter qualities he improved wonderfully — especially after his marriage with one of the best women of the age." This outside judgement reinforces Sarah's own opinion of her betrothed and shows the influence she was already beginning to exert over him. Writing to her grandmother the Dowager Lady Spencer she declares that though she finds his gaiety "so irresistible", she is almost angry with it because "it is the only good quality the world knows, and it is quite, quite the least". She cared very much more that he possessed "real, manly, unaffected piety — It gives me a comfort far beyond all words to recollect the serious attention which quite absorbed him, as he took the sacrament with us on Christmas Day ... and the affecting manner in which he alludes perpetually, amidst his brilliant and superior conversation, to the most serious subjects."

One may perhaps feel a touch of faint regret for the witty, high-spirited young man so soon to be quenched by pious domesticity, but that was the tendency of the first half of the nineteenth century. Nor did Mr. Lyttelton himself have any regrets. One may tell by his diaries how happy and contented he was as soon as he settled down to family life.

Sarah herself was even more blissful in her marriage. She outlived her husband by thirty-one years but though she lived a full and contented life, full of years and honour, surrounded by adoring children, grandchildren and great-grandchildren, a letter which she wrote to her husband's niece, twenty-five years after William Lyttelton's death, shows how much she valued the brilliant happiness of those early years. Caroline Estcourt lost her husband in the Crimea and her aunt wrote to her as follows: "I must write to you; it feels unnatural and painful not to do so. But most deeply do I acknowledge to myself that to you I can do no good by writing or anything else . . . I cannot promise or hope for your *happiness* again. Peace, and patience, and thankfulness, and the power of looking back with softening tears, and with brighter hopes, you will I trust be blessed with. And perhaps earth has no truer happiness — at any rate we have no right to wish for any brighter or better . . . To have been the beloved of such a heart, through weal or woe, for so long, and to have been worthy of the lot, is enough for a woman to live upon, either while the gift is present with her, or remembered and enjoyed in the most private apartment of the soul. So I think, and try to feel comfort for you. But then comes over me the long dreary path you have to travel, the blank, and change — you have not yet *begun* to feel it! One can only pray for you."

She had no doubts from the very beginning. She tried to check her heart's impulse because, as she wrote to Bob, "he is a younger brother, not rich, and I could not for a moment suppose he would think seriously of marrying much less of marrying me". However, the seriousness of his intentions was soon obvious. He came to stay at Althorp for the Christmas of 1812. It was a cold winter and Sarah taking a walk with Gin is eloquent about the loveliness of the frosty world, the diamond filigree outlining branch and leaf under the wintry sun. She tries to chide herself, thinking of the poor to whom the cold means misery and privation while she rejoices in the shining splendour, but the happiness of one who loves and knows herself beloved glows through the whole letter. He must have spoken almost immediately afterwards for on January 2nd she writes again to the Dowager Lady Spencer in a tumult of feeling: "I can collect my scattered thoughts to pray that I may become less unworthy of my happiness."

Everything conspired to bless her. Even Lady Spencer's ruthless tongue was for the moment stilled for she had taken a great fancy to her daughter's lover. She writes of him as "my very dear Lyttelton" and says: "you never did see such delicacy of exquisite feeling as there is in that young man." She adds that really she loves him "as much as my own family *at present*". The last two words are underlined and rightly, for in May of the same year, after Sarah and William Henry were married and were staying at Wimbledon previous to setting off on their wedding journey, we find Lady Spencer writing: "I rather wish for their departure than their continuance here. Oh that my fond hopes should be so deceived."

However, during the engagement all was serene. Mr. Lyttelton had fewer family obstacles to surmount. His only relations were a dearly-loved sister, Mrs. Pole-Carew, and a half-brother, the reigning Lord Lyttelton, who was not only a chronic invalid (he had a rupture) but disordered in his mind. On being applied to for his consent to the marriage he hardly seemed to realize that it was to take place, being much more occupied with the fact that he had to pay one-eighth surcharge on the letter. Lord Spencer thereupon wrote to him, presumably rather sharply, for he replied in a great hurry urging his brother not to delay a moment and in great anxiety lest The Alliance should be broken off. William Henry was so amused by this letter and its contrast with the previous one that, according to Lady Spencer, "he rolled about the floor screaming with laughter".

The certainty that William Henry would succeed the poor invalid George Fulke, would become a peer, albeit a poor one, and inherit the family seat, Hagley Hall in Worcestershire, probably weighed with the Spencers when they gave their joyful consent to their Sal's marriage but it mattered not a jot to her. She was hopelessly, blissfully in love. "What happiness is mine all around me — slippery, dangerous, blinding happiness," she wrote from Spencer House, looking out over the Green Park. "Just at the moment the sun is shining as bright as in the country; the Guards are marching thro' the park, playing a merry tune with drums and trumpets; the air is fresh and reminds me that spring is on its way, and my *intérieur* is so full, so brimful of perfect delight, that it well accords with the happiness of the scene."

Mr. Lyttelton was perhaps less carried away but he did greatly value what he had got. "He talked to me of his Sarah the night before he was married," wrote his sister, Mrs. Pole-Carew, "in terms of rapturous admiration; he said ever since she had consented to be his, he had felt quite another man, that he hoped he was already a better, as he was certain he was a more religious, one from the force of her example, the conformity of their ideas and principles on every subject was something wonderful, and such as must make their union only increase in felicity as it was strengthened by time." The prophecy came to pass and the tribute is a handsome one. It is not quite, however, Sarah's "slippery, dangerous, blinding happiness."

The two were married at the Spencers' seat Wimbledon Park on March 3rd 1813. Mrs. Pole-Carew has left a charming description of the marriage from the moment when driving through "the pretty park" the bridegroom exclaimed: "When she hears the carriage how her heart will beat!" (this remark may strike one as a shade complacent but Mrs. Pole-Carew with greater charity and probably greater truth inferred that the speaker's own heart was "not at that moment very peaceably resting within him") to the time, soon after four o'clock, when she left them side by side on a sofa, "one munching a hunch of dry bread, the other relishing a piece of hard biscuit . . . looks beaming with love and joy."

The first honeymoon was spent at Wimbledon Park but the wedding journey, nearly always in those days taken about two months after the marriage, was decidedly more adventurous. Napoleon still held nearly all of Europe in his grip of iron so the young Lytteltons were forced to turn not to France or Italy but to comparatively unknown regions. On June 29th after three or four very disagreeable days hanging about Sheerness they set sail for Göteburg. It cannot have been a pleasant voyage and it seems to have taken nearly a fortnight but their hearts were light and they were both sunny-tempered. "The navigation was, it must be owned, very trying; at least if narrow quarters, bad air, water ditto, and a thousand awkward circumstances, the least of which would have driven a fine lady mad, can be considered so," wrote Mr. Lyttelton to Lady Spencer. "But the dear girl made light of it all and was always as smiling as ever, after the sea-sickness left her, which it did in three or four days. She was often very much diverted and laughing *de bon coeur*, and when this was not the case it was, 'Oh, how pleasant this will be to recollect'."

They found Sweden clean, prosperous, beautiful, friendly — and rather dull. By August they were quite ready to leave it. But then another plan took shape; they decided to go on to Russia. This was in those days a most startling and even courageous decision. When one remembers that it was only the previous year that Napoleon had been turned back from Moscow, that few British travellers had ever set foot in the northern capital, it seems almost foolhardy. The desire was of course William's not Sarah's. It was the fulfilment of an old ambition. "Don't you remember," she wrote to her sister-in-law Mrs. Pole-Carew, "that before Monsieur *votre frère* ever had cast a wandering thought upon your undersigned humble servant — he used to cast many towards the great city of the Czars and, in plain English . . . did intend to travel to St. Petersburg? And now shall you wonder if, bedogged and bepinioned with a wife, he still is that way inclined. So it is my dear Caroline. He, both his halves I mean, wishes to go to St. Petersburg."

"Both his halves" . . . one wonders. She would never obstruct him in anything he wanted but one senses, reading between the lines of her letters to her family, that she would much rather have returned to the "Refuge" at Althorp. However, it was not in her to resist or to make difficulties. "I am *very very* sorry for the lengthening of my separation from you," she wrote to her parents. "But I must add, that I am sure our return after it will be even more delightful than it would be now — that I shall feel more as if I had left you *for something* really worth acquiring; and I cannot too often assure you, from the bottom of my heart, of my entire and indescribable happiness in my wandering, as far as it depends (and you know best how *very* far that is) upon incessant, *undeservable*, and if possible still increasing kindness and affection shewn me by him who you rejoiced to see me fastened to for life, five happy months ago."

Mr. Lyttelton celebrated the event with some anodyne verses entitled "Farewell to Sweden" inscribed "My dearest Sal, here are some Verses for thee." The first stanza runs:

"Farewell, dear simple land! for aye farewell
　Sweden's grey rocks, & darksome forests green!
Still in your peaceful shades may friendship dwell,
　And chaste domestic Virtues haunt the scene."

Sarah put her thoughts into a letter to her sister, more prosaically but far more memorably: "Farewell from Sweden! God bless you, dearest Gin! Going, going, going a step further! To Russia how very strange!"

They arrived at St. Petersburg on November 5th and found it illuminated from end to end in honour of the Battle of Leipzig which had been fought on October 18th. It was clearly a good moment for English travellers to arrive, with the Alliance in full swing. The Lytteltons were welcomed in the highest circles, presented to both Empresses (the Dowager Empress began "talking about you Papa, your *carrière si brillante et si belle*"), invited to every possible kind of party and "most civilly treated by everybody". Their civility in her opinion, however, hardly made up for their lack of looks. "Men a parcel of figures," she wrote, and again: "Such frights as the men who are still here I never did see. I fancy they must have chosen out all who were not hideous to send them to the army."

Sarah found the large parties formal and dull. There was a new fashion recently imported from Paris,* with "the men and women always in two distant and unjoinable squadrons at the end of the room". Small parties, however, she thought "much more agreeable than the common rule of English society for the want of affectation among women and the general talkativeness and civility among men". There were, moreover, certain gulfs, between the English and Russian outlook on politics. "Went yesterday after dinner to Mme. Palianski's," Sarah records, "and sat agreeably with her & her sister for an hour. No making her understand how English Governments survive the print-shop windows in London. Told her of the Prince of Hessenstein's visit to Mr. Fox when Minister, and of his being desired by Mr. F. to lounge over some caricatures till he was at leisure to attend to him. N.B. Mr. Fox himself being the principal figure in each. Mme. Paliansky [*sic*] to this moment in a hopeless puzzle about it. Said lady in a very dirty white gown, ditto fingers, ditto cap; very agreeable tho'."

Nor did Sarah approve of the fulsome flattery which the Russians bestowed upon "their autocrat".† "He is talked about quite as if he was far above his namesake of old, and called the

* It is strange that this custom now so prevalent in America and so derided by the French should have once been a Parisian fashion.
† Czar Alexander I.

deliverer of the world, with as bold a *bonne foi* as if Lord Wellington and Blücher and Bernadotte had done nothing but obey his orders! There stands his bust opposite me; I declare his soft face makes me sick, out of mere perverseness from hearing him so praised."

Busts of the Emperor and Empress seem to have been part of the standard equipment of the apartment to which they now moved in the Nevsky Prospekt. Mr. Lyttelton apparently had a habit of capering about the rooms and, in one letter, Sarah surmises that he will knock the imperial couple from their pedestals and get knouted. Otherwise they found themselves very snugly installed with a German kitchen maid who could send up a dinner of "roast beef and plumb pudding", a good sofa, many tables and chairs and a pianoforte. There were of course drawbacks; they could, presumably because of the stove pipes, smell the adjoining flats and Sarah complains of the apartment being "infected with much stink from the neighbours, mixture of old tobacco, garlick, and Russian, very overwhelming and sickening".

Their social life continued at a great pace. Sarah's diary records many thumbnail impressions of the Russian aristocracy, put down obviously to refresh her own memory rather than to conjure up a picture for others. Princess Serge Galitzin (with whom Lord Granville, now safely married to Harriet Cavendish, had been in love during his period as Ambassador to Russia) looking "very pretty, in a *huge* black & pink gipsy hat & striped *cotton* gown, with a shawl en draperie". Madame Narychkin, Tsar Alexander's Egeria, "*la belle*—face like the Apollo of Belvedere, exceedingly beautiful. Modest manner, very plain decent dress. Immense figure as to breadth." Admiral Tschitagoff "very shrewd, keen, quick man frondeur", who told her that "the frost did all last year (1812), skill nothing" and that Koutosoff was a sleepy old man, up only six hours in the twenty-four; "always unsuccessful before and unskilful amidst all manner of advantage last year".

The little descriptions are not particularly interesting in themselves but they become fascinating when we realize that the Lytteltons were actually meeting and moving in the society that Tolstoy recreated for ever in *War and Peace*. We almost expect to hear of them meeting Pierre or Prince Andrew at dinner, or attending Anna Pavlovna Scherer's salon.

The weather when they first arrived in St. Petersburg had
been unusually warm, with "incessant warm daily rains and the
ground consisting of slop and mud". By the end of November
however, the frost had begun and by the beginning of January
they were undergoing a particularly severe winter.

Sarah left several very vivid descriptions of the intense cold.
"Snow covered with diamond-dust, columns and spires in the
very furthest distance glittering with frost, all sky very blue and
very sun dazzling." "Dark sky; very few people about; those
mostly mujics, furred up to the eyes; soldiers wrapping their
faces in a bit of their coat skirt; people in sledges not a face to
be seen; horses seem stiff; nobody upright; all look strange and
dreadful." "Carriage wheels creak and whistle on the streets
in a way quite inconceivable, unless one has tried it, like a
knife on a plate." But their most remarkable experience of the
cold took place when they unwisely decided to take a walk,
with the most unpleasing consequences. Sarah records it in her
diary: "This morning [Jan. 4th 1814] thermometer *exhibited*
26 degrees of cold. Sun very bright, sky clear, no wind. At noon
I was seized by a most unhappy fit of curiosity. Proceeded to
teaze and wheedle Monsieur Lyte till permitted to disobey the
doctors and walk.

Ever to be remembered expedition to the Neva. Dress, a
quadruple shawl and fur shuba* over it. Fur boots, wadded
velvet bonnet. Set out; liked it well till we reached the boule-
vards. Then Mr. L's nose froze at the point, turned white. I
pantingly announced it to him. He cured it with snow. We
proceed. All the view the colour like bright cream; rather
hazy but very sparkling and still; awful degree of frost; very
striking. I, however, soon unable to meditate. For at sight of
Neva, where reigned a frost of 30 degrees, I was taken with
faintness, inclining me strongly to lie down; was very near
begging Mr. L to let me so to do! Very odd measure certainly.
Then for one instant had great pain in feet and hands. But these
symptoms gave way to a general insensibility, far from agreeable. Remember only after that being very much frightened,
complaining in a feeble whimper and trying in vain to feel in
my fingers, pinching and biting hard. They persisted in being

---

* Shuba is actually the Russian for fur. Often used to describe a fur
covering. The exact translation of "fur shuba" would be a "fur fur-coat".

like large bunches of very thick icicles put into my hand. Mr. L
hurrying me on all the time. At last making a very unwise
petition to be rubbed with snow, not knowing or understanding
anything, was landed in the snug shop of Feuillette Patissier.
There in a deplorable plight, laid almost fainting on sofa; good
deal swelled, lace obliged to be cut, ditto bootlace, wrist bands
loosened, then recovered my hands, through an absolute agony
of pain, made me almost cry."

Sarah was apparently not much the worse for her adventure;
she describes herself at the end of her diary as having eaten a
good dinner and being "quite snug now, only not absolutely
strong yet".

In February, however, she caught typhus fever and was laid
up for over a month. After that she longed ever more fervently
to return home. Althorp and Gin were both married on April
14th and Sarah must have yearned to be with her beloved
family. It may or may not have been a coincidence that once
Sarah, the confidante and peace-maker, had left home, the
other members of the family deserted it as quickly as possible.
Lady Spencer was her usual outspoken self about her new in-
laws. "That poor silly creature" was how she referred to Gin's
fiancé, Lord George Quin, and she was even more scathing
about Miss Acklom, Althorp's choice. This was a Miss Esther
Acklom, a rather vulgar heiress, who somewhat resembled
Trollope's Miss Dunstable. Sarah, many years later, described
her as "a vulgar person and a spoilt child" and added that
Althorp had made up his mind to marry her "[after taking a
two hours' walk in the Park to bring himself to it] in order to
pay his debts." She admitted, however, that "never was there
a happier marriage, never more sincere and deep affection on
both sides and never deeper grief in any widowed heart." But
Lady Spencer never became reconciled to the marriage and
described her daughter-in-law as being "without a spark of
right-headedness or judgement."

The extreme tact, gentleness and good manners which, in
later years, so characterized situations which must often have
presented difficulties in the Lyttelton family may have been
partly due to Sarah's recollection of the damage done and the
pain caused by Lavinia Spencer's sharp and ill-considered
tongue.

The news of the two marriages was not the only event of

2

importance that came to trouble Sarah in her far exile. Tidings
of the deaths of both her grandmothers, the Dowager Lady
Spencer and the Dowager Lady Lucan, were received by her in
mid-April in St. Petersburg and, as she wrote, "all this news
has quite oppressed me . . . so many feelings and affections are
crowded on me at once!" She was longing to leave St. Petersburg yet, on the whole, she insisted she had been very happy
and even grateful for this long winter. In spite of cold, of
illness and homesickness, she and "Mr. L" during an unbroken tête-à-tête of several weeks had been happy, cheerful
and able to live on their own resources. It was a good augury
she felt for life in "dear England".

The Lytteltons were not able to start for home till the middle
of May. The coming of spring, although it quashed Mr.
Lyttelton's project of visiting Moscow, owing to the badness of
the roads, enabled them to see a little of the country around
St. Petersburg. They visited the Tauride Palace, whose gardens,
in charge of a "scotch and cross gardener", appealed to Sarah
because they reminded her of the English countryside. "But no
grass, nothing green yet [on the 3rd of May] except *leaves* of
crocus and a slight appearance of vegetation on the willows."
They made a further excursion to see Peterhof where they found
"every part of the extérieur in shameful repair, rails broken,
stucco falling, no appearance of its ever becoming habitable."

This was their last excursion. On May 31st they actually set
out and after a most uncomfortable journey via Riga and
Memel they reached the Russian frontier. "Operations here
performed, of greasing the palms of custom-house officers,
showing our pass, and paying and dismissing our Russian
Courier. Then *Passed the Barrier!* at about 12 o'clock on this
morning — 12th June 1814; never to be forgotten glass of wine
to each of the crew* except me, given by Mr. L, on the plain
just this side of the frontier; and 3 cheers performed by him &
Roberts; *faute de* more plebeians, at having left the land of
cheating and got into a gentlemanlike country — changed
horses at Innerath, 1st Prussian inn — very clean and good —
Postboys in smart clothes; very fine, sleek horses — People along
the road looking ruddy, smiling & bold, as if free."

---

* Mr. Lyttelton had been dubbed the captain of the enterprise and the
crew consisted of Lady Sarah, her maid Rowland and the valet Roberts.

AFTER the Lytteltons returned from St. Petersburgh the family records become much sparser. The earliest volume we have of Lord Lyttelton's diary is dated 1827 and all we have to go on are a few family letters mostly to Mrs. Pole-Carew, William's sister.

For some time the Lytteltons seem to have had no fixed home but moved around in furnished houses or stayed with the Spencers at Wimbledon or with Sarah's aunt, Lady Anne Bingham, at Richmond. By 1815 Sarah was pregnant—how lucky she had been to avoid it during her strenuous travelling! —and they were living at Brighton, presumably on doctor's orders. Sarah likened Mr. Lyttelton, who was an active Member of Parliament, to "a thriving linen draper, running down to visit Mrs. L every Saturday, and taking care to be behind the counter again by Tuesday's earliest flying coach". In his absence she amused herself by bathing, though not in the open sea. She frequented the shower baths into which she went bare-headed, taking to a wig when "Mr. L is here. When he is not, I glide about with long, lank, uncurled black locks just parted on the forehead, do you understand? And I look for all the world like the oldest and much the ugliest woman in St. Giles!"*

The sea-air was good for health but Brighton found no favour in Sarah's eyes. She describes herself as living "opposite a bleak, bare, dazzling sea, in the middle of a glaring, tawdy, vulgar town, with no walk but between Dunghill-studded cornfields, all besprinkled with staring coxcombs and parasolled ladies". William Henry liked it no more than she did and Sarah expatiates to her sister-in-law on his "dear kindness and excellence" in staying on at Brighton as long as the doctors advised and never once expressing a wish for a pleasanter

* The quarter of London through which Shaftesbury Avenue now runs, then the most appalling slum.

place. "He does not now admit he wishes to leave it," she wrote in June 1815 the day before the battle of Waterloo, "though there never was such an odious abode for a man like him at this time of the year. It is all my teazing that has made him consent to go away so soon. Now is he not the best husband in the world?"

They were both delighted to leave Brighton for Wimbledon Park. William Henry celebrated the event by composing another of his conventional little poems entitled "Summer at Wimbledon" and dedicated "To my dearest Sally". It starts:

> "How gay, my love, our dear retreat
> All girt with blushing roses round . . . "

and ends:

> "Beyond the World's vain anxious pleasures blest.
> Each wish subdued — each busy thought at rest."

One hopes that their sojourn at "Flora's court" as Mr. Lyttelton termed it, was as peaceful as he made it sound. Lady Spencer knew herself only too well when she said she loved "my very dear Lyttelton", "as much as my family *at present*". As we have seen she was bored with him before he and Sal left for Sweden and after their return she complained to her husband that "Lyttelton annoys me with an early visit every day. I really cannot bear it." Lavinia Spencer was never one to conceal her opinions and Sarah must have had a lot of family patching up to do.

It was perhaps surprising that the Spencers and William Lyttelton got on as well as they did. It was an epoch when political passions ranged strong and deep and they were naturally exacerbated by the strains of war. The Spencers were a noted Whig family but moved by his sense of England's peril Lord Spencer had crossed the floor of the House and became First Lord of the Admiralty under Pitt. With two sons in the Navy the Spencers were naturally fiercely patriotic and keen on the prosecution of the war. Lyttelton on the other hand was a follower of Fox and Whitbread and one of the small minority to vote with the latter against continuing the combat. He joined with the Hollands in their admiration of Napoleon and when after Waterloo he had the opportunity actually to meet the great man he quickly availed himself of it, though, as will be seen, he defended himself and his country with some adroitness.

The *Northumberland*, the ship which was to take Napoleon to St. Helena, was anchored in Torbay and William was a friend of Sir George Cockburn, the Admiral commanding her. On the 7th of August 1815 therefore he was standing on deck watching the longboat belonging to the *Thunderer* bringing Napoleon to his new place of captivity. Lyttelton noted that the top of Bonaparte's head was completely bald surrounded by a fringe of dishevelled reddish hair. His complexion was more than pale, it was sickly.

Lyttelton, who was a little behind the rest of the party which consisted of Lord Lowther, the Hon. Edmund Byng, Colonel Sir George Lowther and an unnamed artillery officer, was not presented to Napoleon on deck but later he and his friends were left alone with the ex-emperor in the Admiral's cabin. This was done on purpose. In the *Bellerophon* Napoleon had occupied the best quarters using them as his own. In the *Northumberland* it was to be made clear to him that the Admiral's cabin was for the use of the Admiral and his friends.

Bonaparte looked suspiciously at the slim young man in civil dress. He obviously had no idea who I was, says Lyttelton, and may have thought I was a servant of the Admiral's. He lifted his chin and said in a severe tone,

"Who are you?"

"Monsieur le Général" (Lyttelton, obviously on instructions, kept to this form of address throughout the interview), "my name is Lyttelton and I am a relation and friend of the Admiral's."

"Are you one of the ship's company?"

"No, I am not a sailor."

"Then you are here out of curiosity?"

Lyttelton replied that there was no object worthier of curiosity than that which brought him here. This seemed to go down fairly well, and Napoleon questioned him and Lowther about their estates and showed a rather unexpected interest in the subject of fox hunting.

This exhausted, however, a terrible silence ensued. Bonaparte turned his back and looked out of the window through his spy-glass. Bingham whispered to Lyttelton: "For God's sake say something. Talk about the weather if you like but say something."

Somebody managed to mention that Lyttelton was an M.P. and this revived the drooping conversation. Bonaparte was keenly interested in the Opposition in England; he knew that Fox and Whitbread had always been against the war. He asked Lyttelton if he were a member of the Opposition. Lyttelton answered that his conscience had often made him vote against Ministers. "We are a free country," he added, certainly intending a covert dig in spite of his admiration for Napoleon, "and one must act in what one thinks are the country's best interests."

He was questioned about Whitbread's suicide. "Was it from what you call the spleen?" Lyttelton answered that foreigners were apt to attach too much importance to what they called the English spleen. Whitbread was mad and that was that. Bonaparte also questioned him about possible successors and Lyttelton managed to slip in a neat compliment. "You know, Monsieur le Général, that it is not so easy to replace great men."

In spite of the quick glance with which Bonaparte acknowledged this, the interview dragged terribly and Lyttelton tactfully went to find Sir George Cockburn to say that since the point had been made about their right to occupy the cabin they surely should now retire. They were just settling down to a little cold luncheon (presumably in the dining cabin) before going on shore when Bonaparte passed through with Bertrand on his way to the upper deck. He spoke to them and they followed him and resumed the conversation. Out in the open air the interview flowed much less lamely.

Bonaparte seized the opportunity to complain bitterly of the English government saying that they had disgraced their flag and their national honour in imprisoning him in this way.

Although Lyttelton was a member of the Opposition and had always been anti-Pitt, in this crisis his English patriotism came to the surface and he acquitted himself very ably.

"We have broken no promise to you," he told Bonaparte, "and the National interest demands that you should be placed in a position where you cannot re-enter France. You are subject to no more restraint than is necessary to fulfil that object."

Bonaparte went on insisting that he only wished to live as a simple English citizen and that his career was finished.

Lyttelton, rather daringly, reminded him that he had said as much on Elba.

Bonaparte. "Then I was a sovereign. I had the right to make war . . . I made war on the King of France with 600 men!" After a short discussion of the Hundred Days in which he stressed how much French support he had received, a point which would have invalidated his argument if anyone had taken it up, he went on to blame the English and wished he had given himself up to the Austrians or the Russians.

Lyttelton. "The Austrians—perhaps—but as to giving yourself up to the Emperor Alexander you will give me leave to doubt it." (Lyttelton had good reasons for his unbelief. The previous evening Lord Keith, on remarking to Bonaparte that he could have surrendered to the Russians, had received a shrug of the shoulder and the reply *"Dieu m'en garde"*.)

Bonaparte sulkily went on affirming that the English knew his character and that they ought to have believed his word of honour.

Lyttelton. Dare I tell you the exact truth?

Bonaparte. Speak.

Lyttelton. Ever since the invasion of Spain there hasn't been a single person in England who wouldn't have mistrusted your word.

Bonaparte. I was asked into Spain by Charles IV to help his son.

Lyttelton. But not, I think, to put King Joseph on the throne.

Bonaparte. It was necessary to establish a counterweight to your enormous power, and anyway, it was only what the Bourbons did.

Lyttelton. But you must admit that France under your rule was much more to be feared than she was in the last years of Louis XIV. Besides her territory has expanded.

Bonaparte. England on her side had become much more powerful. There are her overseas possessions and India.

Lyttelton. Plenty of intelligent people think that England loses more than she gains by the possession of these distant unaccountable powers."

At this point Bonaparte suddenly harked backwards and said: "So it seems the English don't think much of the Emperor Alexander?" Lyttelton replied that though the Emperor was popular with some ladies on the whole the English had a poor opinion of him and that for his part he could never admire a prince who had absorbed Finland and Poland in such a disgraceful fashion.

Bonaparte possibly feeling that the subject of conquests concealed another covert dig asked William about his time in St. Petersburg. The latter in his reply said that he had often heard Napoleon much praised by the Russians, more than as an Englishman still at war, he quite liked. Bonaparte replied in a very revealing sentence.

"Eh! Why should they hate me? I made war on them, that was all."

The conversation then ranged over military subjects, the projected invasion of England, Beresina, Belgium and finally Waterloo, which drew out the flattest exchange of platitudes that can ever have been enunciated.

Lyttelton asked what Bonaparte thought of the British infantry.

Bonaparte. The British infantry is very good.

Lyttelton. In comparison with the French?

Bonaparte. The French infantry is very good.

Lyttelton. With the bayonet?

Bonaparte. The French infantry is also good with the bayonet. It depends on how it is used.

Lyttelton. What about the engineers and the artillery?

Bonaparte. All that is good, very good.

After this the conversation revived a little and took a turn oddly relevant to today, when Bonaparte said that though France's trade had suffered as a result of the war her interior resources had been revealed as adequate and chemical discoveries had produced many products which before this had come from abroad. For example beetroot sugar, which he had heard of as excellent, was much less dear than sugar from outside on which he had placed a heavy tax.

Finally, Napoleon terminated the interview with great brusqueness. Lifting his eyes to the sky he said suddenly: "It seems to me it is getting rather cold," and on the tips of his toes, with little affected steps, and a slight balancing of his shoulders, he went down below. The little group of Englishmen, taken by surprise, stood watching him and had much ado not to laugh.

Sarah by no means shared her husband's enthusiasm for Napoleon. "The horror of the Napoleonic Wars never faded from her mind," wrote one of her grandchildren, "& she taught us to hold him in greatest dislike & disapproval."

Although Sarah, as a born Whig, sympathized with William over Reform, it is probable that she looked on him as a husband and father, rather than as a politician; and indeed he figures more and more in the former character as the years flowed by.

"Your brother is quite altered about zitis," Sarah wrote to Mrs. Pole-Carew when Caroline Lavinia Lyttelton, who made her appearance in January 1816, was a year old. "He is as good a nurse as you could wish to see; and dandles and courts and converses with Miss Lyttelton full as much as I do."

Before Caroline's arrival Sarah had not been overjoyed by her pregnancy. "I daresay you are [as I well remember being] not so glad as you ought to be," she wrote to her eldest grand-daughter, Meriel Talbot, when the latter was expecting her first baby, and she firmly told her sister-in-law that though she thought the Pole-Carew children exceptionally "nice zitis" she did not "*mean* or *wish* to have as many by about half."

Nevertheless Caroline was only a few months old when Sarah was once more expecting. "I shall be sure to affront the family with another daughter," she wrote on February 8th 1816, "so break down your pride and your temper Mrs. Carew and be prepared for such an humiliation." She was not called upon to apologize, however, for on April 3rd 1817 George William Lyttelton was born, "immense and very strong hitherto; he is not nearly so pretty as Caroline was, which I don't at all quarrel with him for; I have always been wishing for a manly, stout, ugly son."

It is pleasant to reflect that perhaps George's birth moved his father to consider the plight of other little boys, for on June 5th Sarah wrote: "Mr. Lyttelton is going to town today to try to do some good to the poor chimney sweepers," and it was partly owing to William's efforts that legislation was passed, though much later, to prohibit the use of "climbing boys" like little Tom in *The Water Babies*.

Sarah's intention of limiting her family did not seem at first to be meeting with much success. George William was followed in quick succession by Spencer, born 1818, William Henry in 1820 and Lavinia in 1821. But after that there were no more children and she achieved her object of having a smaller family than her sister-in-law, five only to Mrs. Pole-Carew's seven.

There are not many letters preserved between 1815 and 1826. The Lytteltons had no permanent home and probably destroyed most of their correspondence. There are the usual baby anecdotes. George is very ugly though a fine boy and Sarah finds she is very fond of him "which is new, for I used to prefer his sister sadly". Spencer is "a *very* pretty man" and has an "exemplary good temper. I believe he is going to be the meek person of the family." Later he is described as a "funny little sort of Puck with a great deal of mischief and some waggery in him". The baby, Billy, is "*too* ugly, immensely fat, and exceedingly good-tempered as yet".

They spent the first of many, many Christmases at Althorp and there was a traumatic incident when Caroline stuck herself in the eye with a sharp pair of scissors. She managed to hit the insensitive middle of the eye and suffered no pain but there was of course an irreparable injury to the sight of the one eye from which she never recovered.

In 1826 there was a change in the family fortunes. For some time William Henry's half-brother George Fulke, the reigning Lord Lyttelton, had been failing both in body and mind. Now the latter had almost given way. He had delusions and suicidal tendencies. There had long been a breach between the brothers but now William decided he must go to Hagley, and take charge. His brother received him and it was plain that the poor man was no longer capable of looking after his own affairs. From all the accounts in the diaries and letters the younger brother seems to have acted with the greatest kindness and delicacy. It would not have been impossible one imagines to have the poor lunatic (who kept desiring the doctor to cut off his right arm since it pained him after a bleeding which had taken place several weeks previously) put away in an asylum; but William arranged for surveillance to take place at home and left the owner in full possession of the great house, while the heir and his family occupied a small sham Gothic house in Hagley village called Rockingham Hall, which had been built in earlier less strait-laced days by an illegitimate, though distinguished scion of the Lyttelton family, one Admiral Smith.

Hagley Hall is very close to Birmingham, less of a drawback in 1826 than it is today; on the other side, however, it looks out over the Welsh hills. At the back of the house is Clent Hill and the Lytteltons were always sauntering up it on an evening stroll, or rushing to the top to get a breath of air. The house is in the Palladian-Inigo Jones tradition, severe and plain with a tower at each corner, each tower surmounted by a low pyramid roof. On the garden side of the house is a broad terrace, called "the perron", on which the family often sat on summer evenings and below which the Lyttelton coffins were laid before being transported to the church, about 100 yards distant. The gardens which were laid out by the first Lord Lyttelton in 1747 are full of walks, of "peeps", of monuments, such as a small copy of the temple of Theseus at Athens, a slender obelisk, a ruined castle and an Ionic rotunda.

William, like all Lytteltons, adored Hagley, and was only too happy to be back in the well-loved scenes of his youth, but Sarah seemed at first a little overpowered by the new situation. Rockingham Hall had to be done up before they could fully enter into possession, and though the children could go straight there, the parents were obliged to take up residence in the back part of the great house in two rooms looking over the stables, near the book-room. "The said book-room," Sarah wrote to her sister-in-law, "is a favourite snuggery of mine; for to own the truth the lofty awful rooms below with all their crimson damask, old china, japan cabinets, tapestry and carving, are not fit for a poor lone body to sit in of evenings, when her chicks are far away with all their merry noises and her husband gone to dine out, and she left in a strange disunited tête-à-tête with another poor, *poor* lone being!" In another letter to her brother George, she describes the beauty of the scenery and setting and adds: "But, as if to show how far that alone is from sufficing, there in the midst of it all is, tottering along on his melancholy evening walk, the *owner*!—talking loud to himself, afraid of all human beings, and occupied only by gloomy delusions, unsatisfying wild pompous fancies." Lord Lyttelton saw his brother occasionally, but hardly came into any contact with Sarah though he liked to watch the children playing about the Park. When they were learning to ride his bald head would appear at a window in the big dining-room and if he met them in the Park he would stop and speak to them, particularly distinguishing their governess, Mdlle. Quignon, for he liked to show off his French. He always wore a white hat, Caroline remembered, and being lame, walked about the Park with a stick occasionally giving vent to a loud shout.

It was after the move to Hagley that William Henry Lyttelton began keeping a diary. It is a very innocuous record of

country life. On the left-hand page every day he painstakingly
chronicles the weather. Barometer, temperature, winds, rain or
sun. Otherwise it is largely taken up by observations on things
growing in the woods and garden, the first fawn seen in the
Park (Hagley had a celebrated herd of deer); the moss-roses
flowering about the middle of June, the other roses rather
later; flights of starlings alighting, and rising together and
wheeling about in the Park and on Obelisk Hill; a remarkable
season for mushrooms; the first appearance of "Harry
Longlegs".*

The pattern which shaped Lyttelton lives for many generations was already taking shape. On June 18th 1827 the foundation for a village school-room was laid, and that on July 3rd the
"First stone of New Aisle to the Church" was laid by William.

The new era was certainly setting in, though there was
rather a jolly Regency flavour about his entry for the 23rd of
June 1829 when he attended the S.P.C.K. District Committee
at the Lyttelton Arms. "Too many toasts and Nine drunk
though the Revd. Gents were not actually toxicated."

Spiritual health was not the only improvement brought to
Hagley from the new régime. Mr. Lyttelton's diary of Feb. 19th
1828 records briskly: "A child . . . having died in the Village
of the natural smallpox, I went round with Mr. Turner, and
found near forty persons, one or two grown up, who had never
been vaccinated or inoculated. Took a list of them, got their
consent to have vaccination performed on themselves or their
children, and wrote to, and made an agreement with Mr.
Freer, a Surgeon at Stourbridge, to vaccinate all, and attend
them afterwards. One man, Tompkins the Wheelwright, had
four children unvaccinated — & on my asking him the reason,
he said as how 'the people in this Country did not much have it
done, & therefore he didn't'."

William had been taking up the reins of Estate management

---

* In addition the diary contains many passages sedulously blocked out
by a later hand. Erasures always interest a biographer but William's life
appeared so particularly blameless that there seemed no possible reason for
such excisions. A contemporary letter however provided a clue. In it there
were some words erased which, from the context, plainly indicated an
attack of diarrhoea. William's health was poor and he possessed the temperament of a hypochondriac. The erasures, which grow longer in later
years, probably cover up what the Victorians regarded as indelicate bodily
symptoms.

and government ever since the move to Worcestershire but, in November 1828, George Fulke died, the hatchment was erected over the front door, to remain there a year, and the new heir entered into his inheritance.

It was not all plain sailing. The old Hall had not been repaired for many years and the drains and flues were in a sad state. One of the earliest entries runs: "the bad smell broke out in the library and rooms beyond, sometimes in one, sometimes in the other, with great violence." And a few days later he records: "A vast quantity of filth found under the privy at bottom of the back stairs — the clearing away of which infected the house with such a strong and prevailing stench, that Sarah was all but sick."

Henceforth the diary is punctuated with accounts of repairs and plumbing. The flue in the steward's room was cracked and the house was nearly burnt down. The new alteration to the boiler, which was supposed to provide hot water all day at a moment's notice, sounds extremely modern, "but alas!" when William attempted to take a bath, "the pipes were obstructed, the servants were obliged to bring the hot water in buckets and the cold [I can't yet tell why] came in dirty". Worst of all the "great Pipe of the new Water Closet at the top of the Stone Stairs was found to be defective". The continuing health of the inhabitants of Hagley was something of a miracle.

The stench, however, seems to have abated sufficiently for a visit from Lord and Lady Spencer, George and Fritz in the month of September. Lady Spencer's advent was always regarded with trepidation by any member of her family. Sarah's sister, Georgiana Quin, once wrote when expecting her parents to stay: "All day I was upstairs making up the fires, looking out of the window, pressing my face against the glass, and really in such a state I never shall forget . . . After a bad night I was up and dressing this morning when, at half past ten, in rumbled a jingling carriage, and Lord G.* called out, 'Lord Spencer is come.' I became more dead than alive, for I thought she was there too, and I not dressed."

Sarah, who was older and had been married for fifteen years, was probably not in such a state of alarm, but both she and William were obviously much relieved that all went off well.

---

* Her husband, Lord George Quin.

"I believe," Sarah wrote, "that all our little arrangements to receive them and help on the visit did please them, and that even my mother was *nearly* as comfortable as at home;" while William retails in his diary Lord Spencer's admiration of the place, the success of a fireworks exhibition and ends with a charming period picture which might form the subject of a Morland engraving. "On Sunday she [Lady Spencer] gave A Bun a-piece to all the School-Children, who were assembled after Evening Service in the Servants' Hall: it was a pretty and entertaining sight: some of the little folk scarce being able to hold their buns, which were very large Two Penny ones with some currants in them."

The Spencers concluded their visit just in time. In November a "grand stink" broke out in the library, so violently that it drove the Lytteltons out of the room.

Although the diary is mostly a chronicle of household events there are several intimations of the wider world. The years 1831 and 1832 were overshadowed by the Reform Bill which doubly implicated Lord Lyttelton. As a Lieutenant-Colonel in the newly-formed Yeomanry he had to keep order in a countryside seething with discontent, and as one of the few Whig Peers he had to go to London to support his brother-in-law Lord Althorp, who was in charge of the Bill in the Commons, and Lord Grey who led the Party in the Lords.

The latter House threw out the Bill on the 8th of October 1831 and the county, which had been fairly quiet up till then ("the Machine Breakers and Incendiaries had not done any mischief or attempted any in any parts of Worcestershire: and only some few threatening letters, signed *Swing* received," wrote Lord Lyttelton in 1830) now began to show signs of disturbance. Worcester rioters apprehended by the Constables were rescued by the mob, the Yeomanry with ball cartridges were sent to Derby where it was feared the colliers would revolt.

In his other capacity as a prime supporter of the Bill Lyttelton went to London early in December and left a vivid account of his first dinner with Lord Grey and the Whig peers. "The Duke of Sussex was one of the party. He showed the usual bad taste and faulty principles of his Family in conversation, telling stories that were little short of blasphemous, and uttering profane oaths frequently: and I hear he is very often gross and indecent. His manner to us was half buffoonish, and contrasted strongly with Ld. Grey's highly gentlemanlike demeanour. On the other side of Ld. Grey was the Chancellor* — as dirty, as acute, as droll, as easy, as natural as ever. As I was opposite him, he gave me sundry nods and winks, as much as to say, 'What a deal of solemn humbug is here!' "

On the next day December 6th, Lord Lyttelton seconded the Address on the Reform Bill and "got through it *tant bien que mal* or rather (I suspect) *plus mal que bien* in less than ¾ of an hour. Lord C† was very conciliatory, and I *meant* to be so, but failed, and the Opposition was galled, which Ld. Grey did not wish; however the effect was good, for the galled jades though they kicked at me, did not kick at the intended Reform Bill, on which I had provoked them — and all they said was favourable as far as it went, not one word the other way."

The next day, December 7th, Lord Lyttelton, with Lord Brougham and Lord Camperdown went in a carriage procession ("alas at procession pace") from the House of Lords to St. James's to present the Address to the King. They found William IV on his throne with all the great officers of State around him. "He looked," says Lord Lyttelton who was no respecter of Royalty, "very dumpy, what is called *sunk in his armour* and did not seem at home in a military uniform, with a Hat with overshadowing plumes."

On the 8th December, doubtless with a sigh of relief William left London and joined his family at Althorp.

This was almost the last emergence of Lord Lyttelton as an active politician. When the Reform Bill finally passed the Lords in 1832 he was at Hagley. He alludes to the "great news" which arrived on Sunday April 15th and notes the figures, a majority of nine (one presumes that he himself was paired or had been able to give a Proxy Vote) but his entry begins: "Went to the School and found a remarkably full attendance. To Church in the morning: a good Congregation."

The Lytteltons spent some weeks of the summer in 1833 in London but this appears to have been more for enjoyment and for the business of bringing out Caroline, than for any political purpose, although William was sworn in at the Privy Council

* Lord Brougham.
† Lord Camperdown who had moved the Address.

on his appointment as Lord Lieutenant of Worcestershire. Altogether this season was a last farewell to the old world in which William and Sarah had grown up. They dined with the Miss Berrys, where they found Sydney Smith, "as uproarious, at intervals, as ever, & as dull in the intervals; & I am sorry to say, not a jot more clerical in his topics, or way of handling them". They went to the Queen's Ball at St. James', where "the King was very gracious. The Queen [I speak of looks and manner only] just the contrary." There was "a display of gold plate against a scarlet Drapery covering one whole side of the room, & lit up with a great number of wax-candles, quite royal; & producing a sun-like splendour." The next day Lord Lyttelton, by himself, rode to Holland House, where he saw "a Portrait of Bonaparte, in his Study, with all his Papers about him, & the very furniture he usually had there. *Gérard* painted the Portrait during *the Hundred Days* and Ld. Holland told me that Louis XVIII had allowed Gérard afterwards to revisit the Room, & to have all the Furniture placed as it was when Napoleon occupied it. — I got upon a Chair," Lord Lyttelton continues, "to examine the Face. The proportions, & each feature appeared there according to my Recollection; but the Expression of the Countenance was not well hit off." On another evening they dined with Samuel Rogers where they much admired the beauty of the house and the "remarkably pretty effect" produced by the lamps and the cut-glass lustres twinkling away; reflected and multiplied in the panes of plate glass in the bay window at the end of the drawing-room.

Nor was culture neglected. William visited Chantrey's studio, where he saw the bust of poor Bob Spencer,* now in the Spencer chapel at Great Brington, and thought it very like. He sat several times to Benjamin Haydon for his portrait which was to be included in the picture of the Great Reform Dinner at the Guildhall. He much admired Pasta in *Norma* though he thought "much of the music was bad" and was even more enthusiastic about Malibran in *La Sonnambula* though there he criticized the music as "downright ugly". The Lady's singing, however, he thought excellent, and "her acting very good

---

* Bob Spencer had died suddenly and quite unexpectedly in December 1830. Sarah was "so afflicted at first as to fall down, and seemed to be almost in hysterics, she sobbed, poor thing! so much". 3rd Ld. L's Diary 18.12.30.

indeed, with the natural spirit and grace which one so rarely sees in an Englishwoman".

The Season ended with one last burst of political activity when Lyttelton had to leave a family party at the Augustus Cliffords' to get down to the House of Lords where he was kept till "near two o'clock, when those impenetrably thick-headed Tories under the Leadership of that acute knave Lord Lyndhurst threw out the Ld. Chancellor's Local Courts Bill".

The next day they all returned to Hagley and from now onwards the London Lord Lyttelton, sharp, mocking and incisive, disappears and gives way to the rather delightful, slightly bumbling country gentleman. He had a passion for statistics. We have already seen how he noted the weather on every page of his journal; he was also very handy with a foot rule and whenever he admired a building, such as St. George's Hall at Windsor, he liked to take its exact dimensions. He kept a weighing machine at Hagley and solemnly recorded the varying weights of his family and of such guests as were amenable. One entry runs, "Weighed the Bishop of Oxford 11 st. 12 or very near."

He did much honest work in the county. In those days when there were no social services and a most rudimentary poor law, a great deal depended on the country gentleman, and William Henry took his full share. It was not only an affair of keeping order by means of the yeomanry. (He is refreshingly unpompous about this, "Put on a regimental Frock, buttoned up to the chin of the unhappy wearer, boots with long spurs . . . and feeling both uneasy and ridiculous, mounted a caparisoned horse and went a colonelling to Hewell." And again: "The only untoward event in the course of the morning was the Fall of the Lieut-Colonel [Myself] from his *Charger* but the gallant officer was not hurt and soon recovered his horse and his seat."

Another enemy, however, more pressing than threats from Captain Swing and discontented colliers was the cholera, which during the summer of 1832 broke out all over the country. It came to Stourbridge in mid-July. On the 16th Lord Lyttelton was summoned to the Cholera Committee; on the 18th he rode into Birmingham and got some "useful Instructions" from Dr. J. Johnstone. On the 21st he helped to form a new Board of Health in Stourbridge consisting of "the chief people of the town and neighbourhood, as well as the medical men", which started to get ready a House of Reception for victims of the disease. The epidemic was slow in taking hold but on August 11th the first case of Indian cholera was reported in Stourbridge and the victim died in fifteen hours. By the 18th of October there were more than 140 cases, and a dispensary was established and the theatre was turned into a hospital. Finally on November 21st the disease seems to have more or less died down. Lord Lyttelton writes that the total number of cases has been 399, the deaths 48 and 5 cases only are left. Typically he concludes the entry by writing: "Observed the *Tulip Tree* on the lawn below the Parsonage, still in leaf, *with scarcely one leaf turned*."

Little was known about cholera in those days, how it originated, how it was carried, and I think it says much for the English sense of responsibility in the governing classes that a rather delicate man with a wife and five small children should neither flee the contagion nor shut himself in his own domain, but should take a leading part in organizing and fighting the contagion. It is sometimes said that it was John Wesley and Evangelization that prevented revolution in England during the nineteenth century. A small measure of credit might go to the unpretending, matter-of-course sense of duty and of obligation which inspired very many members of the country gentry and aristocracy.

During the whole decade of the Lytteltons' married life at Hagley we gain curiously little impression of Sarah Lyttelton. After following her girlhood almost from day to day in her vivid letters to her brother Bob, and her honeymoon weeks in her diaries and letters home, after the birth of the children and the move to Hagley she suddenly almost disappears. This is mostly of course because after her husband's death she destroyed all her letters to him. There is a sizeable bunch of his letters to her, often addressed to "My dearest Partner" or "My dearest Wifie" but what she called the "old musty rigs", with which she must have responded, are no more. Nor do we obtain a very clear picture of her from William's letters. He tells her about what no doubt she preferred to know, his own doings and health. Only in a few letters do we gain some idea of what her answers must have been like. In September he is away staying with Lord Bagot at Blithfield and has been re-reading a bundle of Sarah's letters. "And great pleasure it did give me,—many pretty, many pleasant feelings of thine, and many pleasant and pretty accounts of our children and their goings-on, were in that great bundle. Only some sad and severe things about thyself, which always must give me some pain." A thread which runs through Sarah's whole character is a deep distrust of herself. A loved daughter, a happy wife, and an adored mother yet she remained to the end diffident, unself-confident and easily cast down. This may have been partly Christian humility but it may also have been the effect of being brought up by the snubbing, sharp-tongued Lavinia Spencer. It was a characteristic which somewhat irritated her husband.

Altogether reading the letters and the diaries one cannot avoid the impression that in the Lyttelton marriage *"c'était elle qui baisait et lui qui tendait la joue"*. Lord Lyttelton loved his wife deeply and sincerely but his entire devotion was really given to his home and family life. He writes to her when she is staying at Althorp after her mother's death that he longs for her return, "to find thee, and the house all alive and merry with the lects,* instead of my great solitary Room (a good Room, too, but it proves only half comfortable when so ill filled and always sets me a-wishing for the rest of us!)"

The diary has of course many references to Sarah but she is nearly always coupled with the children. "My dear, dear Wife's 46th Birthday. More than 20 years it now is since she was bestowed on me — and how can I be thankful enough to Heaven for the Gift, and the long continuance of it to me — and the Children!" Or again, more prosaically — "Weighed Children. Lastly Mamma 10st. 12lb."

In fact from the diary one would gather that Lord Lyttelton became almost over-devoted to his children and had a very special relationship with them. The eldest boy George, known in the family as Dodsum, was his peculiar pride and joy. When he took "our dear little fellow" to Eton for his first half it was, contrary to usual practice, the child who was in excellent spirits and the father who could not conceal his sorrow. "It was all holiday to him," wrote Lord Lyttelton — "Not so indeed to poor Papa — yet not much otherwise, except now & then when something irresistible came over his heart & eyes for a minute or so." George William Lyttelton reading this letter forty-five years later annotated it as follows. "While sitting in the

* The Spencer "little language" meaning children.

Christopher" [the inn at Eton at which they had put up] "on this occasion, my father burst into a flood of tears which lasted for some time, such as I have hardly seen before or since."

George was his favourite son but he was almost equally emotional over parting with Spencer, who in the family tradition was destined for the Navy. It is true that this was a more serious affair for the little boy of twelve was to join the *Actaeon* at Portsmouth and to be away from his family for three years. "I was much overcome," Lord Lyttelton wrote, "and could not say half I intended. However what was said was I hope right & that the little man will not attend to it less because it was uttered with so much emotion."

By the time Billy was sent to Winchester the pangs had become less. Lord Lyttelton simply writes: "Took my dear Boy to-day to his School, and with an involuntary heavy heart, left him there." He adds that Billy "was very cheerful to the last and never seemed inclined to shed a tear."

It may be noted that Lord Lyttelton himself took each of his three sons to their school or ship; interviewed the Headmaster or Captain, the doctor or matron. ("She told him to tell her whenever he had a *finger-ache*," he wrote when he left George at Eton.) He arranged about George's bed, about Spencer's case of naval instruments, about leaving Billy in the care of his cousin Gerald Pole-Carew. All these journeys took two days there and back, with a night on the way. Few fathers in the eighteenth century would have undertaken such responsibilities, and not many in the nineteenth.

The diary says less about the girls; in the Victorian tradition they were probably left more to their mother, but we hear of Mr. Hodgson, the surgeon from Birmingham, being sent for to examine Caroline's damaged eye, and of Lavinia's ninth birthday when she was crowned with flowers and ivy and "taken round the house with huzzas".

After reading the diaries and building up such a picture of a careful, loving, almost doting father it is disconcerting to find that his children perhaps viewed things somewhat differently. Caroline Lyttelton reminiscing to a great-niece told her that she adored her mother but was afraid of her father and had very few recollections of him. The man she loved "O! far more than my father" was her grandfather old Lord Spencer. One of her sparse paternal memories was that they were all travelling in a post-chaise, father, mother and children, and Lord Lyttelton, who had very bad eczema, groaned so loudly that they were terrified. Their mother begged him to stop and he said he would try to but afterwards the children went in the chaise behind with the servants as they usually did.

This rather pathetic little anecdote may explain why he was not so much loved by his children as he deserved to be. He suffered during the last ten years of his life both from the eczema mentioned by Caroline, and from a liver complaint which finally killed him. His ill-health made his temper rather uncertain. He seems to have generously offered his orphaned Pole-Carew nieces a home after their father's death, but Sarah Lyttelton finds it necessary to write to them to adjure them not to bring "the Canary birds". "Ld. L. has *no preference* [to speak mildly] for their music . . . We have already one, who undergoes many risks and banishments, and much abuse into the bargain, poor fellow."

William Henry Lyttelton died in 1837. He left a sort of testament partly dictated to his wife and afterwards written down by her from memory. It is a moving document. It begins: "This illness has done me good — my views on religious subjects are greatly altered by it — I feel a much greater repentance for what I have done against God's will — a much greater loathing of my sins." It was obvious that he recognized impatience as his besetting temptation and he describes how he made a rule to look back every night upon the day, to watch for symptoms of it. He never, he said, omitted any of his children in his prayers, but he prayed most for Spencer in the Navy, so far away and exposed to so many trials and dangers. He goes on most pathetically: "The only unpleasant feeling I have, at times, is the uncertainty as to what may be impending over me. Shall I have a great increase of this nausea? Or will pain come on? Or shall I be so weakened as to become helpless at last? May it all be as God wills, but I do feel a wish to be spared such added trials!"

He was spared them. On April 30th he exclaimed on first waking, "Oh what a blessed sleep I have had! Thank God for all my comforts! God be praised! My heavenly Father be praised! Thank God!" He died the same day.

Now the new generation steps on to the stage. The decade of the thirties had swept the boards clean of many of the previous players. Sarah's beloved brother Bob died in 1830, Lavinia Spencer in 1831, William's sister, Caroline Pole-Carew in 1833, Lord Spencer in 1834, old Mr. Pole-Carew in 1835. Pretty little Georgiana Quin had long been in her grave and so had Esther Acklom, Lord Althorp's vulgar, adored wife. Lord Althorp was now Lord Spencer, to be succeeded in 1845 by his brother Fritz, one of the little boys whom Sarah had helped with their home-work in the cold Christmas holidays at Althorp, nearly thirty years before.

In 1837 when their father died the five Lyttelton children were twenty-one, twenty, all but nineteen, eighteen and seventeen respectively. The eldest was Caroline Lavinia, who was to live on into the next century. She was rather a bossy character. "For some years she [Caroline] has directed everybody near her," wrote her Uncle Fritz disapprovingly in 1842 and two generations later her nephew Spencer was to reproach her for domineering over his grandmother. The Queen referred to Caroline as that "not very judicious daughter—who ruled her [Lady L.] completely", and this picture is borne out by a letter of Sarah's own in which she says: "Till Caroline comes back from Blackheath . . . I cannot make up my mind *where* I am to go [for a holiday] . . . perhaps I shall go to Brighton. But all is unsettled for want of king Caroline."

She was probably not a very attractive girl; the Queen and her sister, Princess Hohenlohe-Langenburg used to refer to her in their letters, I fear ironically, as "the beauty". She had a defective eye, owing to the early accident with the scissors, and also developed a crooked shoulder, it was said from over much harp playing. Her début in London was not a success. Unlike her mother and her mother's cousins she had not been brought up in the Whig world of great houses in London and the country. In the nineteenth century, and this went on as late as

44

the eighties, it was considered bad form to effect introductions. Either you were in society, in which case everybody knew you, or you were not, in which case nobody wanted to know you. There was a certain rough logic about the system but it came hard on a girl who had spent the last five years happily immured in Worcestershire. Caroline's first ball was at Devonshire House and her mother's account of it makes one ache for the poor child. "Caroline and I have *gone out*, as they call it, three or four times. Her first and only ball was at Devonshire House, where she went with the highest expectation of pleasure and comfort, and found herself crowded, heated, frightened to death, asked to dance *instantly* by too kind a cousin,* dragged into the first quadrille of thirty-two she had ever seen; and of course she puzzled the figure, got quizzed and pitied, and does not wish to dance again."

She fell in love once. He was a Mr. Spring Rice, a nephew of Lord Monteagle's. On one occasion he sat next her at dinner, leant back in his chair, fixed his eyes on her and said : "Miss Lyttelton, you have a very enthusiastic temperament." "And she thrilled," writes the great-niece who was recording this reminiscence. However, in spite of this somewhat indefinite approach, he married someone else very soon afterwards, and poor Caroline remembered ever afterwards the pattern of the wool she was working on when her brother told her of his engagement.

Her other suitor was Lord Dartmouth. This proposal was regarded as something of a family joke. She was thirty-five at the time and his lordship was some twenty years older. He had been twice married, his second wife had just died and his proposal was couched in the following terms : "There are six little children hoping to call you Mamma." She refused him but she must have had lingering regrets for only a very few years before she died in 1902 she came into Lucy Cavendish's room on her maid's arm saying : "I must speak to my mother! I feel I have been hasty in refusing Lord Dartmouth."

Meanwhile, however, her emotional life had flowed into other channels, treated so lightly and as a matter of course by Victorians. After their father's death the four unmarried Pole-Carew girls had come under the care of their uncle and aunt Lyttelton. Three of them married almost immediately but the

* Lord Morpeth, son of Lady Carlisle, Sarah Spencer's first cousin.

fourth, Kitty, stayed on and became a permanent member of the widowed Lady Lyttelton's household. She was a gentle, unselfish, self-abnegating person and her character complemented the dominating personality of Caroline Lyttelton. They soon began to call themselves husband and wife and their relations referred to them in the same terms. In 1847 Kitty was away staying in Cornwall with her married sister, Caroline Estcourt, and Sarah Lyttelton wrote to the latter: "I don't wonder at the general conspiring of all female relations to entrap dear Kitty—and if a paragon were proposed, I should truly rejoice, either that she or even her present husband should be snapped up—*but* it must be *such* a paragon to satisfy me! and I half doubt whether the best extant, wherever he is, would ensure a decidedly improved happiness to either of our darling old maids."

The association was so close that they were often referred to by the next generation as one person "Aunt Coquitty".*

There is one member of the Lyttelton family still living (1974) who well remembers Aunt Coque on her annual visits to Hagley. She was always pressed to sing as part of the Christmas festivities and accompanied by the thunderous applause of two or three generations, she would, in her faded cracked voice with coquettish archings of her withered neck, oblige with a song of which the refrain ran:

> "What will you have Miss
> White wine or red?
> Mixed if you please
> Said she."

Aunt Coque herself could remember her grandmother coming into the library at Althorp and saying: "Now Lord Spencer, which is it to be, whist or cribbage? If it's whist I come, if it's cribbage Sal comes." The words were imprinted on the child's memory because of the voice, the most charming she had ever heard, low and utterly musical. These two completely trivial reminiscences seem to bear us back over one hundred and fifty years, so that the past seems so close we can almost touch it, as if a door had shut on someone who had just left the room before we entered it.

The most remarkable of the Lyttelton children was un-

* Caroline Lyttelton was always known as Aunt Coque.

doubtedly George William, the eldest son. He was an eccentric in his own time and would have been in any other and his character is so strange, elusive and many-faceted that it is difficult to give a complete picture of it.

Physically he was short, square and rather ugly. The story has often been told how at their double wedding* the villagers of Hawarden contemplating the two bridegrooms and admiring Mr. Gladstone's elegant profile and shining dark eyes said: "Ah it's easy to tell who's the Lord." At four years old his mother described him as "grown as handsome as red hair and irregular features will allow, with quite a striking impression of frankness and manliness in his face, and a very tall stout figure." In photographs of later life George looks rather like a surly young bull and even Richmond who could be relied on to prettify his sitters could not do much with the 4th Lord Lyttelton.

Mentally he was out of the ordinary. In some ways a scholar of the first rank, his acquaintance with the classics was remarkable. Nor was it assumed in order to win academic triumphs; his love for them was genuine and deep. He would recline at Lord's, watching the cricket and reading Latin verse in between the balls, and his daughter records that he kept sea-sickness at bay on a Channel crossing by recourse to Greek verse. Yet in common with many Victorians, all this classical learning that must have given him insight into a past civilization and other worlds never shook the fundamental tenets that he had learnt as a child, never led him to question even for a moment the dogmatic assertions of Christian belief.

But it is his moral character that is the most remarkable part of his make-up. Its basis was a complete sincerity that was almost naive in its simplicity. It never occurred to him to veil any opinion or to put on an act of any kind. This naturally often led to tactlessness and to somewhat unusual behaviour. In his brief spell as Under Secretary of the Colonial Office his chief, Gladstone, had to rebuke him for amending the minutes of senior civil servants; as Chairman of the Commission for Endowed Schools, he managed to put up the backs of every possible opponent and ally; when he drove around the countryside of Worcestershire he frequently amused himself by flicking at passers-by with his gig-whip, which indulgence was

* Mr. Gladstone and Lord Lyttelton married two sisters Catherine and Mary Glynne on July 25th 1839.

greeted with a shower of stones, but it was no more ill-humoured
on either side than the napkin fights with his sons in which he
used to indulge after dinner. Equally, although he annoyed his
colleagues, there was none that did not respect him for his
qualities of honesty, sense of duty and drudging hard work.
These were the keynotes of his character. It will be for a later
chapter to examine the amount of effort he put into the foundation of the Canterbury Settlement in New Zealand, but it is
equally revealing of his character to note that for thirty years
he taught in the Sunday school at Hagley and his family never
knew that he had always hated it until he gave it up. Again, if
he came back from hunting in time for daily Evening Service,
he would slip an overcoat over his hunting pink and quite
unselfconsciously tramp up the aisle of Hagley Church with his
spurs clanking on the stone pavement.

His religion pervaded his whole life but it was not a narrow
or a joyless creed. He was a most enthusiastic huntsman as long
as he could afford to keep a hunter. To his family's apprehen-
sion he loved driving four in hand. His devotion to cricket is
legendary and he was also a very keen billiards player. Nor was
his religion an emotional overflow in words or in preaching. He
was on the whole an inarticulate man. His letters are short and
concise, his diary has the practical directness of an engagement
book. On a particularly remarkable day such as the one on which
he was an accepted suitor, he permits himself a comment in Latin:
"Dies plusquam memorabilis."

He never said much to his sons yet somehow they knew that
any moral failure on their part would cause him an agony of
grief. He was more articulate with his daughters but his deep
affection for them only came out during his fits of melancholia.

His feeling were in fact like some volcano, fiery and very
deep, and only occasionally erupting. On one occasion, when
his little son Edward pulled a marble table down on himself
and was taken up unconscious, his father became nearly distraught with emotion and grief. Such outbursts were rare; his
general outward attitude towards his children was to murmur
"Absurd little monkies", as he passed through the schoolroom
where they were working, but the effort of containing such
extraordinarily-strong emotions may have contributed to the
fits of black melancholy which marked his later life.

The early part of his career was almost unrelievedly happy

except for one thing which probably had some influence on his character. He was subject to ear trouble, painful discharges and abscesses, which led to deafness. It was always being said that this condition would soon be cured; it never was, and in his early youth it probably led to another great drawback, his painful and almost debilitating shyness. Among his own kin he was singularly bright-tempered. "This last quality I don't believe I ever knew him equalled in," wrote his mother to Mrs. Pole-Carew, "it is not only high spirits and glee when all goes *à son gré*, but the cheerfulest endurance of disappointments, and the mildest and kindest receiving of advice and reproof; nothing ever brings a cloud . . . I ought to beg pardon and be ashamed of myself for saying so much about my own son, but I have reasons, or excuses, twain. First and foremost, and sufficient, that it is to *you*, who are a very real auntie and sister. And secondly, that it is his unhappy fate to be praised by none but those who know him thoroughly; his shyness is so excessive, that all strangers suppose him surly, proud, stupid and silent, and with very good reason; I can't wonder at them."

It might be supposed that an inordinately shy, partially-deaf boy would be particularly unhappy in his school life. This, however, was not so. Spencer disliked the Navy, Billy detested Winchester, but George appears to have been devoted to Eton almost from the very start. It was presumably there that he imbibed his passion for cricket, though he never figured in the School XI; it was certainly there that he became devoted to the classics. He had to postpone his first attempt on the Newcastle* because of an access of ear trouble, but he achieved it without difficulty the following year. He left Eton for Cambridge in 1835 but he remained one of her most devoted sons. He was asked to examine for the Newcastle only a few years after he himself had won it, and this was one of his dearest ambitions. In later years he became a Fellow and as eight Lyttelton sons followed one another in and out of the school yard, their father remained in close touch with "the best of schools" for over fifty years.

He was equally fortunate and happy at Cambridge. To enter the University at this time one had to have some smattering of mathematics and since this was not George's forte he was given special coaching by William Brookfield, who was later to marry the lady who became Thackeray's Egeria. Brookfield, "a lank,

* The chief classical scholarship provided by Eton.

lean unearthly shadow", as Sarah Lyttelton described him, was only a few years older than his pupil and became a life-long friend. To him George confided his first impressions of Cambridge. "There is nothing to pump out of the uniformity of this delectable spot but dullness," he wrote, "for I really find it not too unpleasant. We smoke—we read—we become unsocial and narrow-minded—we feel monastic . . . we drink Gesserheim—we pay reluctant Sunday visits to Lord Braybrooke—we talk of books getting through the Pitt Press—we feel like a fellow" (Capital F probably intended here)—"we walk across the grass*—we look at our fair ladies the which you may remember in our study†—we are pious—we are worldly and ambitious . . . we wish for our Brookfield, a man of much facetiousness & dubiousness of futurity."‡

George did not spend his whole time in the lounging way indicated by this first letter. A few months later he writes that he is working so hard that he is becoming "a mere machine for Greek and Latin" and that when he has a theme to write he has "plenty of Latin but *no ideas*. I occasionally rather fret . . . " he goes on, "and do not much pity your entire solitude which I sometimes have a sneaking affection for. But, our nature is two-fold—& my enjoyment of society, & society spirits, are as high as ever, being altogether a super addition to my inner feeling."

In fact, although he was working extremely hard, George, who seems to have overcome his shyness, was also deeply involved in tutorial and undergraduate friendships, which were to remain with him for the rest of his life.

His tutor was the Rev. J. W. Blakesley, who afterwards became Dean of Lincoln. Blakesley was probably a very salutary influence on an enthusiastic young man at the time of the beginning of the Oxford Movement. He had a sense of proportion and a dry wit. Mary Lyttelton observed, possibly with some disapproval, that he seemed more like a lawyer than a churchman, though he amused her with an anecdote of an Evangelical preacher who addressed his congregation as "well-dressed worms".

---

* Only Fellows were and are allowed to walk on the grass in the courts at Trinity, but George as a Fellow Commoner would have had this privilege.
† Pin-ups of some kind?
‡ Brookfield was always longing for some sort of settled appointment and living. At this time he was trying to be a Naval Chaplain.

His dry humour was probably a useful antidote to the other main influence of George Lyttelton's Cambridge days. He had been elected a member of the Apostles and among the brethren his greatest friends were George Smythe and Lord John Manners who were later to become the ringleaders of the political movement "Young England".*

This Cambridge set was not quite the equivalent of Oxford's Movement although its ideals were much the same: romanticism, Gothicism, Church and monarchy. Yet there was a definite difference between the two. The Oxford leaders nearly all stemmed from a parsonical or Non-conformist background, to them the Church, the romantic mediaeval church, purged of Protestantism, of compromise and reform, was the be-all and end-all of their crusade. Their Cambridge contemporaries looked at the world from a more comprehensive standpoint. Their fathers were mostly legislators and they had wider ideas not only of what they wished to accomplish but of how it was to be obtained. This is not to say that they were basically wiser. The list of Lord John Manners' crusades comprises as silly a set of objects as any young man ever set out to achieve (naturally he failed in most of them from the Restoration of Don Carlos as absolute monarch of Spain to the Gothicization of the Foreign Office), but at least while Oxford was lashing itself into a frenzy about Tract 39 he was touring the factories of Manchester and corresponding with George Lyttelton about what was to be done about the Poor Law. It is true that he, Smythe and Lyttelton were uncompromisingly High Church or Puseyite as it was then called. Manners and Smythe were much influenced by a visit in 1838 to Frederick Faber, who then held a cure at Ambleside in the Lake District, a three-cornered friendship, which became a "sort of reciprocal hero-worship", probably with some overtones of homosexuality on Faber's part at least, but as shrewd Doctor Blakesley observed to Lord Lyttelton, "it is quite obvious that the religious views have grown out of the political, and that if we strip off the hide of Newman we shall find Filmer† underneath".

Lyttelton had been far too much exposed to Whig influences

---

* The phrase may have originated with Blakesley who used it of undergraduates in general.

† Sir Robert Filmer, d. 1653. A political philosopher who advocated "the Natural Power of Kings".

to take the same attitude as his friends towards despotic rule and the divine right of kings; but although he never seems to have come under Faber's influence—there was no tinge of homosexuality in his make-up and he was on the verge of getting married—religion and specifically High Church religion was quite as important to him as it was to Manners and very much more so than it was to Smythe. Indeed, it is rather surprising that such high-minded, almost priggish young men as Manners and Lyttelton should have been so deeply attached to George Smythe who was often cynical, always debauched, a compulsive womanizer and continually in debt. Nevertheless his charm in his more idealistic days must have been compelling.* "He was the sun and centre of all my happiness and my hopes," wrote John Manners to Lyttelton when Smythe died worn out in 1857, "and . . . we never tired of auguring for him a dazzling career of glory." More moderately Lyttelton is said to have commented: "Poor George, a brilliant failure."

Smythe's political ambitions were high (he was the original of Disraeli's Coningsby) but there George Lyttelton never aspired to follow him. His deafness was a very obvious drawback and though he was a Tory his later family connection with the Gladstones precluded him from any contact with the charismatic leader to whom Young England pinned its faith. Others, however, predicted for Lyttelton a brilliant political career. "The sort of statesman I expect you to make," wrote Blakesley, "is a sort of mixture of Gladstone and Lord Stanley but with more caution and temper than the latter, and more courage (& I may possibly add more genius) than the former." He coupled his prognostications with a few bits of tutorial advice. He tells George to take care that his "catholicity of taste and capacity for enjoyment of all kinds does not prevent you from devoting yourself to your real duties". Never as it turned out was caution less needed! In a later letter George is also greatly recommended "to limit strictly theological enquiries to the solution of practical questions." "With your occupation," the professional Blakesley goes on, "you have not time to enter into them fully . . . if you *dabble* in theology you may rue the consequences. If you are willing to give up many years to deep study—to subject yourself to many painful

* Although Mary Lyttelton in later years wrote to Catherine Gladstone: "The Smythes go tomorrow. Such a delight, he is like a hairdresser."

doubts and uncertainties which the inquirer into such high subjects must necessarily encounter in his progress towards the region of light and firm ground,—well and good. If not, hold to the rule I speak off: confine yourself to such questions as affect you practically." Here again his advice was either taken or not needed: never throughout his life, even at the time of his deepest melancholy, did the shadow of a doubt as to religion ever cross Lord Lyttelton's mind.

Blakesley's advice was not all on this high level and was perhaps none the worse for that. "People who know you," he wrote, amid his congratulations on the successful result of the Tripos, "are aware that your heart is as good as your head, but those who do not (particularly elderly people, who are sensitive to such things) sometimes find your manner rather rough to them." They are liable, the sensible letter goes on, to impute roughness "either to an indifference to the feelings of others, or to a notion of self-importance; an opinion which, false as it is, is worth escaping merely at the price of yawning or cracking walnuts with an absent countenance while a stupid story is being recounted to one."

The tutor, however, was immensely proud of his pupil and with reason. In 1836 George Lyttelton gained the Craven Scholarship* and in 1837 he came out top in the Classical Tripos bracketed with D. W. Vaughan, the crack Rugby scholar, afterwards headmaster of Harrow. Blakesley later told George that all the examiners except one thought he was a shade better than Vaughan and that the Vice Chancellor's opinion was that the latter had just passed his prime while Lyttelton had not yet come to his "and that if the examination had been put off for six months, he would have had no chance against you".

A more earthy compliment came from an old Eton schoolfellow which must have pleased George for he preserved it. "Another thing gives me great pleasure," wrote one T. Phinn, a student at Lincoln's Inn, "& that is the style in which you have discomfited those cocky Rugby men,† who have done nothing but cry up Vaughan, what with Stanley in Oxford &

---

* The Craven Scholarships were founded in the seventeenth century by Lord Craven, two at Oxford and two at Cambridge. To become a Craven scholar is to obtain the Blue Ribbon of Classical Scholarship.

† "Rugby may be more clever!" Eton Boating Song.

Vaughan at Cambridge they want an Eton Man sometimes to give them a licking."

Lord Lyttelton lived just long enough to see and rejoice in his son's academic triumphs. He died immediately after George left Cambridge and the young man was henceforth his own master. He does not seem to have been particularly affected by his father's death. In his reply to Brookfield's letter of condolence he dwells on his mother's grief but does not allude to his own loss and he sends his first franked* letter to Blakesley with obvious enjoyment. This seeming heartlessness may have been partly a Spencer characteristic. William Lyttelton commented to Sarah on Lord Spencer's "insensibility" after his wife's death, and attributes it to "your Father's never assuming a Feeling, or the appearance of one, when he has it not, which almost every human creature does". This relentless sincerity descended to Sarah and through her to George William.

In 1838 the young Lord went abroad and had a hurried tour in Italy and France which he does not seem to have much enjoyed — at least he wrote to his younger brother Billy who had inherited his rooms in Trinity that "Cambridge is the nicest place in Europe". We have a glimpse of him in Paris where he dined at the Embassy with Harriet Granville who had once been Sarah Spencer's best friend. "If Lord Lyttelton was more aware of what he is about, whom he is talking to, if he were more master of his limbs and tongue, and minded his stops," the Ambassadress wrote to her brother the Duke of Devonshire, "we should be able to get at the quantity of excellent stuff of all kinds which I am sure is in him."

Lady Granville was an unusually intelligent and perceptive woman of fifty-four. It was not surprising that she should recognize his potential. What does seem rather curious is that her opinion should be shared by a lovely, much-courted girl, four years older than himself, who might have been expected to look on him as an ungainly hobbledehoy with uncouth manners, and not to see any further.

George Lyttelton had been in love with Mary Glynne since he was eighteen. We do not know exactly where they first met. It was quite possibly at her uncle Lord Braybrooke's seat Audley End, which is close to Cambridge and where William

* Peers and M.P.s were allowed to send letters free by signing their names on the cover during the times that Parliament was sitting.

LADY SARAH SPENCER

This miniature was given by Sarah to her second son Spencer when he went to sea. She wrote in 1835: "it is not very like now to be sure! But I remember myself very like it . . ."

WILLIAM HENRY,
3rd Lord Lyttelton

MARY, *neé* GLYNNE, wife of George 4th Lord Lyttelton

GEORGE, 4th Lord Lyttelton

brought his son to stay on the latter's introduction to Cambridge. On that occasion his manners seem to have been characteristic. "I think George behaved *very* well," wrote his indulgent father, "allowance being made for his irresistible propensity to lay hold of, occasionally, and bury himself in a Book, whether any Body is speaking to him, or not; & one or two little *neglegences* [sic] & *ignorances* of no moment." It does not sound like behaviour calculated to encourage any ordinary fashionable young lady but Mary Glynne was no ordinary girl.

She was one of a family of four, two boys and two girls. Her father Sir Stephen Glynne had died young of consumption. He had just had time to convert the family seat in North Wales from a charming Georgian house to a crocketted, battlemented, turretted sham Gothic castle, to marry Mary Neville, Lord Braybrooke's sister, and to father four children, when his lungs collapsed utterly and the doctors ordered him to a warm climate. It was of course useless and he died in Naples in 1815. His widow managed to bring her little family — Mary still a baby in arms — back through war-torn Europe and henceforth devoted her life to her children. Stephen, the heir to the title, was an unusually intelligent precocious child with a strong early developed interest in ecclesiology. He was, however, not cut out for a country clergyman, a destiny reserved for his younger brother Henry. Stephen should really have been the Fellow of a college, able to devote his entire life to his overriding interests, Church ceremonies, archaeology and music, and with no sublunary cares. He was not fitted for the management of an estate. Henry, was less intelligent but perhaps even more lovable (they were known as the gentle brethren), and as soon as his uncle Gerald Neville-Grenville retired or obtained preferment, it was understood that he would succeed to the large Georgian rectory, standing almost in the churchyard of the small grey square-towered church of Hawarden and a stone's throw from the Park gates.

After Henry came the two girls with only one year dividing them. Catherine was the dominating figure in the family. Fizzing with energy and *joie de vivre*, she made herself the centre of any circle in which she moved and so much has been written of her that the younger gentler Mary has perhaps been overlooked. But Mary had her own appeal. Quieter, better balanced, less impulsive but just as loving as her sister, she was to all those

3

who knew her the most entrancing and delightful character, and even now to pick up any one of her day-to-day, unliterary, unpunctuated letters is to feel something of her charm.

The two sisters were devoted. Catherine was known as Pussy at home and they were frequently alluded to as "the Pussies". The family was very closely knit and they had evolved between them what was almost a private shorthand language, full of allusions and turns of phrase, which must have been puzzling to a stranger, but which once understood comes to have almost an addictive compulsion. Years later George Lyttelton was to compile a little dictionary of its current phrases which he called the Glynnese* Glossary. He was, he says, standing on the steps of Hawarden listening to Stephen Glynne and his sisters exchanging farewells and he realized that an outsider would hardly have understood a word that they said and was inspired to provide a key to the mystery. Such *jeux d'esprit* are generally delightful at the time and to the persons involved, but the Glynnese Glossary, in its mock pompous style, is so charmingly written and the language itself is so witty and so apropos that it can still be read with pleasure. It is impossible to quote the whole book but where Glynnese turns up in letters the gloss will be given in Lord Lyttelton's own words.

One example may be appropriately quoted here.

FALSE FLASH

A common and popular expression among the Glynnese, and apparently a sporting or military metaphor, as of a gun flashing in the pan: and so used to signify any sham appearance of splendour, power, or the like, when the substance is wanting. Lady Glynne applied it to her daughter's marriage with Lord Lyttelton, alluding to the combination, in that nobleman's circumstances, of respectable rank with comparative poverty: "quite a false flash".

Both the widowed mothers had reservations about the marriage but there were strong influences working in favour of George. During the winter of 1838/39 the Miss Glynnes had also been travelling in Italy though their path does not appear to have crossed George Lyttelton's. It did, however, cross that

* Though actually it should probably have been Neville-ese since it probably started with the older generation, Lady Glynne and her brother, the Rector of Hawarden.

of William Ewart Gladstone. In Naples he fell in love with Catherine Glynne, in Rome he proposed to her, and after they returned to London they became engaged. It is stated in many biographies that Gladstone was a friend of George Lyttelton's. I can find no documentary evidence to this effect though it is likely they met through Lord John Manners. The connection was probably not very close. George was nine years younger than William and though they were both Etonians they had attended different universities. However, George was just the kind of young man of whom Gladstone would have strongly approved. He was a High Churchman, a first-class Classical Scholar and Gladstone had quite enough discernment to appreciate the "quality of excellent stuff of all kinds" which Lady Granville had suspicioned.

The Pussies had always done everything together and when Catherine got engaged it was natural that Mary should wish to be so too, yet she hesitated. "What makes you think I like Lyttelton better than I think?" she asked her brother Henry in a letter written on June 3rd 1839. "You funny creature to wish me so much to accept him, I will very soon put him out of his misery although he begs me not to do it yet, but certainly should it be in the negative it must be done soon for he is in a dreadful state, taking on at nothing."

But if Mary hesitated her relations seemed to be pretty sure on which side she would come down. Her aunt Caroline, the formidable Lady Wenlock, Lady Glynne's sister, had actually interviewed Lady Lyttelton about the match. More pertinently "Pussy" Mary's *alter ego* seems to have no doubts. "Nothing could be sweeter or nicer than her [Lady Lyttelton's] manner about the whole affair," Catherine Glynne told Henry in an addition to the same letter in which Mary had expressed her doubts, "our minds are much more at ease now his Mother knows the exact *footing* it is upon and she said everything that was most satisfactory relative to Mary's conduct & even said that of all people in the world she stood highest in her estimation." (Catherine's pronouns are sadly mixed but the sense is clear.) " 'Her beauty is her least [illegible]' to quote her own words. Meanwhile the poor son neither *eats* or *sleeps*. You will be interested to know about the exact details concerning money matters — he has £3000 a year now to spend — will have £7000 & has some iron shares wh may come to something good" [they never did!] "but Ly L. does not wish this to be reckoned upon there is a debt of £1300 upon the estate wch Ld. L. is paying off by degrees—so much for the money . . . Mary prefers meeting Lyttelton accidentally in the park or elsewhere to *settled* expeditions wch are too marked before she has actually made up her mind to accept him in this *I quite agree*."

But Mary was not allowed to remain or to keep George in a state of uncertainty. Catherine and her William were all in favour of the match and their influence was predominant. On June 17th 1839 in the drawing-room of the Glynnes' house in Berkeley Square Mary accepted Lyttelton while the other engaged pair waited on the floor below. It has often been told how Gladstone seized hold of the young man dazed with happiness who descended the stairs and pulled him down on to his knees so that together they might give thanks to Almighty God.

Neither of the two mothers came to the wedding. Lady Glynne had lately had a slight stroke and had slid into melancholia. "My nights are wretched and the length of the days quite interminable," she wrote to Catherine a month after the marriage. And again in October of the same year. "I poor wretch can do nothing. You have no idea how much the distressed feelings increase and bother."

Lady Lyttelton's reason for non-attendance was more mundane. Caroline and Lavinia had developed measles and she was shut up with them in strict quarantine at Hagley.

In spite of, or perhaps owing to, the absence of the two mothers the wedding was a very gay affair. Three local bands, the Hawarden Castle Lodge of Odd Fellows of the Independent Orders of Manchester Unity Band, the Hawarden Temperance Societies Band and the Benefit Societies Band preceded the white satin brides up the road leading to the small squat church, not in those days disfigured with sculptures and stained glass commemorating most of the principal characters in the bridal procession. The "good feeling" of the inhabitants had led them to cover the path with "rich carpeting" and "beautiful children strewed flowers before the brides". In the church Stephen gave away Catherine and Henry Mary, the promises were made, the vows taken and two of the happiest marriages of the Victorian or any other era were set on their way.

MARY Lyttelton arrived at her new house in a chaise and four at half past nine in the evening of her wedding-day. They rattled along the avenue at full speed, for George prided himself on his skill as a whip,* and were greeted at the front door by Mrs. Ellis, the housekeeper "pale and fussy" receiving those "she had barely learnt to call 'My Lord and Lady'."

Mary's mother-in-law and sisters-in-law were in the house, but they "poor pill-garlicks† with red faces and swoln hands," were still secluded on account of the quarantine of measles. Sarah Lyttelton described how when the bridal couple were safely out for the day she crept into the library "just like the White Lady", to get or return books or newspapers; and "there I found a small pair of feminine gloves lying about, and other little symptoms of a change". The two parties bowed to each other from either side of the aisle in church and notes passed but "till Monday we never heard their voices or saw them near . . . very odd altogether." The meeting when it did take place was exceedingly brief, for Mary and George left almost immediately to join the Gladstones on their Scotch honeymoon.

This tour of the Highlands, though decidedly less adventurous than William's and Sarah's bridal journey in Sweden and Russia, was yet a somewhat unconventional essay; and a passing traveller has left a charming picture of the two pretty young women riding sidesaddle, wrapped in Lennox tartans (to which they had no possible claim) and the young men tramping at the ponies' heads. The tour ended at Fasque, the Gladstone family place, John Gladstone having before the wedding written

---

* He once told his daughter that he was prouder of being able to turn a tandem in the Great Court at Trinity than of winning his Craven scholarship.

† Pilgarlic: A "pilled" or bald head; a bald-headed man; from seventeenth century applied in a ludicrously contemptuous way; "poor creature". Oxford Dictionary.

an old-fashioned courteous letter to Mary, bidding her welcome as another daughter-in-law.

After Fasque there came a round of visits to joint relations, the Gladstones taking in the Braybrookes and Wenlocks, and the Lytteltons the Spencers and the Devonshires. It was from Chatsworth that Mary wrote as follows to her sister.

"My Sweetest: Your precious letter greeted me soon after our arrival, it was as one may think [illegible] nothing cd be more beautiful than dear William's speech to you, and it is only worthy of the delicate and feeling way in wch he petted me in town before our engagement I can fancy it all, and now see you hiding yr. face in his neck, dearest, my pleasure is praying for you; at times I cannot believe it, it does if possible make you doubly dear to me you know I told you I sd love yr babby quite as well as mine own, may God help you, and dearest William. This letter is not to be read to him for I am writing at full speed round a table surrounded by people just going directly but I cd not bear you sd have a blank post on such a subject, it is not quite [illegible] time there is no chance for me yet. The Duke handed me arm in arm to my bedroom wch wd have killed you."

This breathless erratically-punctuated, undated letter, hopping from Catherine's future baby to the Duke, is essentially typical of Mary's correspondence—she must have written just as she talked with an indescribable warmth, sweetness and charm.

What she meant by her penultimate sentence "there is no chance for me yet," is not quite clear but if it refers to a coming baby she was wrong.

Mary's first baby must have been conceived almost directly after Pussy's, just as her engagement had followed her sister's. Returned to Hagley in October she wrote: "I have just written to Ly. Lyttelton to tell her a very simple short note but she cannot bear palaver ... George read ye Encyclopedia [sic] yesterday and read such horrors there that he was quite faint [two words erased] do not let William do ye same."

We do not know if Gladstone did brave the horrors of the Encyclopedia but in his own way he was obviously just as moved as his brother-in-law. He wrote to the latter in the ponderous, well-punctuated style, that was as characteristic of him as Mary Lyttelton's spontaneous outpouring was of her, but which nevertheless betrayed deep feeling. "I am sorry to hear Mary is now suffering so much; it has been very severe with Catherine but from the experience of last week I trust she has now got over the preparatory sickness. We have both the greatest reason to be thankful and not less to be anxious both with a view to the immediate crisis and to our subsequent responsibilities."

Sarah Lyttelton, in more down to earth eighteenth-century style, wrote a month later on hearing of Mary's increasing girth. "I wish you joy of the lengthening of your sash — you will perhaps not *quite* like the symptoms by the time the sash is *very* long, however George may admire it!"

She was able to judge for herself of Mary's size and George's devotion for, in January 1840, she returned to Hagley for the first time as a visitor. It must have been a strange experience for her and a somewhat daunting moment for her daughter-in-law, but the latter was much sustained and helped by the presence of her beloved sister.

Catherine wrote to William describing her arrival at six o'clock on a dark January evening. "The darkness only allowed me just to see an immense mass of buildings, very nervous at getting out having a variety of emotions upon first seeing Mary in her new home wch were not lessened by being *alone*" — William had been kept in London on Parliamentary business — "she and George were awaiting me at the top of the stairs, the latter almost screamed with pleasure at seeing me. Mary was *almost* as trembling as I was. Ly Lyttelton had arrived a little before me our evening not a little spoilt although she is charming and her tact almost unrivalled . . . however I was of assistance to Mary in this 1st evening of Ly Lyttelton's in spite of being tired and sleepy, which made me '*hardly human*'* to bed at ten. Did my Willy miss me as much as I did him?"

On the whole, however, in spite of the spoilt first evening, which must have been a difficult occasion for every one, the visit was a great success. "Mary seems to do all so nicely and to be quite at home," wrote Catherine, "there they sit at the head of their table, like two old married people as sedate as possible I cannot help feeling pleased to see her in such a home but how

---

* *Glynnese*: "not human. It is a favourite phrase of Mrs. Gladstone's and seems to mean only one thing, namely 'very absent', but again it does not mean one *habitually* so, but for the time, for some particular reason."

doubly thankful to be able to think of her with such a Husband!"

On one occasion when George was away for the night the two sisters slept together "like old days different however for little Pussy bounded away much to Mary's delight." "Little Pussy" who turned out to be "little Willy" was a most active baby. In another letter Catherine said "My Pussy resembles a Squirrel at this moment; Ly L. says mine will be a boy and Mary's a girl."

Catherine was obviously becoming very fond of Ly L. whom she admired immensely. She studied the older woman's book of instructions on household accounts and when Sarah offered her and the Gladstones a perch in her rented house in Eaton Square, till they could find something of their own, Catherine was much struck by the tact with which the proposal was made. "She says we shall air it and save her coals! is not this a gentlemanlike way of doing it?"

The way this visit passed off, the good relations immediately established with Catherine and, more importantly, with Mary do indeed show not only "an unrivalled tact" on Sarah's part but a true goodness of heart. For in spite of her honied words to Lady Glynne Sarah's first reaction to George's marriage had been one of dismay. It is probable that with great good sense she never committed her feelings to paper, or that, if she did, the letters were subsequently destroyed, but we get a glimpse of what they must have been in a letter written to her husband's niece, Caroline Estcourt,* in 1844. After expressing her satisfaction with the then state of affairs at Hagley, she adds that it is all "owing to George's marriage to Mary Glynne, just the very thing I used to fancy I dreaded and disliked".

The dread and dislike were far from unnatural. Sarah was well broken in to the harsh but practical law of succession, which decrees that a woman is turned out of the house she had made her home for all or most of her married life, the house in which she has brought up her children, ruled her servants, watched over her husband's death bed, to make way for a complete stranger. She could never have thought of questioning it. But George was only just twenty-one when he married; she might have counted on another six or seven years during which

---

* Caroline Estcourt was the daughter of Caroline Pole-Carew. Sarah was extremely fond of her and she enjoyed her aunt's confidence to a very high degree. Sarah's letters to her are perhaps franker than to anyone else.

she could have remained the head of the household, entertained
for and perhaps married her daughters, and made a home for
her younger sons. She had, however, a strong suspicion that
this was not to be; George had fallen in love with Mary at the
age of eighteen, had made no secret of his intentions, and she
knew that she would have to make arrangements for herself
and her daughters. She was not well off. She had a large debt
to Mr. Baker, the local solicitor, on which she paid interest and
she was worried about the amount she would be able to leave
Caroline and Lavinia. "If I leave it [my fortune] to them
entire, they will be enabled by it, *just* and with difficulty to
maintain themselves in something like their rank in life" she
wrote to George. "If I die in debt . . . it must all be paid out of
their fortune and I shall leave them much poorer than your
Father meant they should be, and in fact in little better than a
dependent situation—after giving them an education, tastes
and habits, fit for rich people, and leading them by their
observation of my way of life, to expect a competency."

When therefore her eldest brother, Lord Spencer, the leader
of Melbourne's Government in the Lords, wrote, immediately
after the Queen's accession in 1837, to offer Sarah the post of
Lady of the Bedchamber, Sarah was really perplexed. She
answers him in a long letter full of doubts and hesitations
putting the pros and cons of the case. One suspects that the
sentence "I agree with all your *private* reasons for my accepting
her offer" may refer to George's possible marriage, but that is
not otherwise alluded to. She places her doubts on the grounds
that she thinks herself "*peculiarly* indiscreet in talk, and wanting
in calm and ready decision in conduct," which seems a strange
view of her own character. She hesitates in case her acceptance
should compromise George who is leaning towards the Tory
side in politics, she wonders "how I am to curtsy and stand, and
drive in open carriages, I don't at all guess," and she feels "ever
an increased bitter regret of the happiness of my past years".
Yet she realizes that the advantages of her children will be very
great and she asks her brother to advise her and promises to
follow his advice. He obviously came down in favour of the
proposal, for on October 2nd 1838 nine months before George's
impending marriage Sarah Lyttelton went into waiting and
entered upon a new life.

It began at Windsor which then, and ever afterwards, was

go on the Terrace and keep quite in sight. *Pray* let me go !' [says Lady L. yes. yes !]."

Her feelings about the Queen in those days were not so very different from those she cherished about the Maids of Honour. She obviously felt most motherly towards her and also in many ways admired her very much, but her attitude, coming as she did from one of the great Whig families, is very different from the reverential romantic one of her granddaughter Lucy when she in her turn came to Court to serve the then widowed Queen.

Sarah frequently refers to the Queen as the "Zit". "If H.M. could wear fewer than *four* different wraps [all to be taken care of and put on] to go there" [to the theatre] "without a bouquet *and* a bag *and* an opera glass, there would be no difficulty at all. But she continues very patient and kind, and a very nice zit altogether." The worst of Lady Lyttelton's trials as attendant on her royal mistress came at the prorogation of Parliament in August 1849. The Queen herself was frightened. "No-one could have guessed it ;" wrote Sarah, "*we* knew by the crimson colour of her face and neck, and a little trembling." And Lady Lyttelton's own duties were unexpectedly arduous. She had to unpin and take off the Diamond Diadem and replace it with the great Crown of England and "*pin it on*! with two Diamond pins through the velvet and her hair at the back of her head." This went well enough but having to perform the operation in reverse, she *could not* she wrote, find the proper place for the last pin on the diadem, and "first ran it against her Royal Head (upon which she looked up with a comical look of entreaty) and then could not put it in at all, anywhere, so she went without it."

Luckily all passed over with the utmost good humour ; Baroness Lehzen was enabled to make an English pun "O! do not mind, do not care a pin for de pin !", and Lord Melbourne, who out of his vast stores of miscellaneous reading always had an appropriate example, quoted Mary Queen of Scots who, when disrobed by her executioners, said, "I am not accustomed to be undressed before so many people, nor by such attendants."

One of the secrets of Lady Lyttelton's success at Court was that she seemed to be able to get on with all of the various sometimes conflicting personalities. She was very fond of the Duchess of Kent but she was also friendly with Baroness Lehzen and records as a pleasing sight the latter's pale face "with her usual half anxious, smiling, fixed look following the Queen from the Castle windows". She appears to have taken no sides in the Lady Flora Hastings scandal except to support the Queen. "What do you mean about the Queen being 'found out' ," she wrote to her son George. "Poor little soul there is nothing to find out about her. She has done nothing and said nothing that I know of, to want hiding or to discredit her—abt. Ly. Flora I mean—only nobody can know or believe the truth." And a week later she added: "I have not seen Sir James Clark's statement—nor do I much care for it. I suppose I may live to the dropping of the subject but I doubt it notwithstanding the greenness of my old age—it grows a dreadful bore."

The Queen on her side immediately took to Lady Lyttelton. She had of course the advantage of being approved by the Queen's guide, philosopher and friend. "Lord Melbourne thinks her a very nice person which she certainly is," Victoria wrote in her journal, "I asked how she was related to him; he replied 'She was my wife's first cousin, and I used to see a great deal of her at that time'." It is fascinating to think of the old man's memories going back to that summer at Ryde, thirty years ago, when he and Caroline had joined the Spencers' sailing parties. He may also have remembered how kind Sarah had always been to poor little Augustus Lamb, his mentally-defective child. She, on her part, though she never wholly approved of him (she found him greedy and probably thought him godless) could not help being fond of him. "I shall," she wrote after he had had his first stroke, "[if I survive him] wear my cousin's mourning with much sincerity, for the strange, inconsistent, but amiable man."

Even without the Melbourne relationship the Queen would probably have liked Lady Lyttelton, who had a quality of ready unfeigned sympathy. "Went and played at battledore and shuttlecock in the Gallery with Lady Lyttelton," runs an entry in the Queen's Journal (Lady Lyttelton was fifty-two at this point which was quite an old lady for those days!) "who is such an amiable person, and felt so much for my losing my dearest Cousins; the remembrance of that merry rainy Monday, when we played at Ninepins etc., together was very painful."

These cousins were not Albert and Ernest but the children of Duke Ferdinand of Saxe-Coburg and Gotha, one of whom became Ferdinand King of Portugal. He was excluded from the matrimonial stakes by being a Roman Catholic.

When, however, the following month Albert did arrive Lady Lyttelton was equally sympathetic. "Out I went with Lady L. on the Terrace," runs the entry for November 11th 1839, "It was a beautiful day and a fine sight, as soon as my Cousins saw me, they rode up close under the Terrace, dearest Albert with that winning angelic smile which I so delight in." And a little further on in the same entry she writes that she has told Lady Lyttelton about her engagement, she is "such a nice clever person".

Since Sarah's opinion coincided exactly with the Queen's (she described Prince Albert as "handsome enough to be the hero of a fairy-tale — and very like one,") it is no wonder that she merited the royal commendation. Her enthusiasm for the Prince moreover was real and never wavered. From the first she augured the very best for the marriage. "The Queen's look and manner were very pleasing," she wrote describing the wedding, "her eyes much swoln with tears, but great happiness in her countenance, and her look of confidence and comfort at the Prince, when they walked away as man and wife was very pretty to see. I understand she is in extremely high spirits since. Such a new thing for her to *dare* to be *unguarded* in conversing with anybody; and with her frank and fearless nature, the restraints she has hitherto been under from one reason or another, with everybody, must have been most painful."

From this time on Lady Lyttelton never ceases to emphasize in her correspondence the affection that existed between the Queen and the Prince and her wifely submission to him. "Not in look or a tone of hers but expresses the most respectful confiding affection — it is the most perfect wife's manner one can imagine." And again: "At bedtime the Queen, evidently much tired and sleepy, won my heart over again by saying to me, 'Tell Lord Alfred to let the Prince know it is eleven o'clock;' [he was at his everlasting double chess; very deep] 'Tell him the Prince should *merely* be told the hour. The Prince wishes to be told, I know. He does not see the clock.' And quite fussy she seemed for fear of a disrespectful message, or anything like a command being sent."

Lady Lyttelton also much approved of the way the Prince was leading his wife towards country tastes and simple, family life.

"By the way," she wrote from Claremont, "I was pleased to hear the Queen making pointed enquiries about the school here; how the master gets on? If it is well attended etc., like a country lady . . . he" [Prince Albert] "is as happy and cheerful now, as he looked dull and sleepy in London. It is only that the poor man likes nothing but *das Landleben* and she is so complying towards him, that it may lead her to like it too at last." He was obviously making progress in that direction. "The Queen is learning trees and plants, and in a very pretty childlike manner when last we walked, told me quite gravely and low, half shy, 'That Lady L. is a tulip tree, you see, a rare tree, but yet hardy, we hope it may succeed, though it is rather large to be transplanted.' Last year she did not know an elm from an oak. 'Love rules the court, the camp, the grove.' "*

It was not, however, solely in his capacity as a husband that Lady Lyttelton admired the Prince Consort.

Unlike most of the English aristocracy she had great respect for him as a man and she found the tone of the Court much improved after his advent. "Many bits of information on naval matters and scientific subjects come up and are talked of very pleasantly at dinner," she writes from Windsor in 1842. "The Prince of course encourages such subjects, and no gossip has been stirring since we have been here, but many things are said daily that I am sorry to forget. The Prince and Queen are reading Hallam's Constitutional History of England together; and for a light book, St. Simon's Memoirs. Very pleasant to find him reading loud to her, while she was very deedily at cross stitch, the other evening before dressing time. Oh what a blessing it is that Love rules the court as he does! What a *mine* of blessing there is, all sent through those potent blue eyes!"

At the very beginning Sarah had a few minor reservations about the Prince; she described his voice as "sadly disenchanting" and she did not care for his enjoyment of coursing. "My wishes for the hares are so troublesome, I could hate Prince Albert for having a greyhound," she wrote, "but that evening the Band of the 1st Life Guards played a most beautiful piece of choral music and the Queen called to me in a low voice and with a great blush, 'Don't you like that? It is composed by the Prince,' and I forgot the greyhound."

* *The Lay of the Last Minstrel*, Sir Walter Scott; quoted by Byron in *Don Juan* Canto 12, v. XIII, but it is unlikely that Lady Lyttelton read *Don Juan*.

Again one evening in 1840 as she was sitting in her bedroom before dinner she heard the sound of music. "It was Prince Albert, dear Prince Albert, playing on the organ; and with such master skill, as it appeared to me, modulating so learnedly, winding through every kind of bass and chord, till he wound up into the most perfect cadence . . . I ventured at dinner to ask him what I had heard. 'Oh my organ; a new possession of mine. I am so fond of the organ! It is the first of instruments, the only instrument for *expressing one's feelings.*' [I thought an't they good feelings that the *organ* expresses]."

Ten years later at Osborne, as she sat looking at the sunset, she records a very similar experience, hearing the Prince's organ "expressively played by his masterly hand." "How strange he is!" she reflected, "he must have been playing just while the Queen was finishing her toilet; and then he went on to cut jokes and eat dinner and nobody but the organ knows what is *in him*, except indeed by the look in his eyes sometimes."

Sarah Lyttelton was fond of and admired the Queen and understood her well. No better description of Victoria has ever been given than the following: "There is a transparency in her *truth* that is very striking. Not a shade of exaggeration in describing feelings or facts; like very few other people I ever knew. Many may be as true, but I think it often goes along with some reserve. She talks it all out, and just as it is, no more and no less." It was Lady Lyttelton too who commented on the "vein of iron" in the Queen's "extraordinary character". But it was "the candour, truth, prudence and manliness" of the Prince, which commanded her greatest admiration and deepest devotion.

Although Lady Lyttelton stressed so much the harmony at Court and the Queen's "wifely submission", she must have been aware that below the surface there was considerable tension. Baroness Lehzen, the Queen's ex-governess who was now responsible for the internal arrangements of the Queen's household, was not disposed to give up her hold on her adored Victoria and the Queen had relied on her for nineteen years. Albert, who regarded Lehzen as "a crazy stupid intriguer", felt that she came between him and his wife and that peace would never be achieved till she went.

The arrival of the children made the situation no better. Prince Albert from the first was a devoted father and he felt the nurseries were ill-managed and neglected. After an illness of the Princess Royal's he wrote a furious note to the Queen which ran: "Doctor Clark* has mismanaged the child and poisoned her with calomel and you have starved her. I shall have nothing more to do with it; take the child away and do as you like and if she dies you will have it on your conscience."

Mrs. Southey, a lady recommended by the Archbishop of Canterbury, who was in charge of the nurseries was certainly not up to the job. "The Nurses and nurserymaids are vulgar and from having no real hand above them — constantly quarelling [sic]!" wrote the Queen. Mrs. Southey herself felt that the situation had got out of control and in a long, rambling letter to the Prince beginning, "Sir, I feel I can express myself more clearly by my pen than in conversation, [for, like Moses I am slow of speech]", she complained that she had lost the Royal confidence and that therefore when "Her Majesty and your Royal Highness can find a more efficient Superintendant of your Nursery dismiss me kindly . . . and no bird can return more eagerly to her nest than I to my own home."

---

* Sir James Clark 1788–1870, Court physician; responsible for most of the trouble in connection with Lady Flora Hastings.

The Queen immediately turned to Baron Stockmar for advice. In their early years the Baron acted something of the part of a wise fairy godmother to the perplexed young couple. The Royal Archives are filled with lengthy memoranda in his sloping spiky handwriting, now to the Queen, now to the Prince, counselling, clarifying, soothing, and it must be said that his advice though lengthily expressed is nearly always very sensible. On this occasion he played his hand with consummate skill. The Queen was averse from having a lady of rank in command of the nurseries; she felt that such a one would be only a nominal head and would have nothing to do with the day to day superintendence, as had been the case in her own childhood when the Duchess of Northumberland had been supposed to be in charge, in that of Princess Charlotte, and in that of her aunts, the daughters of George III. Stockmar thought otherwise and he probably had his candidate already chosen.

His first step was to write to Lady Lyttelton and to ask her advice. She, who apparently took the Queen's view of the situation, wrote back suggesting a Miss Brown, who had been a governess to the Neville Grenville* family, and a Mrs. Boyd, recommended by Lady Denbigh. This was not what Stockmar wanted and his next move was to call upon Lady Lyttelton. He must have then unveiled his purpose for she asked leave to consult her eldest brother, Lord Spencer, on whose judgement in common with the whole of the British Parliament, she placed much reliance. His verdict was on the whole in favour of her taking the post. "Lord Spencer said, and after considering it, still says, that he thinks me as competent as any person he knows, to fill the office in question." However, the post is such an onerous one that he and she would both "feel glad if so arduous a responsibility could conscientiously be placed on other shoulders."

She then suggests two other candidates. The whole tenure of her life and of her correspondence leads one to acquit Lady Lyttelton of any suspicion of double-dealing, but it must be admitted that the drawbacks to the two ladies mentioned would obviously disqualify them in Royal eyes. Lady Frederick Bentinck's family was so much engaged in politics and so

* Brother of Lord Braybrooke, Mary Lyttelton's uncle.

her favourite among the royal residences. Her apartments*
were up a long winding staircase and "if", she wrote, "apartments could *faire le bonheur* would make anybody happy. A
large lofty bedroom with everything a bedroom can contain, it
all to perfection. And the thick walls, glorious breezes and
excellent water belonging to this most sublime of dwelling
houses make one feel so well, so warm and so fresh, that I
wonder our Kings and Queens don't live here for ever in
earnest. Then next to it is the room where I am now — a corner
room very high up, very lofty, two large windows one each way
and a good fire. The view immense foreground a right royal
parterre, a great way down beneath me, rounded with low
battlemented walls and real cannons. Large flower beds,
statues, vases, and a huge round pool in the middle with a
beautiful bright *jet d'eau*, all huge — beyond 'sonnemflutete
weiten'; the well-known interminable valley over the Thames,
loaded with trees, Windsor Great Park, the Forest and to the
furthest distance. The Wind is whistling round the old grey
walls, and the sun brilliant, it is all beautiful."

Nor did she find her duties too onerous. The most trying was
obviously the lady's maid part of it — not because of any false
pride — but because she knew herself to be clumsy and unhandy.
"I had sundry things to carry and many nonsenses to do;
blundered and boggled as usual. The Queen has a strained
wrist, very sad she can't put in a pin, nor undo a string, nor
anything herself, so I *must*; and it don't always answer; she is
perfectly kind and civil and good natured. At first however the
restraint and peculiar frame of society here, was very disagreeable to me. But I have I think got into it, and feel settled
into a proper stiffness."

One of Sarah's duties was to look after the Maids of Honour
who, she writes, "are very coaxy and wheedly with me and
nice zits both of them. 'Lady L, mayn't I walk, *just for once* by
myself on the slopes? I know it's against the rules, but what
harm *can* it do? We used to be allowed but now Lord Melbourne won't let us ... *Pray* let me' [says Lady L. no. no!].
Then another time a gentle knock 'Lady L, *may* I go out? My
feet are *so* cold poking up in my room all morning! I will only

---

* She was probably lodged in the square North tower in the East range
and the view as she describes it, with the cannons and Windsor Park beyond,
is much as it was then.

violently *parti pris* that Lord Spencer thought this would be an objection while as for Lady Morley, "her manner is rough, loud and expresses too much of her talent and wit, and too little of her real tried kindness and good nature". Sarah concludes her letter by saying that if she herself accepts the place it must be offered to her by the Queen; not of course that it could be expected that the Queen should think of it for herself, but that "what I mean is that the Queen should heartily concur in it and make the offer her own". Stockmar immediately got to work on the Queen.

He started off by presenting a memorandum thirty-two pages long to the Queen and Prince on the subject of education. "Children," he states, "shd be entrusted only to the guidance of good, of virtuous and intelligent Persons." After a long disquisition on the sons of George III, he goes on to point out that the peculiar position of the Queen and Prince, and in especial of the Queen, makes it impossible for them to superintend their own children as they would like to do and that therefore they must have implicit confidence in the Tutor they choose. What is most important is that "harmony and union" should exist between the parents and that they should act as one in the choice of governess and in the system of education they select. In this case, he says, with a side glance at the disputes which have so far prevailed, the greater responsibility is on the Queen who must be "constantly on her guard against the temptation which the Constitutional Prerogative puts in her power". Finally he comes back to his original point that the person at the head of the Nursery must be "good and intelligent, experienced in the treatment of children, of good and refined manners, conciliatory and at the same time firm of purpose". The Royal governess in short should be a person of unexceptionable character and she ought also to be "a person of Rank". If she is, not only will it be easier for her to take and maintain her proper place towards the parents as well as the children, but only such a person can have the proper authority over all the staff under her. She will be exposed to the "inquisitiveness and censoriousness of the whole Nation" and it is easier for someone already accustomed to a high position "to resist the efforts of cavillings and calumny". Finally there is tradition. "The English would not relish a deviation from the established rule." Victoria was shaken but not wholly convinced. She applied to Lord Melbourne; "Stockmar says we must have someone in whom we can place *implicit confidence*. He says a Lady of Rank and Title with a Subgoverness wd be the *best*, but *where* to find a person so situated, *fit* for the place and if *fit*—one who will consent to shut herself up in the Nursery and entirely from Society, as she must if she is really to superintend the whole."

Lord Melbourne, possibly previously primed, replied that he "entirely agrees with the Baron and is strongly in favour of a person of high rank".

Three days later Stockmar demurely tells the Queen that: "Lord Melbourne is a man of strong, sound sense, of great knowledge of the world and of men, of long experience, and of a practical tendency."

This was on the 23rd of March. On April 6th the Queen noted in her Journal that a Governess who should be a Lady of Rank was necessary but not *only* for the Title "as with me and my aunts." "We are in consequence thinking who we could possibly take, and we both came to the conclusion that *none* was so fit as Lady Lyttelton, only we feared she never would take the post. Accordingly, when out driving, began to talk to her on the subject, and gradually felt my way, until I mentioned what was in my mind. She was very much flattered, much alarmed though, at the responsibility, and very diffident as to her own qualities. She, however, said she would be ready to devote her life to her duties. I said I feared it might be impossible, on account of her daughters, but she replied that she would be quite satisfied if her daughters lived in a house near her here" [Buckingham Palace] "and at Windsor. She talked most sensibly about everything and wished she might speak to Lord Spencer about it" [she had, as we have seen, already consulted him three months previously] "which I said I would mention to Albert. I told him of my great success, at which he was much pleased, and we both consider it as a great and kind sacrifice on Lady Lyttelton's part."

The Queen's innocent triumph in her own diplomacy is rather touching when we know the guide lines of the affair had already been laid down by Stockmar, a proceeding to which the Prince was almost certainly privy. However, the first of Lady Lyttelton's stipulations; that "the Queen should heartily concur in it and make the offer her own" was met. There were of course others to come. In a long paper, slightly rephrased by Stockmar and presented to the Queen and Prince, she lays down her conditions and very sensible ones they are. She is to have complete authority in the Nursery and to be "the sole judge of the conduct of those persons who serve under her . . . and they all be ordered to consider her *as the only Chief to whom alone they can address themselves in all their affairs, their wants, difficulties, contrarieties or disagreements.*"

She would of course obey the Royal Parents, enter into their views and adopt their opinions, but she asks permission "to ask questions, to discuss doubtful points, and even to maintain her own opinions by argument, without reserve". If the Queen and Prince should find it necessary to find fault or to rebuke her she asks that this be done in complete privacy and not in front of anyone else.

There were various main points. Lady Lyttelton, perhaps recollecting the Prince's injurious opinion of Sir James Clark, says that she should be present at any examination of the Royal Children by Physicians so that she can know exactly what is said and what is proposed and be able to make her own reports to the parents.

Another clause runs: "With respect to the dress of the Royal Infants Lady Lyttelton should first receive her Majesty's orders on the subject and upon this all should be nominally ordered by Lady Lyttelton who would have to render the Account of the Expenditure, and who will very shortly find out by experience how much and how little Her Majesty may wish to be consulted by her." (One feels that Lady Lyttelton's influence was probably salutary in this effect. At the very beginning of her term of office she records the Princess Royal as being prodigiously dressed up, in Garter Blue velvet, Brussels lace, white shoes, pearls and diamonds" and looking "too comical." Seven years later she describes the children as "dressed in coarse straw hats and brown holland frocks and blouses.")

Other sub-clauses in the Baron's memorandum suggest that a special carriage be provided for Lady Lyttelton's use and that a footman should be appointed for the Prince of Wales, then aged six months, who would wait on Lady Lyttelton.

The most important point, however, was of course Lady Lyttelton's own children. Caroline was now twenty-six,

Lavinia twenty-one and the third member of the household —
gentle, self-effacing Kitty Pole-Carew, Caroline's "wife", was
also her contemporary. Lady Lyttelton's periods of attendance
as Lady of the Bedchamber had been intermittent and not too
long, but now she was absolutely committing herself to a full-
time job. "Her daughters are her chief difficulty," Stockmar
wrote to the Queen, "for it is naturally impossible for her to
separate entirely from them — she is anxious that in future they
should not come into closer contact with the Court, than this
has been the case hitherto [sic] and particularly that they should
never be brought into contact with the royal infants." Her own
proposals were that she should sleep, breakfast and dine at the
Palace but spend a few hours at her own home in the course of
the day and receive her children in her sitting-room in the
evenings. The Queen acquiesced in this arrangement but noted
that even when Lady Lyttelton's daughters are with her she
must be prepared "to go to the Nursery unexpectedly (particularly in the Evenings;) — to see that the people (Nurses,
Nursery Maids etc.) *are* doing their duty."

In the event the Queen had nothing to complain of in respect
of Lady Lyttelton's conscientiousness. Her own words to
Stockmar that if she should be appointed she would look upon
the performance of "her high duties" as "almost the chief
object of responsibility of my life" were amply fulfilled. Nevertheless the question of the daughters was never quite satis-
factorily resolved. "I have a sort of pride wh. I don't half
understand in making the best of my position — *besides* the duty
of it, and I fancy a deal of natural independence and good
spirits to help," wrote Caroline to her sister-in-law, Mary
Lyttelton. "I should pity anybody else in the same! It occurred
to me 'they seek a better country even a heavenly' ought to
apply to me, but I am generally much to happy, to let the
one privation i.e. of a settled home, have naturally that effect
on my mind."

Lavinia solved her own problems by marrying after a year's
time Henry Glynne, Mary Lyttelton's brother. She was
probably heartily glad to be away from Court Life and was
perhaps troubled by her ambiguous position. "The Queen
came up to me in the evening," she told her fiancé, "shook
hands and said 'I must wish you joy!' 'Thank you very much
Ma'am' said I, and H.M. said to Caroline 'It will be a great

separation for you,' 'It will indeed Ma'am' this was all that
passed, and we felt very much like two maids as usual." She
got on better with Prince Albert who gave her "a most gracious
bow, and said 'I beg to wish you joy! — It will be a severe separation for Ly. Lyttelton.' I screwed up courage then and said
'Your Royal Highness has been so kind in allowing Mama to
come with us next week.' I almost lost my breath, but I was
glad of it, for he has been so kind, telling Mama she must go to
town when we do on *Wedy.* and stay till Monday!" A holiday
of less than a week for a daughter's marriage does not sound
generous but Lavinia evidently thought it was for she concludes,
"so very nice."

She obviously shared her mother's opinion of the Prince
Consort, for although she was overjoyed by the Queen's gift,
a magnificent red Indian shawl, she appears to have been even
more grateful for a present from Prince Albert, "kind good
man", consisting of a "beautiful little bracelet of light blue
enamel and diamonds, with a locket of the same hanging on it."
He "begged Mama to put a bit of her hair in it; such a pretty
thought altogether!"

Lavinia therefore was safely removed to the Rectory at
Hawarden but Caroline and Kitty Pole-Carew remained in the
position of camp followers for a further seven years. When the
Court was in London they could stay at the Lyttelton town
house, 39 Grosvenor Place, but at Windsor they had either to
stay as paying guests with Lady Grant,* who lived in the
Cloisters or to board at one of the Royal farm-houses in
Windsor Park. When the Queen and Prince built their new
home at Osborne the situation was even more difficult. There is
a memorandum from Mr. Anson, the Prince's private secretary,
to the Queen reporting a conversation he had with Lady
Lyttelton in which he said that there was "every disposition to
consult the convenience of her Daughter and Niece, and that
Your Majesty would provide some place near at hand at which
they could be lodged". (This proved not to be so; in 1849 Lady
Lyttelton was writing to Mary about the impossibility of getting
any lodging for Caroline.) "But it was not wished that they
should *reside* in the Home at Osborne. That your Majesty
always had the object in view of endeavouring to prevent

---

* Widow of Sir Robert Grant, ex-Governor of Bombay.

intimacies between the Royal Children, and those with whom they might be brought in contact—and that this must be attended to when the children were young as if intimacies were allowed then, it was very difficult to break them off when years grew on."

It is difficult to see what harm an intimacy with Caroline Lyttelton, then an unmarried lady of twenty-nine, could have done the nursery party, but presumably it was all part of the Queen's and above all Prince Albert's distrust of the English aristocracy. It was natural that they should have wished for a quiet family life not only for themselves but for their children, especially since the latter were greeted on their public appearances with the tumultuous enthusiasm now reserved for pop stars. Lady Lyttelton, after her appointment, described "the immense crowds, the continual cheers, the fright lest we should smash hundreds at every turn, and all the excitement of wreaths and bonfires, and triumphal arches, church bells and cannons; all the way along we kept flying and dashing, escort panting, horses foaming and carriages swaying with the speed. The children will grow up under the strangest delusion as to what travelling means, and the usual condition of the people, in England! They must suppose one always finds them shouting and grinning and squeezing, surrounded by banners and garlands. 'Where's the Prince? Shew him! Turn him this way! Bless his little face, what a pretty boy! How like his father!' was screamed at us incessantly. And once as I was overheard to say to Mrs. Sly* 'hold up the Prince of Wales,' I was complimented with 'Well done! That's right old girl!' At one place where we had got out, and were returning to the carriage through a thick avenue of people (I believe at Rochester) a great fat lady very smartly dressed, caught hold of the Prince of Wales, and almost dragging him out of Sly's arms gave him the loudest kiss. 'Well done! I give you credit for that!' said an amiable gentleman of the company. Mrs. Sly has not yet cooled down, her rage was such at being taken by surprise."

It is not surprising that the parents should have wished to avoid such scenes and should have valued privacy for their children but it seems a pity that family life should have been quite so enclosed. The Prince of Wales might have shown more

* The head nurse.

judgement in selecting his friends, the Princess Royal might have exhibited more tact in dealing with her in-laws if, in early days, they had been able to work and play on equal terms with some of their little contemporaries, instead of living such an extraordinary domestic life overshadowed by two such towering personalities as their parents.

On the whole, however, as soon as Sarah Lyttelton took over the nurseries things moved more smoothly and far more pleasantly. Baroness Lehzen went back to Germany in October 1842; Victoria naturally regretted her. She confided in Sarah that "it was very painful to me, Lady Lyttelton, waking this morning, and recollecting she was really quite away. I had been dreaming she had come back to say good-bye to me and it felt very uncomfortable at first. I had heard it mentioned to me—that odd feel on waking—but I had no experience of it. It is very unpleasant." Sarah too had been fond of the old caraway-eating German lady, but without her marital friction ceased, and Victoria and Albert acted as Stockmar had advised in "harmony and union". The head nurse, Mrs. Roberts, was replaced by Mrs. Sly. The children regained their health and spirits (Sarah had been of the opinion that they had been "over watched and over doctored") and the Queen became more and more satisfied with her new governess. "So reasonable and sensible about everything that I am sure it will be a great advantage to have her as head of the nursery," Victoria wrote in her Journal in April 1842. A few months later her opinion had not changed. "Ly L. so agreeable and so sensible. She talked of Pussy's remarkable questions and intelligence and the clever way in which she uses her words." And again a year later the journal records that when Pussy had a cold on her chest "Ly. Lyttelton's kindness and devotion to her are beyond everything."

The only point on which the Queen did not see eye to eye with her governess was over the latter's religious opinions. In the eyes of her extremely tractarian family Sarah Lyttelton was almost lax. "The Oxford Movement" wrote her granddaughter in the Preface to the published edition of Lady Lyttelton's correspondence, "caused her considerable alarm; but . . . in her old age she learnt to value Church practices and services which formerly would not have entered into her wildest dreams. She even became reconciled to open seats in church,

though she once said she loved best a corner of a high pew
shut away from all sights and sounds except the voice of the
officiating clergyman; the truth compels us to add that,
though she obediently attended Lenten services, she used to ask
why she might not repent of her sins in August." The Queen,
however, who had been brought up by a Lutheran governess,
married a Lutheran husband, and was by taste and inclination
exceedingly Low Church was inclined to be appalled by what
she described as Sarah's "Pusey" ideas. Her Majesty, minuted
Anson at Easter time in 1843, "could not bring herself to the
Belief that it was right and necessary to receive the Sacrament
on every opportunity . . . (Lady L. having just received it 3
times in 5 days)." Lord Melbourne was consulted. "It quite
grieved H.M." Anson told him, "that Ly. L. should have so
many opinions (good perhaps in themselves but very peculiar
on some points) from which she entirely differed. She could not
help it in some degree shaking her confidence in her—and in
many of the practical concerns of Life she had detected a great
want of judgement still she was excellent and invaluable—and
she felt assured that Ly. L. would not attempt to inculcate into
the children's minds notions which could be disapproved of by
the Parents."

This was the only complaint that the Queen ever made and
the situation was soon straightened out. Victoria (with the
backing of the Prince) resolved never to enter into theological
discussions; and edicts about the children's church going were,
on Stockmar's advice, handed down from above. (The memo
was drafted by him, the letter written by the Queen.) It began
"My dear Lady Lyttelton, as the New Year is approaching I
now wish to inform you of *our decision* respecting the Pss Royal's
church going." The decision was that the Princess should
attend services at Windsor and Buckingham Palace where
there were private chapels but not at Osborne and Claremont
which would have entailed going to the parish church. "It is
our decided opinions," the letter concludes, "that the Prince
of Wales is much too childish to think of his going to any
service for another year."

Sarah herself was not entirely happy during her first years of
servitude. "I am sorry to think," wrote her daughter, "that the
difficulties of her strange situation rather weigh *heavier* on her
spirit than the contrary. Nobody has a true notion of what its

trials are." One of Sarah's troubles was that the diffidence which had been implanted in her in early childhood still oppressed her. "Tomorrow is the day of our journey to Brighton," she wrote, "and I feel sad and dispirited at the prospect of being there without the Queen and in something like a really responsible situation." Moreover, she often felt lonely and cut off from her own natural life. "You seem to have been gone before the memory of man—and I fear it will be long before you return," she wrote to Caroline Estcourt, who had accompanied her husband on a mission to Canada. "To me my own self indeed, it matters less than to any other among us, whether anybody is *at home* or not—though a delusion still hangs about me that if they were, I could and should naturally see them. But all that is *real* in the business is the happiness your return will give to all those outside the *parlour grating*. I must be looked upon as a sort of old and unholy nun, only to peep out at times—So much for sheer nonsense."

Yet there were many consolations. The first and most obvious was the pecuniary one. With her salary and her perquisites she was able to provide for her daughters and to keep up a home in London which would serve for a focal point for all the family. It was a satisfaction to her that she was able to do all this by her own efforts. "I sometimes feel glad, as well as thankful, that I am doing what I used to fancy I wished to do, really *working* for my bread—And yet it is not real work, and it is so much more than bread I get for it."

It was real work, however, and it exacted a quite unusual combination of qualities. In spite of her diffidence Sarah Lyttelton must have known that the situation was one that was much more suited to her than that of a Lady in Waiting, with its duties of shawling up the Queen and making polite conversation to members of visiting Royal Suites. "I know very well I was born to be a schoolmistress," she had written in the long ago days when she had taught her two little brothers at Althorp and it is certain that she had a real flair for teaching. She was also extremely competent over selecting and controlling her underlings and in winning their affection. When she finally left the Royal service the Queen recorded that "all the nurses and maids (were) in tears—she was so beloved." Her post was no sinecure. The three sub-governesses, all the nurses and nursery maids and nursery staff were under her command. She chose, bought and paid for the children's clothes and rendered up all the accounts; and she herself taught the children their first simple lessons.

Then there were the children themselves. Her relationship with the Princess Royal began badly. The Queen (who in those early days was much more relaxed and stood less on etiquette) ran into Lady Lyttelton's bedroom wearing a dressing gown and exclaiming, "Come and look quick, Lady Lyttelton, at the most lovely of all rainbows!" The pleasure of the call and the sight, a double rainbow forming a complete circle, were, however, spoilt, Lady Lyttelton writes, "by the screams and unconquerable horror of the Princess at the sight of me. Nothing could pacify her but my leaving the room." This bad impression, however, was soon erased; the children were speedily calling their governess Laddle and she called them Princey and Princessy. This must have been a concession; the other governesses spoke to their charges as "Prince of Wales" or "Princess Royal". Princessy at this time was a little imp. She was unusually clever and precocious but exceedingly naughty. In Lady Lyttelton's opinion she was "*over* sensitive and affectionate, and rather irritable in temper at present; but it looks like a pretty mind, only very unfit for roughing it through a hard life, which hers may be." Even at two years old much was expected of her. "I do wish," wrote Lady Lyttelton, "that all her fattest and biggest and most forbidding looking relations, some with bald heads, some with black bushy eyebrows, some with staring distorted, short-sighted eyes, did not always come to see her all at once and make her naughty and her governess cross. Poor little body! She is always expected to be good civil and sensible, and the Duke of Cambridge—bless his Royal Highness—tells the Queen to make it better—that it is very odd the Princess should even cry! 'So very odd! *My* daughters *never did* cry!' . . . and Her majesty believed her uncle."

There are numerous charming anecdotes of the little girl scattered through the pages of Lady Lyttelton's correspondence. We see her aged two flirting with Charley Edgcumbe aged four "hiding behind the curtains for him to find her, holding up her frock and dancing up and down before him, and expressing such admiration of him. 'Boy! pretty boy! Legs! Long legs! Knees!' She also expressed much admiration of herself standing before a mirror and exclaiming 'Princessy! darling! Oh you darling! Well I *never* did!' This last phrase," adds her governess, "she has lately learnt and is often using, when much delighted."

She must also have had the most coaxing of delightful ways. "Yesterday," wrote Lady Lyttelton when the child was two, "I was playing with her, when she suddenly took my old head between her tiny hands, and very gently kissed my forehead, before I knew what she was about, and then laughed most slily. It was just as her mother does to her; the very drollest little compliment." And there is another charming glimpse of her aged four and learning to read:

"Princessy (spells) 'H-O-M-E-ly, homely, What does that mean Laddle?'

L. 'It means, not pretty; not *very* ugly, but not pretty.'

P. 'Who is homely?'

L. 'I think Laddle is homely.'

P. 'Oh, Laddle! (very coaxy) 'but then, you are *kind*, and I think you have a very *sweet* voice!'

So pretty it was, it gave me a lump in the throat; so graceful and affectionate her little manner."

Nevertheless she could be as nurses used to say "a regular handful". "The Princess Royal was most tender and touching in her regrets at leaving me: quite like few grown-up friends," wrote Lady Lyttelton when the children were being taken on a yachting excursion. "And if at the last moment she had not quarrelled with her bonnet, and tried to *bite my hand* in her rage, I should take it all for steady affection."

And again, "The Princess after an hour's various naughtiness, said she wished to speak to me. I expect her usual penitence, but she delivered herself as follows: 'I am very sorry, Laddle, but I mean to be just as naughty again.' "

By the time she was six years old the Princess Royal had plainly got beyond Lady Lyttelton. Stockmar was applied to and came up with another of his invaluable suggestions. "Our new governess is a sensible quiet person," wrote the Queen to her Uncle Leopold, "who seems well accustomed to teach children and able to keep up her authority wh. unfortunately poor dear Ly Lyttelton is quite incapable of doing; really latterly Vicky set her quite at defiance and was extremely naughty with her."

The arrangement was that Miss Hildyard should be under Lady Lyttelton but should have complete authority in her own class-room. It worked perfectly, a tribute to both ladies. They were fond of each other; Lady Lyttelton would refer in her letters to "my dear Miss Hildyard," and the Princess Royal with her mind stretched and her intellectual capacities given fuller play became more amenable and easier to manage. "The poor child has been perfectly good ever since we came here," wrote Lady Lyttelton from Osborne, in 1848 when Princessy was eight years old. "I do trust it may please God to complete his work and make her prove really a fine character, as she has always been *all but*, to so strange a degree. She continues to reflect and observe and reason like a very superior person, and is as affectionate as ever."

The Prince of Wales was in many ways an easier proposition. He was perhaps Lady Lyttelton's favourite. "He is very intelligent," she wrote when he was a year old, "and looks through his large clear blue eyes, full at one, with a frequent very sweet smile." At times he was "passionate and determined enough for an autocrat, but he still has his lovely mildness of expression, and calm temper in the intervals." "He is a regular zit, very nice to be with," she wrote when he was three years old. "I asked him 'who is the little boy behind my chair I wonder?' 'Laddle's boy!'—'and what's his name?' 'called Prinny'." She never seems to have entertained his parents' low opinions of his capacities and frequently writes of him as very intelligent and describes him at the age of six as "much improved in size and manliness . . . and continuing most promising, for kindness and nobleness of mind—His sister has been lately often in disgrace and though she is not 'Alee' (Pss Alice his great favourite) his little attentions and feeling on the sad occasions have been very nice—never losing sight of her, through a longish imprisonment in her own room; and stealing to the door to give a kind message, or tell a morsel of pleasant news—his own toys quite neglected, and his lovely face quite pale, till the disgrace was over. *And such truth!* He inherits all his mother's, thank God!"

One thing that appears very plainly in Lady Lyttelton's correspondence during these eight years is the amount of time Prince Albert spent in the nursery. He seems to have been there even more frequently than the Queen, who was of course practically always pregnant.

Prince Albert, however, was a constant visitor. Sitting down

in Lady Lyttelton's chair in the nursery, to the fury of the
Princess Royal: " 'Papa! don't sit there, get up! go away! It is
Laddle's chair! Give Laddle her chair;' till at last 'Papa' gave
way and got up." Building a house with "Pezzessy's" wooden
bricks, so tall that he had to stand on a chair to finish it, "Such
a fall as it made! He enjoyed it much the most." Coaxing his
little son's fingers into a difficult glove and standing by the
child's sick bed. "I thought all the morning that the Prince of
Wales was dying," wrote Lady Lyttelton—"It was only an
aggravation of the poor baby's cough, a sudden cessation of
appetite, and *such* a look of *old age* and dulness, glassy eyes, and
weakness, as made a strange impression indeed on one . . .
Prince Albert was anxious; and I shall not forget his very deep
sigh, as he went up to his little son at the worst time, commanding himself as much as he could, but it would struggle
through; and his pale serious face showed much feeling."

In process of time the two elder children moved away to other
tutors. Lady Lyttelton approved of Mr. Birch almost as much as
she did of Miss Hildyard. "I was so pleased with what Mr.
Birch told me. I must tell it to you," she wrote to Mary. "He
said he was walking with the Prince of Wales, and they passed
a little wheelwright's or carpenter's shop, and stopped to look
at it—the Prince admired the man at work and said he should
like to try—Mr. Birch consented, and actually staid there with
him *above an hour* (how much better than any lessons!) learning
and teaching him, talking to the man, and helping (but not
much) till the Prince had made a monster bungling footstool
with his own hands . . . How I do hope and wish the man may
but stay on! He does seem so perfect for his place."

She herself was still giving lessons to Prince Alfred and
Princess Alice, "which" she writes, "with my present pupils are
as soothing as they used to worrying with les aînés;" but
though she was very fond of them both one does not feel that
they twined round her heart in quite the same way as their
naughtier elders.

Sarah Lyttelton did sometimes complain of the lack of intellectual stimulus which her cloistered life entailed. "I send
you back, at last, at length, your Vol: of Macaulay, which I
finished last evening;" she wrote to George and Mary, "having
been for a few days able to read; with a sort of delight difficult
to describe; it feels like rain upon dry ground—though of no

earlier. "I hear to my great satisfaction," she wrote, "that they are particularly naughty, riotous, disobedient and unmanageable; which will do our poor darlings good in their Mother's opinion."

In addition to Royalties she met most of the leading political figures of the day. There were dinner parties at which she sat next to Sir Robert Peel and others where she was placed beside Mr. Gladstone. "He is so agreeable. I dread their departure, though I cannot *quite* enter into his politics, they are so intricate, and I am always forgetting the principle he lays down."

Nevertheless her days were for the most part occupied with what she described as "my professional business . . . accounts — tradesmen's letters, maids' quarrels, bad fitting of frocks, desirability of rhubarb and magnesia, and, by way of intellectual pursuits, false french genders, and elements of the multiplication table." It almost seemed as if it might go on for ever. "There is a sort of auld lang syne feeling about it," she wrote in 1849 as the Court left Windsor. "so *old* a courtier am I." But the winter of 1849/50 was an unusually cold one. The Prince Consort looking over the quarterly accounts kept doing Scotch reel steps to keep himself warm. Lady Lyttelton caught a chill and was dosed with henbane which brought on a sudden paralysis. On March 25th the Queen wrote in her journal: "Clark . . . came to tell us that she certainly had had a stroke . . . How very sad. Clark feared she never would be fit again to carry out her duties." Sir James Clark, as so often, was wrong. On March 27th the Queen recorded that Lady Lyttelton was quite herself again. On May 27th, however, she had another seizure again brought on by a chill. Her brother Fritz, now Earl Spencer and Lord Chamberlain, had an interview with the Prince urging his sister's retirement. The Prince, however, was loth to let her go. It would be desirable, he said, that "she should not take so much personal share in the education of the children which is in fact an old wish of the Queen and myself repeated to Ly L. very often but transgressed in her zeal". He asked Lord Spencer to prevail upon his sister "to undertake only the general superintendence of the Establishment and that part of the business which nobody else can perform". So it was settled and Sarah described herself in the summer at Osborne as spending her birthday "in deep peace and leisure as all my days go by now". Yet again Fate intervened. Lavinia Glynne died in childbirth leaving four motherless daughters and Sarah felt that it was time to resign her post at Court. The four little grandchildren were surely her first duty besides, as she wrote, "I have a longing to be more with my remaining dear children, after the awful break in their circle, which I feel no reason for resisting."

It was an argument not to be gainsaid. The Queen wrote in her diary for November 18th. "In many respects it will be a great loss, for she was truly attached and conscientious, but her bad health could not have allowed her to remain much longer."

The parting was a sad one; the Queen recorded that "poor Ly. Lyttelton . . . was very much overcome, but full of gratitude and affection for us." Sarah herself says that she "quite broke down" and further adds that the Prince's face was "as pale as ashes". Poor man! He had the previous year just lost his secretary, Anson, and now he must have felt that another of his very few friends at Court was leaving him. The children "all cried and were most touching. The Prince of Wales, who has seen so little of me lately, cried and seemed to feel most." The Princess Royal said "many striking, feeling and clever things . . . Princess Alice's look of soft tenderness I never shall forget; nor Prince Alfred with his *manly* face in tears, looking so pretty . . . At last we got away . . . And it was not till after a *long* nap in the railroad, that I felt my job was done, and woke with a pleasant *subsided* feeling and as if the worst was over; and a beginning of *rest* came into my mind."

Although Sarah was happy to escape from the servitude of the Court she never lost her respect and affection for the Royal Family though her attitude towards them was not at all comparable to the romantic veneration with which future generations regarded them.

After the Prince Consort's death in December 1861 Sarah was one of the few people whom the Queen wished to see and her account of the interview, hitherto unpublished, is realistic albeit touching. She described Victoria as follows: "Her face is very peculiar, so *very fat, large* cheeks and very small sharp chiselled features; quite unlike anybody else—but her complexion I think unaltered, pink all over, and not clear, but as much so as ever I thought. The expression is extremely grave but calm—she smiled once or twice while my visit lasted, which

4

was more than an hour. She kissed me — and then sat down, and conversed without ever breaking down or seeming to struggle against doing so — she soon mentioned her husband — saying something abt. the P. of Wales being 'still childish — quite a boy — not like what his Father was at his age' — which I answd by saying it wd be vain to look for anyone who was so — She dwelt much on the various *symptoms* (one may call them) of her grief saying that she felt still very ill — I believe this is quite a delusion, poor thing! Knocked up by every day's toil — 'I must work *so* hard — all day long — and no one to help or advise me. No one *above me*. People talk to me about *time, time* doing me good. How can it? — Every moment a fresh wretchedness comes on — a fresh need of the support I used to find always ready and near — And the poor children — whom can the boys look to? Who to direct. I am ashamed of myself. I do feel *less glad* than I ought when I see people happy — so *odd* and wrong! I *can't bear* to look at a man and his wife walking together.' She spoke of many other things, just as formerly, only still the same *very* grave look, and perhaps a little severity in opinion. Praised Althorp* 'your excellent nephew' warmly. 'His character is so good — which is rare in the world now, among young people of his rank. I am thankful he is about the Prince of Wales. But it did give me a pang, to see him *in that place* just where he was before!† It is odd, I like best, it soothes me most, to be with the little children. I like their gaiety.' "

* Lady Lyttelton's nephew, now in fact the 5th Earl Spencer but known in the family by his courtesy title.

† Lord Althorp was Groom of the Stole to the Prince Consort 1859–61 and to the Prince of Wales 1862–6.

W HILE Sarah was presiding over the nurseries of Buckingham Palace and Windsor, her heart was perhaps more engaged by what was going on at her beloved Hagley and if the Queen was satisfied with her she was even more deeply satisfied with and devoted to her daughter-in-law.

"It is so pretty to see Mary taking exactly the same interest in all the belongings of her husband's family and home as if it she had been born among it" she wrote to Caroline Estcourt. "Few people can ever have had so much of one sort of happiness as I have," she continued "living to no greater age than mine, to see the whole character and course of the next generation fully established and so exactly what I could wish it to be."

The Lytteltons' life was in fact one of singular felicity. It had only two drawbacks; too little money and too many children, and the second at least George Lyttelton himself would have regarded more as a favourable circumstance than otherwise.

A letter of Mary's to Catherine Gladstone, characteristically unparagraphed and undated but almost certainly written in the autumn of 1841, refers to both these difficulties, but also illustrates some of the circumstances which made life at Hagley so secure and happy.

"Pretty Puss," it begins, "You must indeed miss dear Willy. What indeed would you do without him! It is so curious to feel completely bound up in a person one has known so short a time. I think I shall be able to put off the little Boykin, for he* told me today that it wd be a good thing for 2 months longer. Our bill for next year's Grocery is less than last year i.e. £79 last £70 this on account of not having laid in a large stock of sugar it is expected to be cheaper at Christmas. Oil and candles each cost £22 yearly anchovies, ketchup, mustard and vinegar abt. £5 so that Grocery, lamps wax candles and things for kitchen only came to under £100 wch I think very little. How I envy

---

* Presumably the doctor, but the letter gives no further clue to this.

the old women seeing Dog* sitting pert in his hat through Hawarden."

One of the greatest blessings of Mary Lyttelton's life, coming directly after her love for her husband and the children, was the unbroken and complete companionship and accord she enjoyed with her sister. To Catherine Mary confided everything, even the very faint shadows inseparable from early married life. To her she admitted that she was unhappy when George was out hunting all day; "it is so silly as he has been so good about being back nearly when he says but I believe after being along the whole day one gets nervous and low." She also tells Pussy what she would surely never have told anyone else that she has "now got to beat G at chess so I will give up playing as I do not like to see him annoyed." She adds "do not comment on this." Another sentence obviously meant for Pussy's ear alone was: "I read the Bible every day with G. he asks me questions wh. frighten me to death and says that I understand but have not language to express what I mean."

Mary, however, on occasions could express very well what she meant as is shown in the letter already quoted. "It is so curious to feel completely bound up in a person one has known so short a time." No better comment on the married life of the Glynne sisters could possibly have been made. It was true of Catherine's relationship to William but perhaps even truer of Mary's to George. Catherine certainly was bound up in William but the very circumstances of political life forced them to spend some of their time apart. Besides Catherine was always fizzing with energy, some ploy for helping others continually occupied her mind. Mary was less physically strong and she lacked Catherine's passionate concern with the lives of others. "Pussy always infects me when I am with her with a spark of her energy," wrote Mary when, on Catherine's initiative they had followed a poor girl whom they met in the street back to her squalid lodging; but on the whole Mary's energies were fully taken up with George and her children. Pussy was the only person who could part her from them. She suffered a very uncomfortable August in London in 1849 holding Pussy's hand while William dashed off to the continent in his abortive attempt to bring Lady Lincoln back to her husband. "I do think it is an insane

* William Gladstone Junior, aged about 15 months.

plan," Mary wrote to George "tho' William writes in a grand heroic strain as if great purpose were to be achieved."* But otherwise she was hardly ever parted from husband and children; and though she was a devoted mother it was obvious that it was to George that the main part of her heart was given. "Nothing makes up for being without you," she wrote on one of her short absences in London, and again: "I was so cold in bed without you," and: "To say how I hate my solitary bed is impossible." Feelings like these had their inevitable consequences. "I think I shall be able to put off the little Boykin," she had written but she was able to do nothing of the sort. During the decade of the forties Mary and George Lyttelton produced seven children. Their first baby, given the old Lyttelton name of Meriel, was conceived as we have seen on the honeymoon and made her appearance in the spring of 1840, preventing her mother both from attending George's election for the High Stewardship at Cambridge and appearing with him on a Court visit to Windsor. "The Queen, impertinent little creature! said to me," wrote Sarah Lyttelton " '*so* sorry not to see your new daughter with Ld. L! . . . but I suppose there are *reasons*.' 'Oh Madam!' said I 'such early days! I should not suppose *that*' (no more I *did*: I *knew* it, which is quite another thing)."

Meriel's parents were as foolish about her as parents of a first baby usually are. "Last night baby was wide awake," wrote Mary "and laughing at nine o'clock with a color [*sic*] so I cd. not help taking her down to shew her to George she looked to sweet in her little night cap."

Willy Gladstone (at this period of his life known as Dog since Willy or even old Willy meant his father) preceded his first cousin into the world by a fortnight and from then onwards the Gladstone and Lyttelton families were practically interchangeable. There are many delightful descriptions in Mary's letters of the babies crowing and laughing on the grass while their fond parents cooed over them. "Little babie laughed at the

* "Suzie" Lincoln was the daughter-in-law of the Duke of Newcastle who had provided Gladstone with his first seat in the House of Commons, and Lord Lincoln, an earnest High Churchman was one of Gladstone's great friends. When therefore she left her husband and children and bolted to the Continent with Lord Walpole he thought it his duty to go after her to try to persuade her to return. It was an impracticable plan as Mary so clearly saw.

blue sky," wrote Mary to George, "she gets much less notice
than the Dog, as you are not here, so make haste and come
William doates so on him."

Catherine Gladstone was able to have a gap of two years
between her two eldest children but not so Mary Lyttelton.
Meriel arrived in 1840 and Lucy (there must have been some
disappointment about her sex) in 1841. By 1842 both sisters
were pregnant again. "My own dearest Pussy," wrote Mary
indignantly "*How dare* you have the impertinence to say you are
more sick than I am, why yesterday I was sick again 3 times
besides nausea *all* day . . . I quite think I bear ye sickness much
better than I sd for feeling that we are still the same." This
feeling of simultaneity must have been one of the few comforts
that Mary had; for her pregnancy was a bad one and she had a
very trying confinement, artificially induced, and for some
time it was feared the baby would not live. However, he survived, grew and flourished. His arrival almost coincided with
that of his cousin Agnes Gladstone and provoked the following
typical letter of congratulation from their Uncle Stephen,
whose kindly interest in the sisters' babies came definitely
second to his taste for ecclesiology and church music. "I am
particularly glad you have a son and heir," he wrote to George
after expressing relief over Mary's safety, "Mary and Catherine
have both been gratified this time in their wishes . . . Catherine's
was born on the Feast of St. Luke, yours on the vigil of St.
Simon and St. Jude. I was almost at the very moment of your
baby's birth, at the Vespers of Winchester Cathedral, where
there was delightful chanting, the antiphonal character ad-
mirably kept up, and an excellent plain and solemn single
Chant. There was the Anthem 'In Jewry is God known' — and
the versicles of Tallis accompanied on the organ."

It might have been thought that after three children so close
together, plus a bad pregnancy and confinement, Mary
Lyttelton might have been allowed some respite, and indeed it
was nearly a year and a half before Albert's birth in June 1844.
According to Catherine Gladstone there was a point when Mary
and George seemed "fully to agree that four was enough" but
though to outsiders this might have seemed an excellent plan
they did nothing to implement it. During the forties they
increased their brood by Neville born 1845, George William
Spencer born 1847 and Lavinia born 1849. The children were

real use; all dries up again and is wholly forgotten in a few hours—but still it must be better for one than *only* casting up accounts and keeping peace among nurses, or even teaching the multiplication table."

This gloomy account of her life was not quite accurate. During her eight years as governess she met most of the leading figures who were received at Court. She held Princey on her lap during the review for the Czar of Russia in 1844 and subsequently held a long conversation in French with His Imperial Majesty about the joys of domestic life for Royalty. It was, maintained the Czar, the only happiness "*pour nous autres . . . c'est un dur métier que le mien*". At the subsequent dinner party she sat next the Duke of Wellington who ruminated aloud "Very good-looking man—always was so—scarcely altered since I saw him—rather browner—no other change—very handsome man now.—Don't you think so? All this was uttered in a *very* loud deep tone . . . *just* opposite the Emperor who understood English." Poor Lady Lyttelton had to scream her answer, since the Duke was stone deaf, " 'Yes, very handsome indeed!'—no escape, he waited, wondering why I did not speak sooner."

In 1844 Lady Lyttelton had been present when the Queen received Louis Philippe with all the honours due a reigning monarch. "The Queen having graciously permitted me to be present," wrote Lady Lyttelton, "I joined the court in the corridor, and we waited an hour, and then the Queen of England came out of her room, to go and receive the King of France; the first time in history! . . . From the Armoury, amidst all the old trophies, and knights' armour, and Nelson's bust, and Marlborough's flag, and Wellington's, we saw the first of the Escort enter the quadrangle, and down flew the Queen, and we after her . . . just in time to see the escort clattering up, and the carriage close behind. The old man was much moved I think, and his hand rather shook as he alighted; his hat quite off, and grey hair seen. His countenance is striking, much better than the portraits, and his embrace of the Queen was very parental and nice . . . It was a striking piece of *real* history—made one feel and think much."

Another "piece of real history" came Lady Lyttelton's way, when, in 1848, she had to arrange for the reception of "little Royal refugees", the grandchildren of the old man who had been received with so much pomp and ceremony four years

loved and welcomed when they came but their coming was far from a joy to their mother at least. "I felt very ill all the evening and this morning," she confided to Pussy during her ninth pregnancy, "but it would almost be too happy and peaceful a life for me if I had not these yearly penances."

George's attitude was more carefree. Like many a Victorian paterfamilias he had a curious way of almost dissociating copulation from pregnancy. Dickens wrote of the arrival of his younger children in a fretful, injured strain; rather as if his wife had insisted on adopting stray kittens without his consent. Lord Stanley of Alderley asked his wife when she conceived rather late in life,* what *she* had been doing to account "for such a juvenile proceeding."

George Lyttelton was neither as egotistical as Dickens nor as cynical as Ben Stanley but there is something about his jocular references to his wife as "Mother of Millions" that leads one to imagine that he shared the general attitude of his time in regarding the arrival of children as a happening in which women were concerned and for which they were mainly responsible.

Had he been more worldly-minded he might have been more worried, for the increasing number of little Lytteltons posed not only a physical but a financial problem.

The Lytteltons had never been well off. It was perhaps part of their charm for they escaped the stifling insulation of great wealth which made life among the rich aristocracy so limited and often so dull. They and their cousins the Gladstones knew what it was to go 3rd class on the railways, to make do and mend, and they enjoyed their rare treats and were closer to their fellow creatures because they were for their station in life exceedingly poor. When relatives came to stay at Hagley they came on the footing of paying guests. Sarah, in proposing a similar arrangement to one of her nieces, writes that she and her daughters each paid £1 a week for themselves and 15/- a week for their servants, adding "it may feel odd at first. But remember it is only a part of the trial of confined means — and that it ought to be accepted like any other!"

The other trials "of confined means" are only too obvious as one peruses Mary Lyttelton's correspondence. She and

---

* Lady Stanley got rid of it by the aid of "a hot bath, a tremendous walk and a great dose". The religious Lytteltons would never have dreamt of such a proceeding.

Catherine were continually discussing small economies. "Get your breakfast butter *not* in pats; it saves a good deal and I think cleaner," Mary advises on one occasion. And from her matronly experience she reprobates the Glynnes, obviously preparing for their first baby, "How extravagant of Henry and Lavinia, the pelisses, a pity I think, a white with pink embroidery is the most useless thing they cd. have bought. Albert has only had his cloak! worn by Charles and Lucy! I am thinking of putting a skirt to a little black velvet spencer all the others have outgrown for him to wear in the spring, it will also do for a coat next winter." "I am so afraid of getting stingy from thinking of little things" she wrote wistfully on one occasion, and indeed this necessary parsimony was to leave a mark on her descendants. The Lytteltons got rather in the habit of it and even those who became rich like Lady Frederick Cavendish were renowned for the sparseness of their tips.*

In the forties and fifties, however, economy was a strict necessity.

George Lyttelton was strangely insouciant on the question of money. He was not at all extravagant. "He spent literally nothing upon himself," writes his daughter Lavinia, "not even a new stick—he was very fond of sticks, and yet there was a sort of freedom and generosity and grand Monsieur abt him which never failed." His great pleasure was hunting but he only kept one hunter who died at the age of 26. The other horses (and horses were a necessity in those days) consisted of a grey called "the Maid of All Work", a pony for the children called Charger and various "ungainly cobs suited", like Mr. Bennet's carriage horses, "to various jobs." He was, however, always ready to subscribe and to underwrite good works. One of Mary's first letters to him runs: "Tom Titten† must not pay the Organist, he does more than he can as it is," and fourteen years later she was writing: "£50 seems to me in the state of our overdraft *more* than we ought to give to the Infant School."

Catherine Gladstone, who knew how much the financial situation worried her sister and how she was forced to scrimp

* Even in 1874 when money was so much more valuable a birthday present of 6d given to a nine-year-old nephew by a well-off aunt seems rather skimpy!

† Tom Kitten or Tom Titten was one of the endearingly foolish names such as most young married couples manufacture for themselves.

and save, obviously took George to task about it. He once wrote to Catherine a long letter beginning: "It is not fair to accuse us of extravagance in our general style of living," and concluded: "Here endeth the Humble Apology and Defence of George William, Baron Lyttelton of Frankley, Lord Lieutenant of Worcestershire, High Sheriff of Bewdley, Ex Under Secretary for the Colonies, Against the Fierce Onslaught and Grievous character of Extravagance and Moral Poltrooney Brought Against Him by His Sister-in-Law, Late She Secretary for the Same, Prime Ministress in Embryo, Mistress Ewart Gladstone."

Yet in spite of pregnancies and financial difficulties the forties for the Lytteltons was a golden age. Sarah had left her daughter-in-law a good foundation on which to build. For the happiness and smooth running of a Victorian household depended not only on the character of the master and mistress but on the underpinning that was given to it by faithful and devoted service. Both the Ladies Lyttelton had experience of this. Sarah's early years had witnessed the benevolent domination of the Spencers' head steward "the great Venables", while the rear of Mary's wedding procession had been brought up by a pony carriage containing Mrs. Hand, the housekeeper at Hawarden and Mr. Whiting the butler, who had both been in the Glynne family for forty years.

Sarah's household at Hagley when she turned it over to Mary was headed by Mrs. Ellis the housekeeper and Mr. Clarke, the steward. Her general recommendations are eminently sensible. "Servants' wages," she told Mary, "I believe are good at Hagley but I do not believe all are high. Mrs. Ellis, Betty, and possibly the housemaids may be too well paid—(the 2 former certainly are) but the saving would assuredly not amount to £50 a year and you get better servants, smiling faces, fewer changes and a right to refuse all perquisites, and to look closely at all pilferers."

Mrs. Ellis "always beautifully dressed in black silk with a lace collar coming out to her shoulders and a close white cap with a brown front of little flat curls" had been in the Lyttelton family from time immemorial. She had run the house and taken responsibility in the days of the crazy Lord Lyttelton; but she does not at all seem to have resented the advent of a new master and mistress. Her devotion to the family was absolute. "She

4*

nearly cried in singing your praises," wrote Mary to George
about a year after their marriage, "so good, so clever!" and
Sarah amusedly imagined that her daughter-in-law might easily
become bored with the flow of reminiscence that would soon be
inflicted on her. "I cannot quite endure to think of the dreadful
course we are inflicting on poor Mary just now, through Mrs.
Ellis at dressing time!" Sarah wrote to George when the young
couple first returned to Hagley. "How very dreadful! I suppose
not a basin of gruel ever made for me and not a pot of almond
paste for the girls is omitted in the anecdotes of the family."

Clarke on his side was equally a pillar of the establishment.
Sarah, obviously afraid that Mrs. Ellis' attachment to the past
régime might prove too much for Mary, did gently indicate
that it could be possible to part from her if it was done gradually
and handsomely, but "Clarke is invaluable" she roundly
stated. He had an orotund delivery and choice of words which
amused his employers. "Eggs, my lady, is the *scaircest* things as
is," he once announced impressively and he gave it as his
opinion that the two eldest daughters of the family, Miss Meriel
and Miss Lucy, were "very fine young women—at the least
they will command rectors."

Naturally in such a household the hierarchical system reigned
supreme. Mrs. Ellis was extremely strict with the housemaids
and couldn't bear flowers in bonnets or anything approaching a
flirtation or loud singing. The maids in their turn jealously
guarded their privileges. "It was not Ellis and I who quarrelled," wrote Mary Lyttelton in the first year of her marriage,
"but Ellis and I versus all the servants who wd not wait on the
nursery."

The dogsbody of the whole system seems to have been "the
Usher of the Hall" ('Servants' understood); which title Sarah
wrote "sounds feudal and grand and absurd—but", she continued, "he is a necessary quantity seeing that no other
functionary, male or female, can or will carry coals, water and
huge packages upstairs; or lay the cloth for dinner in the Hall
below, and act as waiter to the others. He is continually hard
at work and in a perspiration, and seems to me worth £10."

The physical conditions under which the servants lived were
Spartan. The housekeeper's room and the steward's room may
have been pleasant enough, but the maids slept in attics with
stone floors and no fireplaces, "really like prison cells". On

Sunday afternoon they sat in the still-room gathered round "a rather rough round table each with her Bible before her," and even at the annual Servants' Ball they had to wear caps and Sunday frocks of "a most quiet kind". Yet it must be remembered at Hagley this was the order of the day for everyone. Bible reading and church almost daily formed part of the stuff of life for the young ladies as well as for the maids and when Meriel had pneumonia as a small child the temperature in her bedroom never rose above 50 F.

The food was plentiful though unimaginative. The staff dinner consisted entirely of joints, potatoes and bread and cheese (Lord Lyttelton allowed $1\frac{1}{2}$ lbs of meat per day per person!) but there were no green vegetables and puddings except on Sundays, when the maids used to retire to their bedrooms after the first course each carrying her plate of plum pudding and glass of beer. (One wonders at the origins of this custom which is also recorded in *The Edwardians* by Vita Sackville West. Was it because that in earlier days after the serious business of eating was over the menservants were allowed to drink their fill and emulated their masters by disappearing under the table?)

The servants were probably better fed than the nursery, for the children only had bread and butter for breakfast and tea, and nothing at all between tea and breakfast the next morning. Nevertheless the nursery was one of the brightest spots in the house. It was a square high room on the third floor facing south and west where "there was always a baby to be washed and dressed before the fire" and where there stood a "towering white wardrobe with a drawer allotted to each child for its things and where the ornamental pin cushion, little basket Xning cup, powder box etc. were always kept before an expected Baby required them". There were shelves for toys, "a large map representing all the birds beasts and fish imaginable" and a picture of the Queen and the Duchess of Kent" standing as if they were about to set off in a polka", a round table and by the fireplace "a little low rocking chair".

This room was the domain of Newman, or, as she was always called, "Newmanny" the Lyttelton family nurse. She arrived when Meriel was a baby and stayed on long after nursery and schoolroom had passed away. At some time she must have been married for we read in 1875 of her daughter dying and leaving four small grandchildren, but it must have been before she entered service, since she certainly had no time for it once she reached Hagley. Child after child passed through her hands, each one taught to wash itself carefully, to fold up its clothes and to "respect the rows of little boots in a cupboard carefully hoarded for some time as the leather lasted much longer if not worn quite new". She sang to them little songs and hymns in a pleasant low voice; gave them their medicines, travelled with them to seaside lodgings and after Mary Lyttelton died more or less brought up the three youngest boys.

There was a dreadful moment in 1842 when Sarah Lyttelton suggested that Newman might transfer to the highest position possible for a nurse and move to Buckingham Palace; Mary was obviously distraught. "Of course," she wrote to her husband, "I would not be so selfish as to think of keeping Newman, if by giving her up it would add the least to Ly L's comfort or be of advantage to the poor little children at the Palace"; but it is obvious that the sacrifice is almost beyond her powers. "Poor babies three" she wrote (Meriel, Lucy and Charles) "you will give up yr Granny and your nurse to the Queen like loyal subjects. Oh! Oh! fancy me looking for a nurse." She adds in a postscript "On reading this letter over it seems to me selfish but I must tell you just what I feel; but remember that it is delightful to me to make any sacrifice for yr. mother who has done *so much* for me, and I also feel I wd do anything for the Princess." Her mother-in-law on seeing this letter must obviously have realized what a blow losing Newman would be and no more was heard of the project. Newman herself does not appear to have been consulted.

Yet if the nursery was a haven of peace and comfort to the little Lytteltons, the schoolroom to which they graduated automatically at the age of seven was considerably less idyllic. It seems incredible that parents as loving and as conscientious as George and Mary Lyttelton can have put up with such very indifferent governesses and have had so little idea of what was going on behind their backs.

They saw a great deal of their children. George gave them simple Bible lessons every day and Mary was the adored and central figure of their lives. "She was of course beautiful beyond all others to us," wrote Lavinia, who was eight when her mother died, "and I can recall her quite lovely face even now with the

soft brown hair waving naturally, lying on her beautiful skin."
Nor was the schoolroom tucked away in an upper storey behind
a green baize door as so often happened in large country
houses. At Hagley it formed a passageway between George's
study and Mary's boudoir, and they passed by so often that the
children were quite undisturbed and "it was seldom," wrote
Lucy, "that they took any notice of us, beyond a smile from
Mamma and 'you little pigs' or 'Absurd monkies' from Papa."
Nevertheless in spite of this supervision it cannot be said that
any of the Governesses at Hagley made a successful job of it.
The first and the worst was Miss Nicholson. She seems to have
been engaged because of her Tractarian views, since Sarah
wrote to her daughter-in-law deprecating Miss Nicholson's lack
of French and music and adding: "But you can't have everything—and with George's opinion as to uniformity of per-
suasion I don't see how you could hope for a governess nearer
the mark." But far worse than any lack of accomplishments was
Miss Nicholson's really horrid nature. Lucy records that she
used to be taken out walking on the parade at Brighton with
her hands tied behind her, terrified by being told it was ten to
one she would meet a policeman. At home her usual punishment was being put into a large, deep old-fashioned bath that
was in one corner of the schoolroom, before which hung
curtains, so that she was partially in the dark. This does not
sound too ferocious but she adds that she was "continually put
between the doors," (those large double wooden doors, which
mitigated the chill of eighteenth century houses) "and often
whipped."

Altogether according to modern ideas there was too much
punishment prevalent in the Lyttelton nursery and schoolroom,
probably more than there was at Buckingham Palace. "Now,
on the subject of Meriel and her crying fits, I can't wonder you
are uneasy about them *j'ai passé par là*!", Sarah Lyttelton wrote
with her usual calm good sense. "But there is no occasion
believe me to suppose they mean *bad temper* at her age. As to
checking them, I fancy taking very little notice is not a bad
thing. I own I am against punishments; they wear out so soon,
and one is never *sure* they are fully understood by the child as
belonging to naughtiness. It is odd that the Princess has
exactly the same cry of 'Wipe my eyes!' all the time she is
roaring."

Mary, however, did not wholly heed her mother-in-law's wise advice. "Meriel has been very naughty today," she wrote to George when Meriel was just two-and-a-half, "I am going to get a rod which she takes in," to which is added a dictated message from the irrepressible Meriel: "Dear Papa Missy's* cold is gone. I am silly ain't I? the rod will bite my hand. Meriel." On the whole, however, Mary depended more on moral reprobation than on physical coercion. "The punishment Mamma used to inflict on us when we had been very naughty," wrote Lucy "was taking us into Papa's room and putting our small tender hands under a thing for pressing letters together; a bronze hand it was, which pinched us slightly, leaving the dents of the fingers on the back of one's hand. This was done very solemnly, Mamma shaking her head at us all the time. I used to think I should never lose the marks of the disgrace." The two younger girls, Lavinia and May, were also subjected to this gentle disapproval. "She (Mamma) used to shake her head slowly, and with such a look of displeasure and sorrow on her face when any of us were naughty she checked hot unkind words or squabbles more than anything else. She was also keen in detecting vanity or conceit etc. I remember when one evening after the early dinners of those days May and I had new sashes on with clean little muslin frocks and we thought to show ourselves to advantage before the grown up party on the perron . . . We ambled along affectedly hand in hand like little peacocks. Mamma only remarked on our return, 'I saw two very silly little vain girls'."

All this goes slap against modern child psychology but it seemed to do the Lytteltons no particular harm. They remained high spirited and exuberant and certainly they never suffered from inferiority complexes. The only one who was perhaps made unhappy in early youth by an over-developed consciousness of sin was Lucy. On one occasion she cut off her eyelashes because she feared they were making her vain and when she was sick on the stairs owing to whooping cough she felt dreadfully ashamed because she had been "dirty". She went so far as to censure the governess who succeeded the unpleasant Miss Nicholson because she was too lenient. "Miss N's rod of iron was better than Miss Crump's broken reed of government," she

* Her family nickname.

wrote, "we had quite our own way with her for she soon grew passionately fond of us and let us get the upper hand." Lucy seems to have much preferred Miss Pearson who was "a woman of stern and upright mind, with a high and stern standard of duty, and little pity for those who did not reach it ... it was well for me," Lucy continued, "to have my faults exposed to me with an unsparing hand, though it cost me many times of almost despairing tears, and a good deal of bitter repentance." Meriel, however, seems to have been less enchanted with Miss Pearson and records a holiday spent without their parents at St. Leonard's when that lady being displeased with them never spoke for three weeks except at lessons!

The children, however, remained wonderfully undepressed by this lowering school-room régime.

Lucy recording her childhood, recalled the Christmases with "bright leaves and red berries" and the "wonderful excitement of the whole number of us going in the early morning to sing 'Hark the herald', at all the doors, beginning with Papa and Mamma, scrambling onto their bed for the kisses and 'Merry Christmases' ... ending with the nurseries, where we all assembled to drink coffee and eat tea-cake, surrounded by the admiring maids, with the holly all round the room shining in the firelight." It was typical of the era, of the Lytteltons and of Lucy in particular, that she lists among the joys of the season: "Uncle Billy's beautiful Christmas sermons."

She is equally lyrical about Hagley summers, "sitting under the trees with the song of birds and hum of bees all around one, or on the lawn, mossy and velvety with age, from whence we looked over the grassy hills rising gently one above the other, crowned with beautiful trees, and where we loved to bring our reading or have tea on summer holidays."

And lest we should think this is a view tinged with the golden hues of nostalgia or imagine that it was only the children who enjoyed such unclouded happiness we have Mary Lyttelton's own contemporary statement. "I do so wish I could look at death with pleasure as Manning does," she wrote after the forties had drawn to a close and she was in the first year of the new decade, "as a Rest and Haven where all will be at Peace, but this life still binds me so strongly to it, not only from what is to be done here, but from its great happiness and interests."

A<small>LTHOUGH</small> Sarah Lyttelton rejoiced in the blissfully unclouded domestic scene at Hagley she did have a few natural
regrets that George, so unusually gifted, one of the best scholars
of his time, should have shone so little in public life; especially
when his career was compared to that of his brilliant brother-
in-law. "I see how rightly, how happily they (George and Mary)
are going on," Sarah wrote to Caroline Estcourt, "and could
not wish anything otherwise than it is—I have had sometimes
a regret that he has settled so early into so quiet and private a
life—a regret I mean, on the *public's* account—But it all goes
when I *see* how useful, how active, how pious a life it is! thank
God !"

It is true that George's public life was not very brilliant. It
began well, for in 1840 he was appointed Lord Lieutenant of
Worcestershire, at the age of twenty-one—this although he had
abjured his family's Whig principles and had become a Tory,
as he scrupulously wrote to tell Lord Melbourne. Melbourne,
however, was never much of a party man and perhaps remembered the kindness always shown by young Sarah Spencer to
his difficult wife and backward son. Lord John Russell was also
an old friend of Sarah's and when she sat next him at dinner at
Windsor Castle she tactfully attacked the subject by saying:
"But let me ask you must a Ld. Lt. be quite with you? because
I believe my son is not exactly a party man of yours—I don't
know much of his political opinions now—but I believe him
not to go quite as far as you wd like." To which Lord John
replied breezily that "*that* didn't signify at all," only that they
could not appoint "a *consistent* and *avowed* Tory".

Mary, who admired George almost as much as Catherine
admired William, told her sister that "George wrote a capital
letter back" (to Lord Melbourne) "saying that he took it with
the understanding that it sd in no ways shackle him . . . It
struck me much", she went on, "ye rapidity with wch he wrote
the letter sitting round ye table in the evening and ye great

strength and manly way in wch he expressed his feelings. Aunt Car takes great rank upon his being Ld Lieutenant!" "Taking Rank" in Glynnese is explained by the supposition that the person to whom it is applied has an imaginary stock of promotions or dignities at command, to one of which he elevates himself as a reward or consequence of some action. Mary was undoubtedly pleased with Aunt Car's satisfaction for the latter was one of Lady Glynne's two rather formidable sisters who exercised a distant but slightly chastening influence on the younger generation. The elder, "Aunt Catherine", once wrote Mary a very stern letter when she refused an eligible *parti*. "Women are not like Men, they cannot chuse, nor is it creditable or lady like to be 'what is called in love'. I believe that few very few well regulated minds have ever been and that romantic attachment is confined to *novels* and novel readers, ye silly and numerous class of idle young persons ill educated at home, or brought up in Boarding Schools."

Unfortunately the Lord Lieutenancy which pleased her so much probably cost George an appointment which he would have far preferred. He stood for the High Stewardship of Cambridge in 1840 in opposition to Lord Lyndhurst, the Lord Chancellor. The latter was much disapproved of, especially by Trinity College, on personal grounds, and George put himself forward as a non-party candidate but a supporter of the Church. He had much support from the enthusiastic young High Churchmen including Gladstone, who wrote that "Cambridge will *disgrace* itself if it selects Lyndhurst and it will be ye consequence of reading Paley's Moral Philosophy".

The mass of county clergymen, however, and the dons who belonged to the High and Dry School were not anxious to vote for someone who had so recently been *in statu pupillari*, who was a member of a great Whig family and had just received a benefit at the Whig Government's hands. "They think you have taken the shilling," Lord John Manners wrote regretfully, and George suffered a resounding defeat. Mary thought it was worth it "to see the beautiful way in which George takes it".

Lord Lyttelton's next essay into public affairs came in 1846 when Gladstone, now Colonial Secretary in Peel's Government, offered George the Under-Secretaryship. The two brothers-in-law were at this time exceedingly close, bound together not only by their marriage but by their common interests, the

Church and the Classics. They collaborated in turning *Comus* into Latin verse and all Gladstone's translations, including his great work on Homer, were scrupulously shown to George who advised on them freely and pungently. "I wish you would put 'lady' or 'woman' for 'female' which may equally mean a cow", is a typical comment. "I am not less obliged by your remarks .... though delighted with your general concurrence", Gladstone wrote on one occasion, and he signed himself, "Yours warmly attached," which from him was an expression of the deepest affection.

Their family ties were of course an even closer bond. George would write giving news of "the babbies", parked at Hawarden or Hagley, twice including the rather surprising information from an upper class nursery that the little Gladstones were well except for their flea bites; and the two men shook their heads amusedly and resignedly over their wives' foibles. "Dear Wm," George wrote in 1842, "A message to be delivered through either Catherine or Mary has some chance, tho' a small one of reaching its destination without serious casualty by the way; but when it has to go through both of them one after the other, they are the most effectual non-conductors of the same."

Altogether at this time the prospect of working together with Gladstone in political life was a happy one to George, not least because of the family connection. He had, however, first to overcome certain scruples which now seem to us totally absurd but which, in the highly-charged High Church atmosphere of the mid-forties, presented a real difficulty. The Government had earlier in the session proposed the amalgamation of two Welsh bishoprics, Bangor and St. Asaph. Anything to do with bishoprics and the authority of the Church was treading on dangerous ground and Lyttelton seriously doubted if his acceptance of a Colonial Under Secretaryship would not be construed as tacit support for such doings. Gladstone had had to wrestle with his own conscience on this point and was able to convince his brother-in-law in eight pages of small writing that his scruples should not hamper him in the wider political field.

When George finally accepted the post Gladstone wrote: "I need not waste words in attempting to describe the pleasure this gives me. There are indeed several considerations," he added gracefully, "which make it go against one to see you in a position of any kind of subordination to my own—but the relation of our ages is such as just to save it from being unnatural."

George could never have entertained such an idea for a moment but "Newmanny", the Lyttelton family nurse, did feel it was *infra dig* that her master should be under Gladstone, and Mary wrote that she had to be told that "butlers were first under-butlers, nurses, nursery maids". George Lyttelton, however, was never destined to climb the steep ladder of political servitude.

He was not by his own nature fitted for political life. During his few months he nearly underwent what we should now term a nervous breakdown. His manic-depressive temperament had always been inclined to swing between extremes of high spirits and deep melancholy, but the strains of office led to a bad bout of the latter. "The attacks," his mother wrote at a much later date, "are brought on by any anxiety and begin by bilious derangement and lowered pulse. The symptoms are loss of sleep, and extraordinary depression of spirits. He suffered worst in 1846, on his attempting to do official work as Under Secy of State."

His own distaste for the *métier* was not the only factor that disqualified George from becoming a politician. He was a monumentally tactless man. A letter from his chief during his brief tenure of office proves as much. "Lest I forget it," wrote Gladstone, "and because so much deference and respect is due from us in the quarter to which I refer, I send a line to say I do not think (though I am not absolutely sure) that it is quite in order for you to correct Stephen's drafts; I think the course is (that which I also think he would follow with a draft of yours) that you should suggest the corrections you think desirable . . . Be so good however as to see whether Mr. Stephen concurs in this view."

"Mr. Stephen" was James Stephen, the father of Leslie Stephen and the grandfather of Virginia Woolf. He had been Permanent Under Secretary to the Colonies since 1836. He had been a prime mover in the drive for emancipation of the slaves and he was known as Mr. "Over Secretary" Stephen. One can imagine Gladstone's horror at finding the drafts of such a man amended by someone who was still under thirty and had been in his job for four months.

When Gladstone joined Lord Aberdeen's Cabinet in 1853 Mary Lyttelton was anxious that George should be allowed another try. He himself, she wrote to Catherine, had "a dread of office" and disliked the idea of coalition with the Whigs. "Lord John Russell" (presumably because of his Low Church views) "sticks in his throat," but she added "I do think I am not wrong in hoping he may get something I do not go on the ground of the good he wd be to the country but the good I think it wd be for him both morally and for money's sake, and the more I see the children require sea, the more in a domestic line I feel having something to pay for it again, what low sentiments."

One can be sure that Catherine sympathized strongly with these appealing "low sentiments" but no office was forthcoming for George. Aberdeen's was a Coalition Government and there was pressure on places. Moreover George had in 1848 become much involved with the Canterbury Association, a Church of England Settlement in the Southern Island of New Zealand. Gladstone was also in sympathy with this cause but he was a politician by profession and by instinct, and he, on principle, kept himself clear of any entanglements which would involve his political career. Gladstone gave it as his opinion that George could hardly in the circumstances expect to return to the Colonial Office. It is probable that for more than one reason he felt his brother-in-law unfitted for political life.

Yet although George Lyttelton had not been an auspicious success in Government office he still had a very great deal of public work to get through, which filled his time but not unfortunately his pocket, since it was all voluntary and as we shall see was to be a drain on his slender resources.

He had of course all the county business to do with his Lord Lieutenantship, in addition to the Board of Guardians. He also was much involved in educational work particularly in the Training Schools at Birmingham. He was on the Governing Body of Queen's College, the first educational establishment for young ladies; he was a member of the Committee which Lord John Manners set up to introduce Sisterhoods in the Anglican Church; he was Vice-President of the London Library and also on that of the Society for the Propagation of the Gospel, but his chief voluntary effort, the one which took most of his time and called most heavily on his pocket, was the Canterbury Association. This Association was the brainchild of two men, Edward

Gibbon Wakefield,* an eccentric but forceful character who was the great authority of the nineteenth century on colonial settlement, and John Robert Godley, the son of an Anglo-Irish landowner. To trace the whole history of the inception of the movement and the various vicissitudes it underwent would require a book to itself so they can only be very briefly summarized. The aim of the Association was to form a community of Church of England settlers, not riff-raff sent out to the Colonies because they could do no good at home, but steady serious men and women, a cross-section of the population who could found a new Utopia. Its plan was to buy land from the Maori tribes, to re-sell it to the settlers at the then high price of £3 an acre, and to employ the profits in making roads, founding a cathedral† and a diocese, and settling up schools and a university. Up to a point these plans were realized. The thriving city of Canterbury with its Christ Church cathedral dates from the time of the early settlers; but there were many problems to be overcome. Financial difficulties were always cropping up and Members of the Association had to guarantee very large sums. Nor could they dispose of enough land at the high price demanded to make the settlement viable. Sheep-farmers from Australia had to be allowed in to farm the land in order to make it profitable. The settlers grew impatient of home control and asked to run their own affairs without benefit of the Association back in London. The passing of the New Zealand Constitution Bill which authorized a federal system in New Zealand with wide powers of provincial self government made this possible and in 1852 the Canterbury Association was wound up. What the settlement owed to George Lyttelton is well expressed in C. R. Carrington's *Life of Godley*.

"Lyttelton's correspondence during the three years of active colonization, and for many years thereafter, reveals the extent of the obligation owed to him by the Canterbury settlers. Not only did he bear the brunt of the guarantees, which, on two occasions at least, saved the undertaking from total collapse,

---

* Wakefield had disqualified himself for public life in 1826 by abducting an heiress, for which crime he was imprisoned for three years. However, he had made himself such a master of colonial problems that nothing in this field could be done without him.

† One of the major difficulties of the Association was finding a suitable bishop.

not only did he subscribe £2,000 to the repayment of the Association's debts, it was he who took final responsibility in all emergencies at home as did Godley in the colony." The debt the settlement owed to him was acknowledged by the naming of Canterbury harbour which was called Port Lyttelton, while the sports stadium is still known as Hagley Park.

Sarah Lyttelton viewed her son's involvement with mixed feelings. She was of course much gratified by his success and by the appreciation that was given him. "I am half ashamed to be so delighted," she wrote when Mary sent her a complimentary letter from Gibbon Wakefield. "I knew didn't I all that it says of my darling?" Nevertheless George's decision to subscribe £2000 to the repayment of debts seemed to her needlessly quixotic. "I am grieved at what you say abt. Canterbury being likely at last to cost you money," she wrote to him. "I *ought* not to give an opinion about it, but still beg to offer the advice of such a miserable old Ph.* as I am—But I cannot help saying, that I doubt whether for the sake of what you call 'discredit', which in this case can only be the discredit of having made honest and generous *mistakes*, you would do right to spend your children's pittances and your own means of usefulness." George, however, was not to be dissuaded—£2000 went to the Canterbury Association.† It is no wonder that Catherine Gladstone sometimes got irritated with her brother-in-law's financial transactions.

One small practical advantage accrued to George from his New Zealand connection—Lord Spencer who had contributed to the Association by buying some land, passed it on to the fourth Lyttelton son, who had had the luck to be christened "Spencer", making him financially independent. There were also many other less tangible benefits. There was the satisfaction of a task well accomplished and the never failing interest which the affairs of the Colony gave him over a long period. He was continually receiving, reading and commenting on copies

---

* *Glynnese*. "Phantod: Apparently a corruption of the English word *phantom*. The sense, however, is essentially different. It signifies generally 'an imbecile person': one incapable of serious or rational procedure . . . But it must be observed that this complete form is not much in use. The authorities generally substitute for it the expressive initial abbreviation 'ph:' not, however, pronounced as one letter, as 'f' but in two: 'p', 'h'."

† It was in time repaid.

of the *Lyttelton Times* as the principal newspaper was called. He kept up, as Carrington mentions, a never ceasing flow of correspondence with the chief men in the settlement, and among them he found two very real and constant friends, John Godley who spent many years in New Zealand putting the settlement on its way but returned to England in 1853, and H. S. Selfe, a police magistrate, who was a member of the Association in England. These two men, whom he would hardly have come across in the normal life of a county magnate, became two of his dearest and closest friends.

On the whole therefore New Zealand was probably more of a source of satisfaction to George Lyttelton than not, but in the early fifties what with the anxieties about the future, the pecuniary losses, some unpleasant comments in *The Times* about mishandling of subscriptions,* it must have seemed at times a heavy burden.

George's troubles, however, were infinitesimal compared with the worry caused to Sarah by his next brother, Spencer.

Spencer was much better looking than his elder brother. He was taller with smooth dark hair with a slight curl in it and large liquid dark eyes. He sported a slight moustache. Unfortunately he had inherited the gambling propensities of his maternal ancestors. They had oddly enough been brought into the family by the very virtuous and pious Lady Spencer who had been Sarah's grandmother. She had been born a Poyntz and had herself in her youth gambled and had passed on the taste, with disastrous consequences, to her famous daughter, the Duchess of Devonshire. Apparently the family proclivity was well known for the Queen's journal records that: "we had great fun with Lady Lyttelton about the Pointzes [*sic*]." Lord Melbourne repeated an anecdote of Lord Lansdowne saying: "I know the Pointzes well; I've known them in the nursery, the Bible on the table and the cards in the drawer."

This unfortunate propensity had descended to Spencer Lyttelton. His naval career had not answered and been discontinued and he spent a year as a lieutenant in the Royal Scots Fusiliers. After that there is a blank in his history (though there is a mention in one letter of a speculation in indigo) till,

---

* As in so many amateur societies insufficient care had been taken over passing assets from one fund to another.

in 1846, he wrote his mother a melodramatically penitent letter in which he declared that he had lost so much money that he had barely enough to live on and had made up his mind to leave England "and pass whatever time I have left to live in this world in some miserable corner where I shall no longer be a curse to everyone with whom I have any connection." The letter concluded "Death or madness wd be the greatest relief I could pray for."

It is obvious that poor Spencer, who was only twenty-six, did not quite mean the last sentence, nor, one imagines, did he suppose that his family would really acquiesce in his living in Teneriffe on £200 a year as his letter later suggested. Nor did they. His mother flew up to London to see what could be done, and enlisted on her son's behalf both the Queen and Uncle Fritz, who was now Lord Spencer. Her letter to the former must have been a difficult one to write and one can sense that she disliked doing it. She explains Spencer's poverty, his desire to marry* and she begs the Queen to ask Sir Robert Peel for a small place. The Queen she says is herself a mother, but not a widowed mother with children who depend on her for "making sacrifices not of money but of feeling, and taking steps of doubtful propriety in hopes of obtaining benefits for them". The Queen did find a small place about the Court for Spencer and the Duchess of Kent to whom she showed Lady Lyttelton's letter wrote: "You acted so well my beloved Child, perhaps if he had a hope for the future it would have a good effect on his character and conduct."

Alas, the Duchess' prognostications did not come true and Uncle Fritz' efforts were equally in vain. Frederick Spencer was a forbidding and rather gruff character not always appreciated by his nephews and nieces. Mary writes of his "pecking" at Caroline Lyttelton, whom he disliked, and adds, "A regular U for an Uncle he is!"† However, in spite of his pecking pro-

---

* He was engaged to Caroline Dawson, one of the Maids of Honour, a niece of Lord Portarlington's.

† *Glynnese*   A was an Admiral
            B was a Boatswain etc.

These expressions, which might be similarly continued through the 24 letters, are taken from an infantile book called the Child's Alphabet: in which it will be remembered that for the assistance of the imperfect memory of childhood, each letter is illustrated by an original design of an individual, of a class or profession of which the first letter is the same as the letter in

clivities he did, on this occasion, do his best to help Spencer and Lady Lyttelton sent him effusive thanks for his generosity,* writing: "As far as I know and believe your magnificent present has *just* turned the scale, and made the settlement possible, which Miss Dawson's family, with tardy wisdom have insisted upon."

Sarah, however, was unduly hopeful; Miss Dawson's family, once alerted to the unpromising position of their future son-in-law, refused to consider him further. Sarah must have been much disappointed for she believed that he was deeply attached "to the charming girl for whom I can't help feeling a sort of motherly affection already"—but it was not to be, and next we hear of Spencer is that he is engaged to a Miss Henrietta Cornewall.† Henrietta's father was dead and her mother must have been less exigent as to settlements for they were married on August 10th 1848. Perhaps Mrs. Cornewall was dazzled by the social grandeur of the wedding, for Lord Liverpool gave the bride away, Meriel Lyttelton aged eight and Agnes Gladstone aged six were bridesmaids, there were a large number of Spencer and Lyttelton relations present and the happy pair went away to honeymoon in the Duke of Devonshire's villa at Chiswick.

All this, however, was very much "false flash". The young couple had almost no money, and, what was worse Spencer, could not refrain from gambling. In December 1848, four

---

question. And inasmuch as the said individuals are represented in the full appropriate costume of their class or profession, and inasmuch as, from the homeliness of the execution, their countenances and appearances are invariably of an inexpressive and indistinctive kind, after the manner of the waxen busts in the barbers' windows, these phrases are used to describe real people, who in the view of the speaker are *mere* generic specimens of the class to which they belong, neither rising above it nor falling below it by an peculiar characteristic; bare types, in which the individual and original has been repressed and rubbed out by the conventional and professional. . . .
Example: Mrs. Gladstone to Lady Lyttelton:
   'What sort of person is . . . ?'
   Lady L. 'Oh, C was a Clergyman.' "

* Family tradition says that the 3rd Lord Spencer (the Lord Althorp of the Reform Bill) had on his death-bed in 1845 forgiven Spencer his wild ways and left him as a sacred charge to his brother, which may account for the latter's really great concern.

† She was one of the Cornewalls of Delbury, a family descended from Richard Earl of Cornwall, brother of Edward III.

months after his marriage, Princess Hohenlohe-Langenburg
wrote to the Queen from Baden: "I forgot to answer your
question about Lady L's son. I was told he gambled *dreadfully*
here lost all his money, and that which was sent for his poor
wife's journey back to England, they sent some more and she
left this place in the 'diligence' without him, he was *not* in
prison, and now he has gone."

Spencer was always having to be baled out by his long-
suffering relations. In 1861 he had to retire to Ostend till a
settlement was contrived by his brother George and his uncle
Fritz which Sarah Lyttelton hoped would provide a clear
income of £600 a year for "the wretched couple. Wretched
from their footing together and their future responsibilities,
which one can trust to *neither* of them for meeting honestly."

For Henrietta found no favour with the Lyttelton family.
She was thought by them to be flighty if not worse. (She was
known in the family as "fast Henrietta".) One hot summer in
London Mary Lyttelton writing to Billy describing their common sister-in-law, as fanning her white face and going about at
night "with as little on as may be, looking like a decorous
statue". Sarah Lyttelton prefixes the word decorous by the
prefix "in" and adds two exclamation marks."*

In fact Henrietta's faults were legion — she insisted on having
a wet-nurse; she tight-laced; she was in high spirits after a
visit to Melton where "she met a proper lot of scamps". In
June 1850 Sarah Lyttelton decided (in consultation with
Caroline) that she had better *write* to Henrietta to tell her
"the report abt. Lord M.† so that she may be warned as soon
as she comes to London." One wonders if the warning was
effective. Henrietta had rather a power of checking her
interlocutors. Sarah thought it better to write than to speak "as
she would perhaps throw me over by her silent smile."

One of the main bones of contention was of course the baby.
(Luckily there was only one.) Grandmother and nurse wagged
their heads over him when he had convulsions during his
teething and decided that the illness was chiefly due to mis-

* Judging by Mary's somewhat incompetent drawing which decorates the
letter, Henrietta seems to be wearing nothing worse than a sleeveless rather
decolleté night-gown.

† There is no knowing who Lord M. may have been. I fear Lord Melbourne would have been too old by 1850.

management and "an obstinate resolution of Henrietta's that on no occasion is physic to be given". (When one thinks of the amount of blue pills, black doses, James' powders etc. that Sarah and Mary Lyttelton and Catherine Gladstone rammed down their children's throats one cannot help sympathizing with Henrietta!) Meanwhile the errant mother had been out for a walk and when she came in "hardly admitted she had been frightened, and certainly did not look anxious".*

One's sympathies sometimes veer towards the wayward Henrietta but the truth was that the Glynnes and Lytteltons had a very strong code of good manners which Henrietta continually transgressed. And good manners in this connection are not so trivial as they may sound. For any close, corporate life, particularly a family one, they are essential. If physical distance cannot be maintained then there must be moral restraint to prevent the wounding word, the intolerable aspersion, or life becomes impossible. Henrietta was not brought up in this tradition. "Mrs. Cornewall after inviting Henrietta and the baby for a fortnight," wrote Sarah "first threw over the baby . . . and has now put off Henrietta for a week . . . without evident reason—and some angry notes have passed between the High Powers quite enough to have made anybody else wretched for life—but they are used to it like eels to skinning; and nobody cares."

The Spencer Lytteltons carried on somehow, always in debt, always borrowing money. In 1855 Spencer asked his cousin the Duke of Devonshire for a loan of £500 and the Duke replied that he never lent money but would make a present of it, thereby, perhaps wisely, protecting himself from further inroads.

---

* The poor baby did not turn out well. "His father and mother are nice to him now," his grandmother wrote a year later, "but I cannot help feeling a painful pity for him." It was not misplaced. He seems always to have been hanging about on the outskirts of that boisterous, close knit family life. "Poor unfortunate Harry Lyttelton," they called him; "Harry" tout court being reserved for Harry Gladstone. His cousin, Lavinia Lyttelton, commented in her diary that his rooms at Oxford were pretty "but he is too odd a person." Perhaps his rooms were, in Kipling's phrase, "more like a whore's than a man's," since poor Harry was sent down, disowned by an indignant father, found wandering penniless in Rome, and finally packed off to New Zealand. A curious young great-nephew asked his Aunt Lavinia what was the truth about Harry. "My dear," she replied, "I believe he did something nasty" (using the Victorian short a) "with men."

In 1869 his mother was annoyed at his trying to borrow
money from his brother-in-law Henry Glynne, adding bitterly:
"I only wonder he didn't do it before." The letter goes on: "Oh
dear! I am to call for Henrietta to take her for a shopping drive.
I only hope she will decline for *her* talk on things in general, as
they are now, would go far to driving me mad." None of the
Lytteltons much liked Henrietta, and Spencer must have been
an enormous liability but they remained part of the family,
staying at Hagley, attending family festivities, referred to in
family correspondence. Sarah never became in the least fond
of her daughter-in-law but as a personal memento bequeathed
her a miniature of the family ancestor Sarah Duchess of
Marlborough. Henrietta seemed touched, but somewhat
shocked her in-laws by being infinitely more concerned about
the correct degree of mourning she should wear. Even her pet
dog was ornamented by a large crêpe bow.

The third Lyttelton son christened William Henry after his
father but known to all the family as Billy* was very different
from Spencer. He was a high-minded, delicate, good-tempered
boy, "the sunshiniest person I know," in Blakesley's opinion,
and had always been intended for the Church and the family
living; yet he too presented his problems. His health was pre-
carious and after his ordination he went to Germany to rest and
to recover where unfortunately he imbibed a dose of German
philosophy becoming as he put it himself "sadly Low Church".
This did not worry his mother but she certainly wished he
could keep his ideas to himself. She was "very sorry he wrote
to George a long account of certain opinions of his on religious
subjects," she told Caroline Estcourt, "which though as I need
not say, most beautifully pure and pious, and to my mind
almost correct if not quite, even as to inessentials, are not
George's. Dear George is incapable of looking upon any such
difference in a bitter or uncharitable spirit. But he has answered
him, and got Mr. Gladstone to write down his views too — and
all this controversy, kindly and mildly as it is carried on, is I
am sure as unwholesome to Billy as raw turnips or lemonade to
a gouty alderman. And I hate to think of it, interrupting his
rest . . . We are in fact living in sad times as to Church matters.
Dire schisms splitting every parish and family into sects, and

* George generally wrote to him as Bull or Bühl.

infesting every plan, book, conversation and sermon.—I trust
real religion will not suffer in the scuffle."

"Church matters" seemed all important at this time to
George Lyttelton. The High Church tenets which he had
imbibed at Cambridge had been reinforced by contact with the
Glynne family and above all by the influence of Gladstone. In
his correspondence with Billy he is continually citing Gladstone's opinions or quoting long passages from his book.*
Billy's tolerant oecumenical outlook was frowned on by his
brother who held that "to a very large extent Dissenters are
in the same category with heathens or infidels or Socinians".†
A long and impassioned correspondence was carried on for
nearly a year and at last matters reached such a point that
George almost felt that it might be his duty to refuse to install
Billy in the family living which had always been intended for
him.

"I do not at all mean to say that I have altered my views
with reference to this living" he wrote, "but I have thought it
fairer and more satisfactory to have some further explanation on
this matter." It must not be assumed that George was applying
sanctions in order to bully his brother. He truly did feel that if
he allowed dissent into the parish and permitted the school-
children to be, as he thought, mistaught, he would be doing a
great wrong. His postscript which was absolutely sincere shows
how much his conscience cost him. "You will not suppose," he
wrote, "because I do *not* talk pathetic, that I have no *feelings*
on this subject. Of course it would be a matter of infinite distress to me for my whole life not to have you here; but the
object must be both for you and for me not to let the feelings
have anything to do with the determination of the question."

The feelings, however, would of course creep in. George
wrote to his mother and she answered with a supremely tactful
letter to the effect that the decision was his and that though of
course nothing could make her happier than to see Billy at
Hagley, yet it must be with the provision that he is there with
"no sacrifice whatever of principle in either of you; and at

* *The Church in Its Relations with the State,* 1838.
    † Lelio and Fausto Sozzini ("Socinus") were an uncle and nephew who
in the sixteenth century rejected most of the basic Christian doctrines. At
the Confession of Rakow 1605 their followers held that Christ was not the
Son of God but a prophet of God's word.

none either of comfort". He must not be appointed in the wish to please her.

Yet appointed he was. Probably when the brothers actually met the acid doctrinal questions were submerged in the contemplation of Billy's obvious goodness. In 1846 old Mr. Turner died and Billy became Rector of Hagley; by 1847 George's letters show how completely he had begun to rely on his younger brother. From that day onwards there was no more closely knit relationship. The brothers were very much alike in some ways. They were both somewhat manic-depressive, but in their early days the manic quality was much more prevalent. Both had very loud voices and used to roar with laughter on very little provocation. (One is reminded of their father, whom they probably remembered only as a stiff rather strict invalid, rolling about the floor screaming with laughter at Wimbledon Park.) Their relationship was one of deep devotion, spiced with humour and rather schoolboyish teasing. George's letters to Mary and to his mother have been destroyed but we have the whole of his correspondence with "Dear Bühl", "Dear Güggen-bühl", "Most Ignorant", "Monsieur L'Eveque", "Foul Heretic", as he addressed his brother at various times. The letters are interspersed with lively little drawings and doggerel verse, on the composition of which George rather fancied himself. (He is said to have laughed so much at his own creations that he had to lean out of the railway carriage windows so as not to upset the other passengers!) Two examples of drawings and verse may be given here. The first shows that Billy was (like all the Lytteltons) very bad with money and that his mother was understandably worried. The second, though not the best example of George's rather indifferent muse, gives a good picture of the relationship subsisting between the two brothers.

Duns with Bills   Bühl   Dowager

"Güggenbühl, Gig-a-bühl jolting together O,
Parson and Peer in facetious confab,
Peer King of puns in the dullest of weather O,
Parson in laughing and roaring a dab."

Uncle Billy's shattering roars of laughter were, it may be
explained, famous in the family. "About dear Billy," wrote his
sister Caroline, "his laugh is as often from real tearing spirits as
from shyness. There is no baby joke of his own that fails to set
him off laughing." His other sister, Lavinia, said that she was
sorry that "the moment he comes out of church . . . the
servants shd. hear him shout with laughing after *elevating* the
minds of all and sobering them as he does." His mother wrote
that on one occasion she was staying at the Rectory and by a
slip of the tongue mentioned that her eldest grandson, Charles,
had shot "a three-legged bug" (instead of buck) "in the Park".
Billy was so immensely tickled by this fancy that not only did
he keep laughing throughout the evening but he could hardly
control himself over the breakfast table.

At one time Sarah thought her youngest son would never
marry, he was so devoted to his sister-in-law (he once dreamt of
her wearing her nightgown) and Mary Lyttelton was the
repository of his hopes and fears and false starts in the matrimonial direction. "Bye the bye," she wrote to him in 1851, "I
pumped the Bishop of Birmingham about Miss Pepys. He said
she was not particularly clever but nice and not frivolous." By
1853 Billy seems to have been drawing back since his confidante
wrote: "As for Miss Pepys, I do not think it at all difficult to
show her you do not mean to make her your wife, because there
is no reason for her ever having thought so, and I do not like
young ladies making up to young gentlemen." But the following
year Miss Pepys' tactics had obviously been successful for Mary
wrote: "What it must be to you to find such a congenial heart
and spirit as you describe your dear little bride to possess few
can imagine as well as I can, and to find her so willing to talk
of the deepest things must be a great additional blessing to you.
I have often wondered what made you like living with us as
much as you did, because it is very true that it is not either
George's or my way to do this. Don't let her talk Glynnese,
because it is not her, and is always forced in others' mouths,
and I want her as she is; as for loving her there is no doubt of it,

you know how well I can do that." Aunt Emy, or "the little aunt" as she was often called, never did attempt to talk Glynnese, and one somehow gathers from the letters that she found the Hawarden atmosphere and in particular Aunty Pussy rather frivolous. Aunt Emy herself could never be so described. "She had," wrote her eldest niece by marriage, "strange limitations and a narrow rigid outlook on life." The boys got rather bored with Aunt Emy, and, in a confidential letter to Mary, Sarah Lyttelton, using an unusually slangy expression, opined "that the little grey mare is too decidedly the authority—she will in time make him into a complete Jerry Sneak". However, "the Rectors", as they were generally known, became an essential part of the family and Aunt Emy's rather narrow views were mitigated by the open warm-heartedness of Uncle Billy.

QUEEN VICTORIA receiving Louis Philippe 1844

*ft to right: The Duke of Wellington, Sir Robert Peel, the Earl of Aberdeen, the Marquess of
:eter, the Earl of Jersey. The Countess of Gainsborough, the Dowager Lady Lyttelton. The
ichess of Kent, Nurse holding the Duke of Edinburgh. The Princess Royal, Princess Alice. The
teen holding by the hand the Prince of Wales. Louis Philippe. The Duc de Montpensier, the
ince Consort.*

*Vinterhalter has taken artistic licence in staging the ceremony indoors. As we see from Lady Lyttelton's
ount, the Queen actually received Louis Philippe in the courtyard at the foot of the stairs leading
the Armoury.)*

MARY CATHERINE
LYTTELTON
daughter of George
4th Lord Lyttelton
*This drawing may have been
copied from a photograph as
it was done in 1875, presumably after May's death.*

HAGLEY HALL

T HE fact that Sarah's peculiar life at Court had to be shared by her daughters, had naturally been a source of anxiety to her self-doubting mind. Caroline was already twenty-six when her mother became Governess and had Kitty Pole-Carew as a refuge but Lavinia was only twenty and her mother must have worried considerably about her future.

She was, judging by the engraving of her picture by Richmond, by far the best looking in her generation with a calm wide brow and black hair, banded across the forehead in the fashion of the 1840s. She had great simplicity and something of her brother George's transparent honesty, but what struck everybody about her was that she was quite different from other women. "She is peculiar," wrote her mother, "unlike anybody else but very like herself for all the years she has lived."

As a child she was naughty, kicking the doors and the paint of the old nursery at Hagley, marks which survived till the next generation. During the rather unsatisfactory Court life that she was forced to lead under her mother's wing, she took her own line. Asked to dine by the Duchess of Kent she was perfectly capable of coping with Baron Stockmar at dinner but when after the meal she was left with a young man who had presumably been invited for her,* while the rest of the company played whist, they "flew apart to two remote sofas, and devoted themselves separately to annuals, in determined silence till the evening broke up".

It might have been anticipated that when Henry Glynne, Mary's brother, the Rector of Hawarden, showed unmistakable signs of being attracted by Lavinia, maternal anxieties would have been at rest. He was a gentle, sweet-natured man. The living was worth £3,700 a year. They would set up house in the

---

* "He is much improved in abbearance, the young man," the Duchess said kindly in her thick German accent to his mother, Lady Cooper.

red brick Georgian rectory, with its terraced garden sloping down to the river, a stone's throw from Hawarden church and two minutes from the gates of Hawarden Park. He was, it is true, eleven years older than Lavinia but this probably worked in his favour; she had not much use for younger men. The Glynne family was all in favour of the connection. Their only doubt was if Henry could conquer his shyness and be brought to the point. "He is always slow in his movements from modesty and caution," wrote Mary Lyttelton to her husband, "and he seems to have great difficulty in getting beyond common topics, but he looks at her as if he could eat her." Mary was frantic because her mother-in-law let the cat out of the bag before Henry had actually proposed, but in time he managed to bring it off—giving Lavinia a rose out of the garden, which was found among her papers after her death. Mary and Catherine were delighted, but Sarah, like many mothers, more romantic than her daughter, had her reservations. "Henry Glynne is not the man I had dreamt of for her husband," she wrote. "But he is I doubt not at all, most excellent, most exemplary in principle and spotless in conduct, and perfect in temper, and highly gentlemanlike, and deeply attached to her, his first love, albeit he is 33 years old! If he were a few inches taller, and had darker eyes, and more firmness in manner, and a little more of the kind of talent or strength of mind one wishes to *lean against* in ones journey of life, I believe he would please *me* better but not *her*, for she sees no fault and wants no change and though not in love she thinks she is, and laughs and dances and sparkles and chatters about her happiness, and her Rectory, and her village, and schools, and curates and old women so that it lights up the room she is in."

One sees what Sarah means about not being in love when one reads Lavinia's letters to her fiancé. There is none of that iridescent trembling happiness that shone through Sarah's own letters and through those of Catherine and Mary Glynne during their engagements. They do not begin "My own own" or "My own precious" but "My dearest Henry"; they are loving and affectionate but they might be written by a wife to a husband of thirty years' standing.

Yet Lavinia knew very well what she was about. Her brother George might compose one of his doggerel verses faintly mocking at her limited life:

"In Babbs,* clubs and churches, school, physic and toys,
Old men and old women, small girls and big boys,
In squallings and crawlings, in ponies and dogs,
Poor people's allotments, broth, dripping and hogs,
In squabbles of servants and grumbling of Curates
In looking up tithes and complaints of too few rates
    Poor Binks† lies spell bound
    Like a cow in a pound"

But Lavinia had no time or inclination to spend on self-pity. Her first child was born in August 1844 and "ever since", wrote her mother, "her happiness has indeed been beyond the common lot. She nurses like a cottager and looks really beautiful."

Two more little daughters joined the first in 1846 and 1847 and Lavinia seemed ideally happy; the Rectory, the Church, the gentle, beautifully mannered little girls seemed to make up an idyllic life.

However, the Nemesis that lay in wait for so many Victorian wives did not spare Lavinia. In 1848 a son was born, but as the bells were ringing for his birth (for he was the probable heir to Hawarden), he slipped out of life, lying by his mother's side. After that fears began to be entertained for Lavinia's health. Sarah Lyttelton and Catherine Gladstone got together in a tacit conspiracy to prevent or at least to suspend further pregnancies. "My dear Catherine," wrote Sarah, "I am anxious to let you know how fully dear Henry and Lavinia answer one's best expectations as to taking advice—not one of our easiest of oftenest performed duties!—Lavinia writes today: 'we *both* entirely approve Locock's‡ prescription—indeed Henry says, he had already prescribed the same measure for me in his own mind—so you see how ready he was to accede' ... Now dear Catherine," Sarah continued, "I must remind you that I did not hint at *your* having had any share in this wise advice, and that I hope you will keep to the same story; which I hope is not a *fraud*, but only a *silence*."

Locock's prescription was a cure at Ems. Lavinia went out there with her cousins the Estcourts and returned still "thin and brown" but better than her mother had found her on any

* Presumably babies.
† Binks was her family nickname, Lavinia—Win-Winks-Binks.
‡ Sir Charles Locock Bt. 1799–1875, the foremost gynaecologist of the day.

former visit. Catherine, however, was not to be consoled by Sarah's optimism. "Pussy is quite out of heart about Lavinia you see," Mary Lyttelton wrote to George, "on account of the doctor not having given a directions [*sic*] about beginning again."

Lavinia was only too anxious to "begin again" and there was the almost inevitable result. A fourth little girl arrived in October 1850 to join the Glynne nursery, but her mother died a few days afterwards.

Sarah was in charge of the younger Royal children at Osborne while the Court was at Balmoral when she heard that Lavinia was in danger.* She hurried up to Hawarden but she was too late to find her daughter alive. In a rather curious letter to Caroline Estcourt she disclaims undue grief. She dwells on Lavinia's peculiar fitness for heaven "after so tranquil, so flowering, so pure an earthly life"; and on her own advanced age and the "necessarily short time" she will have to live on (actually she survived for twenty more years). She admits that consolations "could be vainly addressed to one of really soft and warm feelings—these I never had—and I think they belong less and less to me—so that I have all along felt calm, and fully equal to common life and occupations, and undisturbed in health." This unsentimental truthfulness comes almost as a shock even to the modern reader. It is a throwback to the eighteenth century; so might Lavinia Spencer have written. Her children, Sarah wrote, were much more greatly affected. "George was torn and harrowed, by grief so deep and strong that it was awful and I trembled for his nerves—then Billy looked ghastly; pale and thin beyond example—and each hour seemed to make him worse—and poor, *poor* Caroline!—Alas!— *there* you may pity and weep!—for so crushed a poor tender creature never was—Sleepless, and in unceasing tears, and constantly trembling and cold, I can't bear to think of her state."

The sisters-in-law were almost equally affected. Lavinia's tranquil brightness had so much endeared her to them. "It is

* Sarah never accompanied the Court to Balmoral and obviously did not wish to do so. When the Royal family returned from their annual holiday she was bored to tears by their enthusiasm. "Scotch air, Scotch people, Scotch hills, Scotch rivers, Scotch woods, are all preferable to those of any country in or out of this world," she wrote, "deerstalking is the most charming of amusements etc. etc. The chief support of my spirits while it is going on, is the comfortable recollection that I shall never see, hear, or witness these various charms."

better not to talk or write about one's feelings," Mary wrote in a letter to George, when she visited the desolate Rectory five months after Lavinia's death, "but I was almost frightened with myself for finding how little I realized that she was gone nor how much I yearned for her, the tones of her sweet voice rang in my ears and her books and ways, and now nothing is left but her picture which Henry truly says almost makes it worse 'it is so like, and yet what is it to me'."

Henry and the four motherless little girls were of course the chief object of everyone's care. It seems that all did not run quite smoothly. "Many little and great trials there have been" wrote Sarah Lyttelton, "among so numerous a family party, all kind and loving—but not always *quite* judicious—not feeling as others expected they shd—besides great *mechanical* difficulties as to plans and arrangements—which have been uncomfortable. This of course I say in strictest confidence."

We cannot be certain as to what Sarah refers, but it probably reflects a slight impatience with Catherine Gladstone who was only too ready to manage everything for the benefit of her loved ones. The difficulties and trials seem to have been straightened out and Sarah, now released from Court life, spent a great deal of time at the Rectory superintending the health and education of the four little girls. They were all good and gentle but they were delicate. Mary, the eldest, was not quite normal, possibly epileptic, and Katie and Nora both died in childhood. Under the peculiarly ugly window put up to commemorate Lavinia in Hawarden church there is a charming bust of a child with chubby cheeks and hair tumbled about the rounded marble brow. It is Nora Glynne. Only the baby grew up quite healthily, to become the beauty of the family and to marry Lord Penrhyn, who had already seven children by his first wife and was to have eight more by Gertrude Glynne.

Sarah was a most loving and conscientious grandmother (she spent several months at St. Leonard's-on-Sea in 1854) nursing the ailing Katie who seems to have had some kind of rheumatic fever;) but it was necessary for her to find a home and to make a life of her own. Although she had spent most of her life in the country she was too wise to settle down near Hagley or Hawarden and she came to the conclusion that it would be best for her to take a small house in London where she could provide a home for Caroline and Kitty and make a

centre for the rest of the family. The family discussions and
arguments over where the home should be are amusingly
summarized in one of George's doggerel poems entitled "The
Doubting Dowager", which neatly takes off some of the
family characteristics:

"O Doubting Dowager! what chance of peace?
Beset by brother, daughter, sons and niece!

*   *   *   *

Belgravia ho! the fast Henrietta cries,
To walk alone, uncheck'd by prudent eyes!

*   *   *   *

Out on thee! Mary shouts, the peeress poor,
Mother of millions: how from door to door,
Shall I then carriageless and weary walk,
To elder sister for an endless talk?

*   *   *   *

Henpeck'd (unconscious) in his wedded life,
The Marshal of the Court* supports his wife

*   *   *   *

The tyrant Caroline has many a care,
Districts and duties, friends in every square,
One drags her east, another pleads for west;
One thing alone is sure, 'Whate'er is best,
'Tis I shall govern, *I* shall fix the place,'
And shakes her conquering fist in passive mother's face."

The poem goes on to list other members of the family; Kitty
Pole-Carew, whose "gentle lungs sound scarcely heeded in the
war of tongues;" Uncle Fritz, "the wise Earl", casting gloomy
doubts on everything; and bossy Catherine Gladstone who
exclaims:

"Dare ye go
Beyond the limits of St. James's? No!
Dare Doubting Dowager! But dread the wrath
Of her who never fails! Before whose path
Quails he, the leopard-eyed!"†

---

* Spencer, "Marshal of the Court" was the "small place" Sarah had
asked for and the Queen had found for him.
† Gladstone.

Pussy got her way. The house eventually selected was in Stratton Street and provided a family gathering place and staging post for many, many years.

George's poem, which was incorporated with his Dictionary of Glynnese and privately printed in 1851, provided a pleasantly light note in a decade which was for the most part a sadly depressing one. It opened badly with the death of the Gladstones' little daughter, Jessy, from meningitis. Mary, who was eight months gone with child, was almost as anxious as the distraught parents. "I get sick when there is no letter from London," she wrote, "and tempted not to open one when there is. Shall not teaze Pussy any more by offering help as she knows she has but to summon me and I shall be there." Any human help, however, would have been unavailing. There was a glimmer of hope when the dreadful screaming ceased and the child opened her eyes and asked for her feeding cup but it was soon extinguished and she died on April 5th.

Then in the autumn came the death of Lavinia Glynne, and Catherine Gladstone, worn out by nursing her sister-in-law, suffered a serious miscarriage in Naples where William had taken her to recuperate. She had not wanted to go. She felt too tired to make the effort and she hated leaving her babies who were parked at Hagley. Nor did she much care for sight-seeing; "She does not much enjoy pictures and churches as William does," Mary told George, but William liked such things, and when William and George wanted anything, Catherine and Mary saw that they got it. William in Naples became deeply involved with the question of political prisoners, one of the landmarks in his career, but Catherine felt ill and lonely and deeply disappointed when she lost her baby. "I do feel for your disappointment," Mary wrote, "for even I with so many should feel it very much more particularly as you felt yr baby would have been so associated with blessed Lavinia." For the two young women had been pregnant at the same time and while Catherine nursed her sister-in-law during the summer and autumn of 1850 they must often have talked of the coming babies.

Catherine's illness after her miscarriage was so bad that William, called back to England by the resignation of Lord John Russell's Government, had to leave her in Naples under the charge of her brother Stephen. However, by the spring she was recovered enough to come home and to recuperate at Brighton, which was at this period the favourite Gladstone-Lyttelton resort. (Later they changed to St. Leonard's-on-Sea.)

While she was at Brighton Catherine made one of the very few friends who penetrated the Gladstone-Lyttelton family circle in Mrs. John Talbot. John Talbot was an offshoot of the Shrewsbury family, he was consumptive and was at Brighton for his lungs. While there he suddenly died and Catherine with her instant empathy, her quick vigorous sympathy, was of the greatest support and comfort to the widow.

Mrs. Talbot was a remarkable person in her own right. She had been Mary Stuart-Wortley and readers of the *Life and Letters of the first Lady Wharncliffe* will find her there as a somewhat spoilt and very self-possessed little girl. Her doting parents took her on a visit to Welbeck and her mother recorded that Missy (then aged four) "came in *singing* and not the least shy. She stroked the heads and faces of the two youngest Bentinck girls, and then said, 'I like these little *Babies*.'" She developed into an ardent Churchwoman and almost more ardent Conservative. Gladstone was still to her mind on the right side of the fence when she made the acquaintance of the family and by the time he strayed over nothing could shake her love and devotion. "You will let me say *us* as if I belonged to you" she once wrote to Catherine "though it is by other bond than blood."

Mrs. Talbot had two sons Johnnie and Edward, with nine years between them. They too were swept up into the "Glynnese" orbit, spent many of their holidays at Hagley or Hawarden and, in time, married two Lyttelton daughters; but that was well into the future and we must return to the early fifties.

Public events were at this time deeply exercising the Tractarians. The Church seemed to its ardent supporters to be in a perilous state. In 1850 came the much discussed Gorham judgement.* It is doubtful if this caused much pain to Catherine

---

* This was the judgement given by the Judicial Committee of the Privy Council supporting George Gorham, an elderly Devonshire clergyman, in his action against the Bishop of Exeter who had refused to induct him to his living because he held (in the Bishop's opinion) unsound views on the Doctrine of Baptism. By 1850, however, the issue had come to turn not on Mr. Gorham's views but on the right of the Privy Council, a State Tribunal, to lay down laws for the Church. This was a bitter pill for the High Church party and led to many conversions to Rome, including Manning's.

or Mary. "Mr. P (Phillimore)* full of Gorham, but I now can't think of anything but Jessy," the latter wrote; but it strongly affected the men of the family. "William's lowness about Gorham has quite affected his temper," Mary told George, "distracted at small things if I only cd understand it dare not ask him for fear of shocking him." While Stephen Glynne writing New Year's Greetings to his brother-in-law in 1851 dismissed Lavinia's death (although he had been very fond of her) as less shocking than "the terrible prospect of the future as regards the Church".

Another public event which cast its shadow over the fifties was, of course, the Crimean War. It did not directly affect the Lytteltons, but Colonel Estcourt, the husband of Sarah's favourite niece, was killed; so was Hugh Seymour, the much beloved brother of the new Lady Spencer, and so were two of Mary's first cousins, the sons of Lord Braybrooke, Henry and Grey Neville. They had both written home the very day before their deaths, Mary told her brother-in-law Billy, "Henry full of joy at the trench work being over, little thinking the next day he would be a mangled body, having been killed in a most frightful way lingering 11 hours in torture, the circumstances of his death the Queen told Pussy, are so dreadful the poor parents must never know it—Grey wrote to say he was going on quite well 'and hoped before long to go home to see the faces of those he loved so well' the next day bleeding of the lungs came on and he was gone both in their youth and manliness, and I now see them before me the fine little boys we used to nurse and be so fond of. The Queen feeling [*sic*] is most striking talking of little else and taking in all the separate griefs of her subjects." It was a cruel war and probably an unnecessary one but one cannot help feeling with the Queen and with Sarah Lyttelton who wrote that she could not help being somewhat annoyed by "the deep regret which every *success* of our troops wakens in Mr. Gladstone".

But to women public events are never as worrying as private anxieties; and Mary Lyttelton had her hands full with her own immediate troubles.

Poor Lady Glynne died in the spring of 1854. She had suffered a stroke before her daughters' marriages and she had been afflicted with melancholia. "I feel more and more

---

* Afterwards Sir Robert Phillimore Bt. a well known lawyer and scholar.
5*

moribund" she wrote, "I poor wretch can do nothing. You have no idea how much the distressed feelings increase and bother." She took a dislike to Hawarden which she said was too full of memories and for the last ten years of her life she and her companion, Miss Brown, lived almost entirely at Hagley. It must have been a great strain for Mary. "I was obliged to make Mama dine at a quarter past 6 and our dinner at a quarter to 7 so with great bustling I got the nursing and dressing over in time tho' it shewed me how great help you had been to me besides pleasure," she wrote to Pussy after a visit from the latter in 1848; and again to George: "I have such a deal of accounts to do I can scarcely spare a moment for the children with nursing of Mama."

Sometimes Lady Glynne's mind was reasonably clear and she was able to talk over past times recalling "Horace Walpole and the wicked Duke of Queensberry," but sometimes, as Mary confessed in a partially erased sentence, "it is uphill work explaining to Mama who is who." She impinged hardly at all on her grandchildren's lives; just a distant rather formidable figure with a black patch on her nose, near whose room they were forbidden to make a noise, but her own children cared for her to the end. One of the effects of her illness was that she was unable to convey emotion. " 'I was trying to cry when Henry went out of the room'," she told Mary, " 'but I couldn't', which shows how much she does feel" her daughter added.

Her death was very easy and peaceful. "She was quite herself" wrote Mary "and her voice the same as in old days when she used to say a little hymn to us before we all three went to sleep."

Lady Glynne's death must in some ways have been a relief. Yet, as a charming letter of condolence from an old admirer, who had known Mary Neville in the days "when the admiration of her beauty was such as to be troublesome to her," put it, "It is sad to think that what I remember so good, *so* lovely and so gay should have passed first into affliction and then have ceased to exist."

Mary at this time had much to contend with. Meriel became seriously ill with a pleural infection and all but died. Mary herself had a lump on the breast which had to be removed though it was fortunately not malignant. Above all there were her continual confinements and her own increasing debility and weakness.

Sɪʀ Eardley Holland, the well-known twentieth-century gynaecologist, gave it as his opinion that, if a woman were young and healthy and circumstances normal, for the first eight children pregnancies became less dangerous and confinements easier.* After that the pattern sharply reversed itself. The vital forces slackened, the muscles were exhausted. Each baby after number eight was a steadily growing risk.

Mary Lyttelton's case certainly seems to bear out his views "I am rather weaker than usual," she wrote when Arthur was a month old, "but perhaps it is this air" (she was in London in what she described as "a mutton broth atmosphere") "and perhaps the 9th begins to give warning that I have had enough babies."

The salutary warning produced no effect. Less than a year later she had a miscarriage. "I hope you will not move about too soon," wrote her anxious mother-in-law, "it is of great consequence, quite as much as if it were a baby. If you *could* avoid beginning again *quite* immediately, it would be the making of you."

Sarah's adjuration was as useless as the symptoms produced by the ninth baby; less than a year went by and Mary was writing once more to her brother-in-law Billy; "Take in that this last baby was one of the very worst bouts I have had, also take in that I have no megrims before hand, as to thinking I shan't get over it, but a lowness about everything, anticipating you in jail, Charles a scamp etc."

This tenth baby was Bob, born in January 1854. In July 1855 he was followed by Edward "the tiny 11th".

The confinement was a comparatively easy one but after it Mary became seriously ill. Sir Charles Locock said that having another child would endanger her life. There is a conflict of

---

* He was discussing Jane Austen's sister-in-law, Elizabeth, the wife of Edward Austen-Knight, who died in childbed with her twelfth child. I believe the present view is that the safety factor lessens after the fifth child.

family evidence about this, not about what he said but to whom
he said it. Why he did not say it to Lord Lyttelton, who was of
course the obvious person, is incomprehensible.

Lord Chandos (the son of Alfred, Mary Lyttelton's twelfth
child) writes in his autobiography that it was Sarah who had
received the doctor's information and that she had not passed
it on because she said: "we never spoke about anything so
nasty" (employing the short a which was then considered the
U pronunciation).* This sounds altogether unlikely. Sarah was
perfectly able to talk about such things; she had done so in the
case of Henry and Lavinia and indeed people at the time of her
upbringing were far less mealy-mouthed in discussing the facts
of nature than the Victorians. Another theory is that Catherine
Gladstone was the recipient and this is perhaps more likely, but
the question still remains if Victorian delicacy prevented her
tackling her brother-in-law on such a subject could she not have
asked William to do so? We do know that in November 1855
Mary had a slight attack of congestion of the brain and it was
considered that it was due to over-nursing. Catherine wrote
both to her and to George saying that weaning was essential
and Sarah weighed in with some very sensible advice. "I can't
help being still fussy," she wrote to George, "from the fear that
you will not be careful enough as to quiet which you may be
sure is of the greatest importance for her getting really well—I
mean quiet of mind and body, as total as can be arranged. She
ought not to be asked a question, or order dinner, or hear a
lesson, or be told a piece of news, in several days—and be
spared as much as possible for weeks." After which a paragraph
is erased by another hand. Mrs. Talbot wrote to Catherine
Gladstone that she hardly dared hope the nursing must come to
an end lest there should be another baby. Catherine wrote to
Mary and said that it was time she and George had separate
rooms.†

It was all to no avail. The three ladies seem to have been
like the chorus of a Greek tragedy, hopelessly aware of impend-

---

* Lucy Lyttelton complains of her brothers coming back from their first
half at Eton talking about "harf" and "clarss".

† Mrs. Battiscombe saw this letter at Hawarden when she was working
on her life of Mrs. Gladstone, *The Story of a Marriage*. Since then the papers
have been transferred to the Flintshire Archaeological Society and I am
unable to trace it.

ing evil and unable to avert it. In the autumn of 1856 Catherine wrote to her husband, "Alas, there is a secret at Hagley which has come upon me quite as a blow; what think you of Number Twelve on the way?"*

One of the strangest things is why Lord Lyttelton, an un- usually religious, self-denying man, with a strict sense of duty, who adored his wife, should have been unable to restrain his natural appetites. Perhaps the doctor had not put it to him in so many words but the truth was only too obvious for any who cared to look. It is true that George Lyttelton was still a young man. He had married at twenty-one and was four years younger than his wife. In 1856 he was only thirty-nine. It is quite obvious that he was strongly sexed and at that date it was hard to satisfy sexual urges without procreation. Contraceptive methods were rough and ready, and to the deeply religious would probably have been considered wicked. Any form of sex on the side was unthinkable. It was connubial intercourse or nothing. It should of course have been nothing, though this would have been hard. Yet after Mary's death, for thirteen years George almost certainly lived a chaste life. I think that the main fault was not a lamentable failure of will power but a failure to connect cause and effect. Victorians especially in any matters to do with sex sadly lacked realism. They could accept the fact that the wages of sin is death, but not that a specifically non-sinful act (such as sleeping with one's wife) could by inadvertence or ignorance have exactly the same effect. Since they believed in an all-wise Providence they were inclined to think that all that happened must be done for the best. It was hard for them to realize that bad drains produced cholera and typhoid, that a completely free economy led to overworked factory children, that too much child-bearing killed women. They preferred to think that calamities were arranged by a Higher Power for some inexplicable but valid reason.

George Lyttelton seems almost to be arguing in favour of Mary's death when he writes in her Memorial: "there is a Christian sense to the heathen saying, 'Whom the Gods love die young.' But apart from the religious sense, I am disposed to

---

* Alfred Lyttelton must have been conceived in May. This long interval before telling Pussy is very unusual; as a rule the sisters exchanged news of impending confinements at once. Mary must have known how much her sister would disapprove.

believe, that she was not physically fitted to struggle with suffering or adversity bodily and mental. She could have borne it with entire meekness and holy resignation but her bloom and brightness and elasticity would have gone."

Incidentally one cannot feel that the plan of life indulged in by the family was one calculated to prolong the life of an overtired pregnant woman with a heart condition. The winter of 1855/56 was spent at St. Leonard's-on-Sea, firstly on Meriel's account, but also very much for Mary "as a person in delicate health and requiring particular care".

It cannot have been much of a rest cure. The Lyttelton family, Mrs. Talbot, her elder son, and an assortment of nurses, maids and governesses were all packed into a very small house. The three eldest girls according to Lucy's diary shared a tiny bedroom where there was "nothing wherein, and little whereon to put anything . . . Next to this is Mrs. Talbot's room. On the third floor are Baby's and Newmanny's slip of a bedroom, next to that a small apartment containing Amelia's bed, and answering the purpose of sitting, washing, and day nursery. Next to it is Papa's and Mamma's room . . . and next to them a bedroom for two maids." So much for separate rooms. Lucy goes on to say that: "the tight fit is great fun. So are the beds, which are perfectly unparalleled for hardness," but then she was fifteen and in perfect health. Matters were further complicated by three of the children getting scarlet fever. (Their convalescence was enlivened by Auntie Pussy coming every day and regardless of onlookers dancing in the Esplanade before their windows.) In April the whole family returned to London and Mary took the children to the Queen's Ball, rapturously described by Lucy. By June they were back at Hagley, and Mary must have known that she was great with child.

She had very strong suspicions of what the end was to be. She told George that the twelfth baby "was as the last gallant effort of the high-mettled racer", but her courage was high and her heart was perhaps hopeful.

So life went on in the comfortable old house, the boys came back from school and the click of cricket balls was heard just outside the drawing-room windows. A new governess, Miss A. N. Smith, arrived and for the moment won everybody's hearts. Matthew Arnold came to stay and was scorned by the pious Lucy because he did not kneel in church, lacking a hassock, "rather horrid for a strong man". In December the new plans for the church arrived, showing how the galleries were to be pulled down and the windows to be renewed. The chancel was to be "perfectly restored, with encaustic pavement, stained glass, seven steps, sedilia, and straight altar-rail. The obnoxious monuments to be stowed away in less glaring places." In fact as Sir John Betjeman writes:

> "Church furnishing! Church furnishing!
>   Sing art and crafty praise!
> He gave the brass for burnishing.
>   He gave the thick red baize,
> He gave the new addition,
>   Pull'd down the dull old aisle,
>   —To pave the sweet transition
> He gave th' encaustic tile."

In January the "whole tribe of Gladstones poured into the house," which was "choked overflowing echoing with children". There was a fairy play acted by six Gladstones and nine Lytteltons and a week later there was a lecture at the school on Longfellow's *Hiawatha*. There was also a servants' ball.

Later in the same month the whole party moved up to London and Alfred Lyttelton was born on the morning of February 7th 1857. He arrived quickly and for the moment, the confinement safely over, relief spread over the house. The two elder girls and Auntie Pussy all had a good cry together "with a gushing overpowering sense of thankfulness". William Gladstone called and "seemed hardly to imagine that she (Mary) could be so well, with good reason as we heard afterwards." Only George seems to have been unaware of the pressing terrible danger. Miss Smith and Lucy raced down the stairs to tell him about the baby's arrival. "He made a curious pucker with his mouth, opened his eyes wide and said, 'A boy! Why was I never told?' and stamped upstairs with a terrible noise . . . on the top he said to Miss S. and me with a delighted chuckle, 'Another boy! what in the world shall we do with another boy!' and went into the room."

His mother wrote to him on the day of the birth and her letter shows that the horrible anxiety which had hovered over the past nine months had not been shared by him. "What a bit of road we have all passed through!" she wrote. "It seems impossible to feel it enough, though one's whole mind is full of thankfulness and *wonder* at such a presentation — I am glad you did not know the worst at the time. It would have been so great a trial, to have behaved calmly as you must have done."

Catherine Gladstone speaks somewhere of George's "unearthly* manners in the sickroom," so it was probably a wish to preserve Mary's peace of mind as much as a desire to spare him which produced this conspiracy of silence.

After Alfred's birth his mother's health seemed to improve a little. Sir Charles Locock had said that she was so weak that she must be put on a particularly strengthening diet of port wine and steel. For a while this seemed to succeed. She went down to Brighton and seemed to get stronger, but the gain was a temporary one. George Lyttelton thought that the "strength that accrued was an artificial one, and the constitution rebelled against it. The high stimulants may have excited the circulation, and so caused the disease of the heart, which, we cannot now doubt, shewed itself as established, at Falconhurst."

Falconhurst was Mrs. Talbot's country house, set among the deep woods and valleys of West Kent and it was there Mary went after her sojourn at Brighton. Although it was then that she suffered the first attacks of breathlessness which showed that the heart was damaged it was not felt that her health was seriously imperilled. There were one or two expeditions to Penshurst and to Tunbridge Wells where, with her unspoilt childlike nature, she much enjoyed her dinner at the inn and the long drive there and back. She was able to attend Lucy's Confirmation, that immensely important event in the life of a High Church family. "I know," Lucy wrote, describing the occasion in her diary, "that I shall never forget the touch of the hand on my head . . . and the glorious rush of trembling calm that followed the indescribable feeling. And then I went back and knelt down . . . And the new Life had begun."

Altogether the period at Falconhurst was a happy one. "The

---

* *Glynnese*. "*Unearthly*. The word is well known in the mother-tongue, in the sense of something above, transcending this world and human nature; in the Glynne language it signifies something below them. An English Poet would mean by an unearthly noise or sound, something heavenly or ethereal; a Glynnese, something strange, not reducible to the rules of experience, but apparently proceeding from some gnome or fiend. . . . "

last," wrote George Lyttelton, "in which pleasure and hope predominated. We did not doubt that on the whole she was making progress. After her return to Hagley" (on June 13th) "tho' there was occasional hope, it was on the whole a constant decline." William Gladstone sent over his horse "Budget" (named after the budget of 1854), for the Lytteltons were unable to afford carriage horses, and Lucy was allowed to drive her mother out; but she grew steadily weaker and soon had to be carried upstairs. On July 7th she went to the Flower Show held in the Park, which gave such great pleasure to the local people that she liked looking back on it; but the effort tried her. The weather became very hot; she was sleeping badly and was plainly exhausted. July 14th was the last day she spent downstairs. Catherine Gladstone and the "invaluable Mrs. Talbot", as Sarah described her, both came down and divided the nursing between them, aided by Meriel and Lucy, aged seventeen and sixteen. There were no professional nurses that could be trusted in those days, but presumably there were housemaids. All the long accounts of Victorian illness compiled by loving relatives, though they chronicle minutely every change of breath and temperature, never allude to a bedpan.

The worst was still being kept from George. On the 12th August, "with the doctor's explicit sanction" he went to keep a two days' engagement at Birmingham and slept there that night. (They may have been glad to get him out of the sick-room.) But on his return he "for the first time observed what I thought even an inexperienced person could hardly mistake in thinking bad and formidable symptoms . . . On that day I first said to myself, and said to my mother and Mrs. Talbot 'I think it is drawing to an end.' "

If we were asked what was the main difference between ourselves and the Victorians we should probably pitch on our attitude towards sex. Yet an almost equally great division yawns between our differing feelings on the subject of death.

We do not of course in the main hold the same opinions about an after-life. Most of us nowadays think of ourselves like Archytas as "a little dust on Matine shore,"* whereas most Victorians were fairly, if not wholly, confident in the prospect

* Archytas was a Pythagorean philosopher and the quotation comes from the XXVIIIth Ode, Book 1, of Horace.

of a heaven where Christ would receive them and loved ones be reunited. But it is not only in matters of doctrine that we differ so greatly from our forebears. It is in the treatment and trappings of death and of dying that we find ourselves almost incomprehensibly remote.

We think of death nowadays as a private affair. It takes place mostly in a hospital or nursing home. The last days are soothed and tended by professional care. We do not hang around to watch the spirit leave the house of clay; we are told it has happened. We do not wear mourning. We think it the proper thing to rejoin the stream of life as soon as possible. Our grieving is done in private and not inflicted on others.

With the Victorians things were very different. A death bed was a great set piece. All the near relations were present or waiting about in the wings. The children were not exempt. They were hoisted up for last kisses and taken to see the corpse in the coffin. We are inclined to think of such a display as barbarous; and indeed it must have inflicted a very great emotional strain, not only on the relatives but on the dying person, him or herself. One can perhaps agree with old Lady Stanley of Alderley who brought a breath of eighteenth-century realism to her daughter-in-law's description of a sick bed. "I want to hear more of the dear Child's bodily state and less of her mental or spiritual . . . it is incomprehensible to us all that she should have been allowed to be so surrounded and to talk to much . . . keeping her hearing and feeling on the constant strain. I really think you must all have lost your wits.—have got into the seventh heaven of enthusiasm and forgot every-thing sub-lunary." Mary Lyttelton was probably too far gone to recover after mid-July 1857, but the terrific strain she was under during the last three days of her life must have seriously lessened any chance there might have been. And yet—and yet—the Victorians were only acting in the tradition of all civiliza-tions which have held that man must be accompanied on his last journey with pomp and ceremony, with wailings and lamentations. They were endeavouring to express some sense of the great mysteries which surround us, and the overstrained emotionalism with which they did so was perhaps a comfort to them. Great grief may reject a show of grief as affectation or it may find release in expressing what is after all a sorrow common to all mankind. We could not endure such a scene as Mary

Lyttelton's death bed nowadays; is this realism or cowardice?

We are able to follow all that was said and done during those long, long August days because George Lyttelton in a pathetic endeavour to embalm every last remembrance of his loved one wrote an account of them, asking everyone who had been at the death bed to contribute their memories. Although this crystallization of last hours and words was frequent in Victorian days (Gladstone wrote a long and minute account of the illness and death of little Jessy and Archbishop Benson wrote one of the last hours of his son Martin), it was not so usual to ask others to contribute to the Memorial and some distaste was expressed by Mrs. Talbot and Catherine Gladstone. "He (Lord Lyttelton) was so anxious for it that I did the best I could," wrote the former. "I share your dread of it being shown to people, it makes me almost *shudder* to think how your poor sister herself would have shrunk from that, and I used the strongest language of caution I dared to him abt it."

The Memorial is long, very long. It hardly seems possible when one has finished reading it that the main events took place in a space of three days, and this dragged-out feeling probably represents accurately the emotions of the watchers by the bedside.

On August 14th Mary was told by the local doctor, Dr. Giles, that she was in great danger. He had his hand on her pulse and the effect was that the pulse grew quieter. "It acted like a tonic," he said. But she was not quite reconciled. She told George that the thought of the children was almost too much for her: "They do so bring me back to life." Yet the next day she braced herself to take leave of them.

"The room got full; most of the children were there; some half awake, with their night gowns on; and much moving about and the confusion. But that she did not seem to heed. She said very little. 'Bless you dears. Mammy is going away.' "

She said to little Arthur (aged six) to whom she had taught the first rudiments of religion " 'Arthur dear, I am going to heaven I hope.' He just understood it, and cried very much; and said afterwards he should like to go with her, or that she might remain with him."*

---

* She had devised the plan of giving each of the younger four boys to be the special charge of one of the elder brothers, but this did not work out and was abandoned.

She took leave of the governess, of Agnes Gladstone and of those two pillars of the household, Newman and Mrs. Ellis, and then she and her husband, her two elder daughters, Mrs. Talbot, her brother Henry and her sister Catherine received the Holy Communion. (It was eighteen years since she had written to Pussy on her honeymoon to enquire if she was to take the Sacrament on Christmas Day. Mary herself would rather have postponed it till the following Sunday when she would be less tired but she would like to feel that she and Pussy were celebrating it together.)

After the Sacrament Sarah Lyttelton describes the scene: "She sat up, supported by pillows—white and thin, grave and altered indeed; but looking grand and gentle too, and like a Christian Matron soon to leave us. I spoke to her after she had communicated she was holding herself up, and shewed no weakness. Her appearance and expression were most striking, full of a calm holy dignity—as if her mind were raised above this world. Her voice was firm, eyes large and clear. It was not her usual countenance tho' beautiful. The look was grave— less young, it inspired confidence, and heavenly hope. Her extreme simplicity and her words were so striking. She said to me 'Now don't fash yourself about the children; you are too old for that. Your province is to look after him (George) and comfort him.' "

Before the service she had said to Billy who was of course officiating: "I don't pretend that I am not sorry to go, you know," but after it when she was told she was rather better: "I don't think I am glad to hear it. I don't wish to go back now."

She said goodbye to her eldest son; "You will make a friend of Papa, Charles; but remember that if ever you have anything in which Aunt Pussy can help you, always tell her as you could me, don't be afraid." And she added: "Well Charley dear, you see how everything seems to have gone wrong in little things. I was so anxious to see you play at cricket; and then when I was at Eton I could not stay for the match as Papa did. Then I thought it did not much signify, for I should have plenty of opportunities of seeing you play at home and now—I shall never see you." After her farewell to her eldest she said goodbye to the youngest, taking little Edward and Alfred in her arms and making cooing noises to the baby. It was hard to leave her sons but she bore up stoically; her greatest pangs were felt when she contemplated two other partings.

One of the few times when emotion was at all visible in her was on August 16th and was recorded by William Gladstone who had come down that day. " 'Take care of her,' she said, looking at Catherine . . . 'for it will make a great change to her and after a time she will feel it more and more.' " Mary could well imagine what the loss would be to her sister. The previous day she had said to Pussy, looking at her "so lovingly", " 'Oh if I were to see you in this state. I think it would break my heart.' "

Another moment when emotion broke through is recorded by Sarah Lyttelton. "Rather suddenly she said 'There is only one thing except . . . ' (She paused, turning to George) 'My eldest child — Meriel my eldest. I can't look at that child . . . ' I believe she stopped as if overcome, so as not to finish the sentence, 'and think that I must leave her. Not that I don't love the others as well — it isn't that; but my first baby — how I remember her as I saw her first — little black thing! Lady Lyttelton, *you* know what I mean don't you feel it about Caroline?' "

It may perhaps seem strange that the two cries of unforced emotion were directed towards her sister and her eldest child, not towards her husband. I think, however, that, knowing the depths of despair to which his mercurial nature could plunge, she did all she could to shield him. She once said wistfully to him: "How you will miss me! We have always gone on so well together"; and her mind dwelt on the time so long ago when he had brought her to Hagley as a bride: "I remember Papa showing me this room, and how lovely I thought the place," but she did all she could to lighten his burden, for as Catherine Gladstone put it: "She who would lean on others with childlike trust, was really filled with inward strength." She made little jokes to make him laugh and when he helped her to sit up she murmured: "So snug to have you here." Above all she talked to others of what they must do when the inevitable separation came. She said to Meriel: "You know what sort of things you can be useful to Papa in: things like Mackie and the pines* —

* Mackie was the gardener and the pines were presumably the hot-house pineapples.

what is to be done with them. And try to get things round him as he used to have." And on one of the few occasions she was left quite alone with Catherine in the dawning of August 17th the latter records briefly: "We had some talk—chiefly about George." It must have been on how to comfort him. Mary probably advised he should marry again.

Religion of course wound like a thread through the two days. She frequently asked for hymns or for special bits of the Bible to be read to her and she once dwelt on the possibility of seeing her Saviour, feeling, perhaps even a little doubtfully, that the prospect "ought to make up for all one is leaving". But on the whole as the first long, long day wore on, she spoke mostly of small practical kindly things. She said to Meriel: "Mind you are kind to the neighbours; I don't mean just now, but afterwards, the little civil things I used to do." She planned for the girls' coming out, asking Catherine and Mrs. Talbot to look after them; "I should not like them to be buried in the country, but to go to London occasionally, and make acquaintance with nice people: *good* people, people I like." And: "You'll take them to the Queen's balls, Pussy dear." And turning to the girls she added: "You must always go to Papa dears, always tell him everything, when you are older; whatever happens." She was even able to laugh at the situation; at one point she asked Lucy who was in the next room and on being given a catalogue of grief-stricken relatives she commented: "Dear! What a grim party," with, Lucy writes, "all her old fun in tone and look." Yet for a great deal of that Sunday she seemed poised on the edge of departure "with a serenity which passed understanding," "gazing beyond us all as if looking at something far away," but in the evening came an anti-climax. Her pulse was stronger and she seemed better. She was almost distressed at it. It was as if someone having made up their mind to a distasteful and uncomfortable journey had it put off and dreaded to return to the unpacking and the cares of everyday life. But this was not to be. The next day, August 17th, was physically a much more distressing one. Her breath was shorter, her heart beats accelerated and she was exhausted. She had a strange ringing in her ears and she thought that it was the Hawarden church bells of her girlhood. About half past seven in the evening she fell asleep. Suddenly in her sleep "she gave a piercing cry, loudly, clearly and strongly, like a frightened child. " 'Pussy!' "

Lucy takes up the tale: " 'Here I am darling,' said At. Pussy . . . 'did you think I was gone? I am always close by you.' Mamma answered in her usual voice again, quiet, and gentle and tender, all the fright gone in an instant: 'I thought you'd gone away, you wouldn't go away from me.' And she shut her eyes again."

A little later she had her only spasm of severe pain, which lasted about four minutes. She could not lie in bed so the old armchair, in which she had always sat opposite to George in the library, was brought in and she was lifted into it. When she was sitting up she said in a low gentle voice: "Let me go, let me go." She was not kept waiting long. There were a few last goodbyes to be said. Her brother Stephen, her sister-in-law Emy, the faithful Mrs. Talbot, her eldest son Charles. Then she kissed Meriel and Lucy with lips so icy cold that Lucy could not get the feeling out of her cheek at night, and whispered: "Good-bye dearies — you have been so good to me."

All this time her husband was holding her up with his right hand, supporting her head with his left. He called to her in anguish: "My darling, you can smile on me once more?" She had gone a long way on and she must have been very tired but she had never denied him anything. She turned her head and looked at him and smiled.

A few seconds afterwards she died.

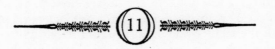

Mᴏᴜʀɴɪɴɢ was a serious business in Victorian times. Charlotte M. Yonge, whose family novels mirror with an almost uncanny directness the circumstances of the Lytteltons in real life, describes a new nurserymaid coming to a motherless family and being invested with "the universal blackness of the household". Queen Victoria wrote after her brother-in-law's death that she thought the dislike of mourning "positively wrong"; and added that "Darling Beatrice" (then aged just three) "looks lovely in her black silk and crepe dress".

Mary Lyttelton did not share the Queen's almost ghoulish delight in the trappings of woe, but it never occurred to her that the customs of the time could be flouted. "How sad it will be," she exclaimed the day before she died, "to see all the children in mourning. I remember the look of them so well after Mamma's death."

The week between Mary's death and her funeral was filled with the bustle of the maids getting the mourning ready. Lavinia and May were still so young that they were able to enjoy the great event of having two new frocks each. Black silk frocks with three broad bands of crepe for Sundays and stuff frocks with no crepe for weekdays. Writing years afterwards Lavinia said that "the smell of crepe has always taken me straight back to those August days". The poor children were taken to see their mother in her coffin and Lavinia was frightened and cried bitterly. Every blind in the house was drawn, no-one went out, and the great hatchment was hoisted over the hall door.

It must have been almost a relief when the day of the funeral came at last and the children, walking in pairs hand in hand crossed the lawn and the cricket pitch to reach the half restored roofless church and saw the coffin lowered into the grave. "I can remember," Lavinia wrote, "the delight of (having) the house light again and hearing the boys whistle."

The children had of course suffered an irredeemable loss.

142

"Their grief" wrote E. M. Forster of the motherless Wilcoxes of *Howards End*, "though less poignant than their father's, grew from deeper roots, for a wife may be replaced; a mother never."

The Lyttelton boys were reserved and never mentioned their loss but it deeply affected the elder ones. Meriel and Lucy found alternative mother figures in Mrs. Talbot and Auntie Pussy but the memory of their mother was always with them. "I went in the twilight," Lucy wrote two years after her mother's death, "to look at Mamma's beautiful E. window shining thro' darkness, as the thought of her does, in all that happens." The very little ones of course could remember nothing, but "quite young children," wrote Lavinia, "are feeling things deeply and unknown to the 'elders' and I recall bitter tears when alone, and a most real and dreary sense of loss and perhaps I hugged a rather morbid feeling that no-one cared for me. They were kind but not loving, not Mamma at all."

Nevertheless after a great calamity the young are resilient and recover, even if they are marked for life. With George Lyttelton it was otherwise. He had been so wrapped up in Mary, so utterly dependent on her for eighteen years, that no-one could imagine how he would manage without her. His mother in particular was deeply apprehensive. He saved himself at first by a total abandonment to his grief. "He seems like a child in simplicity and trustfulness," wrote Sarah, "relies upon every-one's kindness — weeps openly — talks of his feelings — and seems *sure* we are all feeling alike and will help him. The very first day, he came here to me, and sat sobbing as long as he could, and then wandered about, as if calling for pity. Now he is wonderfully quiet and able to occupy himself, and take some interest in other things." A little later she wrote to the same correspondent, her niece, another Lavinia, the daughter of Georgiana Quin: "Dear George looks very ill, *so* thin; his face quite altered, and very pale, almost always deeply grave, and ready to talk of what is past — and weep and muse and pine. He is not ill; sleeps and eats well and takes great exercise, his powerful health supports him, but it looks like a shattered spirit, always gentle and kind to all." In spite of her recognition of his loss there is almost a note of relief in some of Sarah's descriptions. "I ought to have said George's almost first uttered words, and after he has said them since, were a thanksgiving that he had *no temptation* to repine or murmur — never for a moment has he felt *bitter* grief, it has all been soft and kindly. He *accepts* it all, with loving patience. *This* is indeed *my* comfort." Knowing as she did her son's manic-depressive temperament, his tendency towards deep melancholia, Sarah must have been greatly relieved that his grief-stricken spirit was able to keep on an even keel.

On her death bed Mary, with her usual sense of proportion and realist attitude had said: "I know how it will be — dear George will feel it very much. He will grieve deeply for me — but I know his buoyant spirits. He will soon recover — and *then*" (turning very earnestly to Mrs. Talbot and Catherine) "don't be angry with him." She had, however, underestimated the part she played in her husband's life; he never truly recovered from her loss.

One of the first tasks was to go through all her old letters to him, range them in order and date them (Mary and Catherine hardly ever put a date on their letters). From the earliest ones starting "My own precious Tom Titten" to the last one which ends: "Bless you my precious, oh how I wish for your sake that I was well," they are a loving chronicle of every little facet of daily life. They are never high flown in language. They deal with mundane matters; the children, the servants, the governesses, money affairs; whether to sell the cart-mare or to breed from her; into which meadow to turn the sheep. There are characteristic turns of phrase, one letter is written from "Stinking Waiting Room, Wolverhampton Station," another compares Pussy's photograph to "a drunken landlady," but as she said "I like so writing to you just as I should talk." It is no wonder that the last two letters are blotted with tears and the last of all written on July 14th 1857 is endorsed: "She died 17th August 1857 L. O My God help me."

His two great consolations, besides his religious faith, were of course his mother and his eldest daughter Meriel, who, at seventeen moved into the headship of the house and did what she could to take her mother's place. 'She was a great companion to Papa," wrote Lavinia. "I do not think we smallies particularly liked her. She seemed a long way off and she was called the 'Old one' . . . She seems to me in memory to have been nearly always sitting in Library or Gallery reading and never rode or knocked about out of doors as Lucy did . . . But she was always gentle and just and wise, and was everything to Papa in the terrible loneliness and depth of his sorrow."

But in May 1860 Meriel became engaged to Johnny Talbot, Mrs. Talbot's eldest son, in the rather unpoetical surrounds of the long covered way leading to the station, after an expedition to the Crystal Palace. Johnny had at one time been attracted by Agnes Gladstone, but she was rightly considered too young to be told of it (she was only fifteen) and in the intervening three years he had switched his attention to Meriel. Her father doubted her being much in love but Lucy records her as "so radiant with the new happiness, that she looked quite pretty in her blue silk". It was, however, agreed on all sides that the person who most rejoiced was Mrs. Talbot who seized hold of Lucy exclaiming: "I couldn't have believed that I could be so happy."

To George Lyttelton, however, it was a serious blow. The loss of his favourite daughter (in Lavinia's opinion "he loved Meriel the best of his daughters though Lucy loved him best") and the awakening of old memories precipitated that crisis which might have been anticipated in 1857.

"George has been unwell — I believe, Bilious," wrote Sarah to her daughter-in-law Emy — "but the effect of whatever was the cause has been one of his terrible fits of depression which really alarmed me. No mental reason assigned, except that the marriage preparations reminded him of his own — and that he felt how sad it was for a bride to be motherless — All sadly true! However, after several bad nights and day he has slept well — and is today more like himself, tho' not *quite* right yet."

In these days of course George Lyttelton's melancholia would be regarded as an illness and treated if not cured by drugs. It is true that it was in part an hereditary legacy. His brother Billy wrote that: "I have still the strange complaint (which Caroline tells me Fanny Yorke* and the Carews* also have often) of *alternate* days of 'up and down' and the downs some-times are terrible," but Billy never came near to committing suicide. George's melancholia was part of an inescapable temperament but one cannot avoid speculating whether events in his life influenced the onset of the attacks. One bad fit was

* His first cousins.

attributed, as we have seen, to anxiety over his abortive Parliamentary career. The death of his wife and his daughter's marriage perhaps brought on the crisis of 1860; especially as in addition to these losses, he may have been burdened with a sense of guilt. We do not know when he heard that Sir Charles Locock attributed Mary's death to over much child bearing but he did hear it and, not unnaturally, it preyed on his mind. Lavinia, then a small girl, remembered walking between him and Newmanny and his enquiring of the nurse whether she thought that "the children" had had anything to do with her ladyship's death. Newmanny replied stoutly: "No, my Lord," and in fact there seems to have been a general conspiracy to keep the truth from him, as is shown by the following letter written to him by Mrs. Talbot in February 1858:

> "Miss Lyttelton mentioned that your Mother's impression of the long trial of Lady Glynne's state having had much to do with the break down of that health on which your life's happiness hung, is rather a satisfaction to you instead of supposing it to be simply the result of the twelve children — My opinion is of course worth little on the subject but such as it is the more I have heard & thought the more strongly I feel persuaded that the number of children had but a very secondary share in the cause of it — (indirectly of course whatever exhausted her powers may have contributed in some degree to the development of evil) — It was indeed because Locock fixed his eyes so exclusively upon that cause and *concluded* that all was to be attributed to it that he was so fatally blind to everything else. You may remember that when Dr. Evans saw her in the autumn of /55 though the fact of her eleven children was pressed upon his attention he made quite light of that & evidently did not think that there was the appearance of serious evil from *that* cause. Mrs. Gladstone though always herself at the time inclined to take the other side strongly often told me that — I own myself that I would rather not look on the children as having cost us her — & I can enter into your feeling it so — that is why I have said all this, which you will take for as much as it is worth."

Yet Mrs. Talbot in October 1855 had written to Catherine Gladstone: "I feel I dare hardly wish the nursing" (of Edward) "to come to an end lest there should come another Baby" and whatever anyone else might think Catherine in her heart was sure that overmuch child-bearing had caused her sister's death.

This unuttered certainty may have affected George Lyttelton's relations with the Gladstones. Catherine did her very best. As soon as the summer school holidays of 1857 were over she swept the remainder of the family off to Hawarden, though she herself was ill and pulled down. "You are indeed most certainly fulfilling her wishes — *petting* him," wrote Mrs. Talbot and in spite of her frantically busy life Catherine managed to write to her brother-in-law almost once a week during the next three years.

The Gladstone and Lyttelton children were shuffled about indiscriminately between Hawarden and Hagley and Catherine brought out the two eldest girls, as Mary had wished. Any rift was probably quite imperceptible to the younger members of either family. Yet after Mary's death there is not infrequently a note of criticism among the Lyttelton letters and the most definite evidence that all was not as it had been is that, when George Lyttelton made a new will after his wife's death, he appointed as guardians to his children two of his associates in the Canterbury scheme, John Godley and R. S. Selfe. They were close friends and he liked and admired them both, but they were far from the intimate circle of friends and relations which was so characteristic of the Lyttelton milieu. Godley, an Irish landowner's son was distantly related through his wife to George's cousins, the Pole-Carews, but Selfe was a police magistrate, a professional man having no connection with George Lyttelton's world. The latter's letter to Selfe shows that he was aware how strange the decision would seem. "I have only told my mother of my wish that you and Godley should be guardians," he wrote, "and I strongly prefer not telling anyone else. It is impossible that near relations — or *their* near relations should not feel a little surprise that persons not related should be preferred to them for such a function. I have not made this proposal without consideration; but as it is possible and not improbable that nothing may ever come of it, I may prefer not incurring the almost certainty of giving some slight dissatisfaction. In the event of my death I am sure there is not one of my relations whose good feelings would not lead them to perfect acquiescence, and to co-operate cordially with you if the occasion arose."

Luckily the occasion never arose; by the time that George Lyttelton died most of the children were of age and the younger ones could be left in the charge of their elder siblings, but there is no doubt that Catherine Gladstone would have been deeply and irretrievably hurt if she had ever known that Mary's children were to be entrusted to comparative strangers rather than to her loving heart. "Some slight dissatisfaction" is an extraordinary understatement!

George's melancholia at the time of Meriel's marriage led him to seek some sort of alleviation. "I was glad lately to hear," he wrote to his brother Billy, "that my mother and Caroline had spoken to you . . . I had rather have no secrets of this kind among my near relations, but still I do not readily mention it as I know it is a thing to which I do not mean as to myself, but generally some persons have a great aversion. I mean the idea of my ever marrying again. It is hardly more than an idea, it is hard to look forward to perhaps 30 or 40 years without some real hope in prospect." The difficulties he admits are very great and "a poor substitute for the past it wd needs be." She must not be young, for 12 children are enough, she must not have children of her own "wh. is always inconvenient", and she must have some money. "There is one person whom I might have vision of," he concluded, "who unites all the above, and I believe is of great merit; but . . . " The rest of the letter is lost but in one written a week later he says: "I believe I might as well think of the moon."

The unnamed lady was Louisa, Marchioness of Waterford, who had lost her husband in a hunting accident in 1859. She was a daughter of Lord Stuart de Rothesay, a remarkably beautiful artistic and pious girl, and there was some surprise when she became engaged to Lord Waterford, who had never seemed to care for anything but racing, hunting and practical jokes. "Ld. Canning told Ly. de T. Miss Stuart had just accepted Ld Waterford Oh!" Mary had written to George in 1842. Nevertheless the marriage was a blissful one till its unhappy end. Lady Waterford certainly fulfilled two of George's conditions. She had no children and her husband had left her extremely well off, endowing her with his Northumberland estates, including the beautiful old Ford Castle. Yet there is a strange naiveté in his even contemplating the idea that she should give her hand to a comparatively poor man, deaf, with twelve children, whom she scarcely knew. He did not venture to approach her direct but wrote the following, covering twelve pages with his scrawling untidy handwriting, to her sister, Lady Canning, and it must be one of the oddest proposals of marriage ever made.

> 10 Great George Street
> London S.W.
> 29 May 1861

Dear Lady Canning,

When you have read this letter I trust you may not either wonder very much, or think me much to blame for having ventured to write it.

I should not presume to do so on the strength only of the slight acquaintance with you of which I had formerly the pleasure. But there are several of my near relations & connections with whom you have long been on much more intimate terms, & on this account I will rely upon your kindness to excuse what I am about to write.

It is concerning your sister Lady Waterford. Long years ago I knew her, I may perhaps say, pretty well. I believe that if I had not, at the age of 18, fallen into my first & only love, I could not have escaped being captivated, as no doubt many others were, by her singular grace and beauty, & dignity of character. Circumstances are much altered now. She, as well as I, has gone through the heaviest of human afflictions.

I am not going to trouble you with any talk about myself. Second marriages must always be very different from the first: but I hope it is not strange, or wrong, or inconsistent with the enduring affection and regret which I must ever feel, that after the unbroken happiness & habits of 18 years I should, at my age, yield to the thought "It is not good to be alone". What I venture to ask you, is your judgment whether it is out of the question that your sister would, at a future time, listen to such a thought as I have suggested.

Pray understand the limited extent of the question I have (illegible). Except for a moment about 10 years ago, I have not seen her, I believe for 20 years, till I saw her for a few minutes, not to speak to, some days ago. I do now know that she is much altered: but I doubt if I should have known her again; & she probably had no notion who I was. At my time of life & after all I have gone through, it would be ridiculous to talk like a young gentleman of 20. But day-dreams of whatever kind, if they are but dreams, are best destroyed at as early a stage as possible: & before having any serious thoughts on the matter I have wished to learn, if I could, if it is wholly idle to do so.

I must admit that looking at her great position, at mine, & on the whole, I can hardly entertain the idea as a possible one. I feel as if I might as well think of wooing the goddess Juno. Indeed, I hardly know how I am ever likely even to see her, little in the world as I am.

But I may also be forgiven if I imagine some few considerations of a favourable nature. She has a great place to attend to: in which some aid might not be unwelcome. At some future day she must be left, as it may seem, rather lonely. She may be fond of children : & though I feel strongly that such a family as mine must naturally be looked on as a serious charge, even for the qualified responsibility which a step mother undertakes, still I do believe that there is no family of children equally numerous who give less trouble, perhaps who are much pleasanter, than mine are.

Lastly, looking at my very inadequate means compared with my position in some respects, it would certainly not be unnatural in her, or in others, to suppose that I was thinking less of her than of her wealth. Now it would be very foolish, in my circumstances, to deny that such a point *must* have some weight. Indeed I *could* not marry any one without any fortune. But I may perhaps trust that my character is decent enough to protect me from the idea being seriously entertained that I formed such notion, should I do so, without being determined by other motives than that.

I say "should I do so", for I could repeat that I had not even formed a wish on the matter at present. Before being led on to do so I wish if possible to be warned by a friendly voice, if I am entering on a hopeless attempt. I must again apologise for intruding on you, & the more so now I see to what a length my letter has run. But I have long known and heard of your kind nature & on the whole I feel some confidence that you will not be displeased with me for what I have written.

I am here in a house that I think you know. My eldest daughter and her husband have the use of it & here she expects her confinement in a few weeks.

The character of a grand-papa goes oddly with the subject of this letter. But I am still young even as a widower, & shall be rather strangely so as a grand-papa. Hoping that Canning as well as yourself is in good health
I am ever.

Yrs faithfully
Lyttelton.

The exact terms in which Lady Canning answered we do not know. In fact, except for the two letters to Billy, there is no allusion to this incident among the Hagley Papers. Sarah must have destroyed her own letters on the subject. We can deduce, however, that George met with an unqualified refusal, concluded in the nicest terms, for there is among the Harewood Papers a further letter from him thanking Lady Canning for her "very great kindness and friendliness much beyond what I had ever right to expect." Later he says that since he last wrote he had for several reasons come to the conclusion that it was a very unlikely prospect and had been turning his thoughts in other directions. "My circumstances and the number of my children make the thing so difficult from the small range of selection as to be almost impossible. I well know that if I were more of a hero I should remain as I am. But I am no hero : and I am very sure that there are few men of my age to whom long years of widowhood are not 'a sore burden too heavy for us to bear', . . . Forgive all this egotism, it is a tiresome consequence of the condition the extreme longing for a companion, which is laid upon me."

We do not know if, as this letter seems to hint, George Lyttelton made any other attempts towards marriage. He may have done though there is no trace of any such among the Hagley Papers. It is nevertheless obvious that not only the loss of his dear companion but the exigencies of a celibate life weighed heavily upon him. In one of his letters to Billy he writes of "the continual discomforts of single life" ; in another of "the heavy chain and burden of widowhood" [*sic*] ; and later he describes himself as "being of the earth earthy". There is no doubt, however, that he resisted temptation. He left among his papers a draft of a letter which he apparently sent to his sons as they approached manhood. Part of it runs : "You may sometimes hear from vicious and profligate men, that there can be no sin because it is simply unavoidable. Now I wish to assure you in the strongest way that this is not so : it is a delusion of the Devil to destroy souls. There are greater and lesser temptations of all sorts in this life : and greater and lesser differently to different people. But this particular temptation can be resisted by any one, like all others. I should not say this, if I did not know it from my own experience. I dare say I had as strong passions as any one else : but I never fell into vice, not once, nor did it ever occur to me as a *possibility* at all."

George Lyttelton strove manfully not only with his temptations

6

but with his grief. The latter was perhaps therapeutically aided by the extraordinary openness with which he was able to refer to it; not only among his intimate family but to friends and neighbours. In 1862 he gave a lecture at Hagley on the English Poets in which he not only referred to Cowper's "horrible mental delusion and melancholy" but quoted *in extenso* the poet's lines to Mrs. Unwin in which every stanza ends with the words: "My Mary." He also quoted Hood's poem: "We watched her breathing thro' the night." The references to his condition were obvious and were taken as such, but perhaps partly owing to the fact that he allowed his wound to bleed openly it did not at this time fester, and he was able to guide his motherless children through a boisterous and to most of them a blissful decade.

After the violent seizure of 1861 and his abortive attempt to woo Lady Waterford there seems to have been a long calm interval. It would be untrue to say that he recovered from Mary's death. "Never," he wrote in 1863, "for these six years, in a single moment of any day has my loss been out of my mind." Nevertheless it could be said that his natural ebullience of temperament reasserted itself. "I heard Papa whistle (softly, and half to himself) for the first time since '57," Lucy recorded in her diary for 1862. Outside interests began to crop up. In 1861 Lyttelton in conjunction with William Gladstone published a book of *Translations*, Gladstone rendering passages from Latin, Greek, German and Italian into English, while George Lyttelton, more unusually, translated Milton, Tennyson, Dryden, Goldsmith and Gray into classical tongues. One of Gladstone's choices was an ode of Catallus on to which he grafted a line from Sappho. George Lyttelton seems to have objected that Sappho was invoking a different kind of love, which appears to have surprised his brother-in-law since he wrote: "Re Sappho. I have known it" (the ode) "for more than forty years but your objection has never occurred to me . . . I think it is better to fall back on the construction, not in itself unreasonable, which I suppose is conventionally put upon it viz. that Sappho spoke in the person of some youth."

Public work also made its demands on George. In 1862 Lord Granville, on behalf of Lord Palmerston, offered him the chairmanship of a commission on secondary education. There had been two previous commissions, one on elementary education and one on the Public Schools. This third and most important one was to deal with "education given in schools not comprised within the scope of the two former Commissions"; and its province was the essentially middle-class education provided in endowed private and proprietary schools. These categories contained over 3,000 schools and ranged from Marlborough and Clifton on the one hand to Thame Grammar School on the other, which supported two masters and one backward pupil on an income of £300 a year.

The need for drastic change was only too clear; the subject, never having been touched, was a thicket of preconceived ideas, vested interests and outmoded legal statutes. The Commission was not so much a breath of fresh air as a strong gale, blowing among the accumulated dust and debris of the past. It has been called "the most determined and unceremonious of all educational inquiries". While another commentator has described its report as: "One of the most impressive public documents of the 19th century."

George refused the chairmanship of the Commission which went to a dullish Liberal peer, Lord Taunton, from whom it took its name, but he became one of its most active members. There were twelve Commissioners in all, a distinguished list including Lord Derby, Sir Stafford Northcote, Dean Hook and W. E. Forster. There were also eight Assistant Commissioners employed to make a special survey of eight districts chosen because they contained sufficient variety of population and occupations. One of these Assistant Commissioners was Matthew Arnold. The report was issued in twenty-one closely printed volumes in 1868 after four years of gruelling work. It was in all probability in great part the work of George Lyttelton, Frederic Temple, Bishop of London and afterwards Archbishop of Canterbury, and Sir Thomas Dyke Acland.

Its conclusions were radical and far-reaching. It proposed to set up a central authority over which a Minister of Education might preside. This authority would reorganize educational endowments, appoint inspectors of endowed secondary schools and set up a system of inspection and annual examination for all secondary school pupils. It would also examine candidates for the teaching profession and only grant certificates if they came up to standard.

There were many other recommendations, including a system

for grading secondary schools into three categories. First grade which would take upper middle-class boys up to the age of eighteen and provide a classical education together with mathematics, modern languages and natural science; second grade schools which would take boys up to sixteen and would teach Latin but not Greek; and third grade schools which would provide "a clerk's education, namely a thorough knowledge of arithmetic and ability to write a good hand". These boys left school at fourteen. In addition there was what was called "a ladder of education" by which a clever boy could rise from a low grade school to a high grade school and thence to a university.

It is of course impossible in a joint report to pinpoint the various contributions of the members; but we do know that George Lyttelton was unexpectedly liberal in his opinions. It is true that he thought that parents should if they could pay for their children's education and should regard it as a privilege to do so, but he also thought that any clever boy from any stratum of society should have his chance and should have every opportunity to rise upwards. He was a believer in an élite, but it was an intellectual élite. Nor, although he was such a passionate devotee of the classics, did he hold that they were a necessity of education, thus differing from the great majority of Victorian schoolmasters. But the most surprising stand that he took was on the "Conscience Clause". This enabled dissenting or agnostic parents to withdraw their children from religious instruction. Lyttelton felt that this compromise was preferable to the completely secular education called for by the Nonconformists since it would enable the children both of Church parents and parents who by and large were indifferent to obtain religious teaching, but he greatly alienated many of his Church supporters.

His open-minded outlook is also seen in his attitude towards girls' education. We know from a *jeu d'esprit* of his, written in 1867, that he was mainly responsible for the chapter in the report dealing with that subject. In a typically boisterous style the paper begins:

> Births
> At 21 Carlton Terrace, on July 11th, after a painful and protracted labour, Lord Lyttelton of a chapter on Girls' Schools. Friends at a distance will be glad to hear that this

long expected event has taken place & that parent and child
are charming well.

The Infant Chapter has a strong likeness in features and
deportment to its parent. It is uproarious — squalls incessantly —
and hopes to make much noise in the world."

The "Infant Chapter" does not today strike us as very
revolutionary, but we must remember the background against
which it was written. "There is a long-established and inveter-
ate prejudice," Lyttelton truly asserted, "that girls are less
capable of mental cultivation, and less in need of it than boys;
that accomplishments, and what is showy and superficially
attractive are what is really essential for them; and that in
particular, as regards their relations to the opposite sex and the
possibilities of marriage, more solid attainments are actually
disadvantageous rather than the reverse."

He set himself to combat this view on three fronts. The
Assistant Commissioners had reported that though girls were
better at Scripture and essay writing than boys they were
inferior in grammar, science and mathematics. Yet how could
they compete when they had no teachers capable of grounding
them in subjects which require a trained mind and the applica-
tion of reason?

The existing Special Training Institutes for schoolmistresses
were quite inadequate, and Lyttelton advocated very strongly
that teachers in girls' schools as well as boys' must pass the
proper Examinations and obtain "the definite credential of the
Certificate" which would be "a declaration of competency in
the art of teaching."

He then turned to the Endowed Schools, pointing out that
whatever the intention of the founders "it is evident that the
endowments for the secondary education of girls bear but an
infinitesimal proportion to the similar endowments for boys."
This was a state of affairs that must be remedied.

He concluded with a tremendous philippic directed towards
the new rising class of middle-class families who ought to have
wanted secondary education for their daughters as well as for
their sons. He castigated their "apathy and want of co-opera-
tion, often their active opposition . . . They will not pay for
good teaching when they might have it, they are themselves
the cause of deterioration in competent teachers . . . and their
own want of cultivation hinders it in their children."

This sort of language was not calculated to endear the Taunton Report to the mass of rate-payers, and it had already made many enemies among the vested interests of endowed schools and the formidable array of Victorian headmasters. But the pioneers of female education, Miss Buss and Miss Beale, Miss Emily Davies and Miss Annie Clough, future Principals of Girton and Newnham respectively, supported it (if an Irishism may be allowed) to a man!

Although he was so much occupied with the education of other people's children, and although the Taunton Report was probably his most important contribution to public life, George's main preoccupation during the decade of the sixties was of course with his own family.

After his two elder daughters were married he concentrated chiefly on his sons. "Our elder sisters," wrote Edward Lyttelton, afterwards Headmaster of Eton, "told us how when he was bowed down with grief in the darkest hour of his bereavement he said, 'This is the worst blow that could have befallen me except one of the boys going to the bad.' No-one will ever measure the amount of good those few words did, spoken as they were at one of the most sacred moments in the speaker's life and with the weight of all his moral power behind them."

After their moral welfare came their cricket. One after another of his sons succeeded each other in the Eton XI* and on the grass of the famous playing fields, their father would sit "just out of the line of sight, with a pocket classic in his hand reading and murmuring the lines to himself, but, as long as a son was batting, *never missing a ball*, and continuing to read between the balls." "He one day seriously alarmed his mother," Edward Lyttelton wrote, "when, bursting into her room in the London house and flinging himself into a chair, he groaned aloud, 'O Charles, Charles, I never dreamt he could have done it.' My grandmother hastily concluded that some barely mentionable tragedy had occurred and said, 'O George, tell me the worst,' but after close questioning the horrow was disclosed. Charles had 'run out to a slow and been stumped.'"

Sarah must indeed have been puzzled by this outburst. "It is amazing," she wrote, "how all our plans and arguments are mixed up with *cricket* nowadays — and all the time I understand

* Except Albert who strained his back and had to be taken away from school. He shared a tutor with Edward, Mrs. Talbot's younger son.

no more of the subject than an owl." The little girls got very bored being fagged by their brothers to pick up balls and stand at long-stop for hours and hours, but for the boys cricket was king; the pitch was immediately outside the drawing-room windows between the house and the church, a space which in other houses might have been utilized for flower beds. The little boys played in the upper corridor of the house with a ball of wash-leather stuffed with bran and a big paper knife for a bat; the elder brothers on wet days used the long gallery on the ground floor, oblivious of the rare early Georgian plaster work, the dim Venetian mirrors made for the house, the priceless pictures. For in matters of art the Lytteltons appear to have been complete Philistines. There is a family legend that the boys were only just prevented from sawing off the edges of the pie-crust Chippendale tables in order to obtain a flat surface which they thought more practical. They all loved Hagley but not one of them seems to have been aware of its visual beauty. The house, wrote Lady Wenlock, Mary Lyttelton's formidable aunt, "is as complete and as fine comparatively as either Stowe or Holkham, having nothing wrong about any part and being exquisitely finished in the correct and chastened style of its day". But that was an eighteenth-century appreciation; the nineteenth century cared nothing about the superb Georgian art and architecture. There is a faint sigh of regret from Lucy when "Papa sold 'the Rubens'," but otherwise they all seem to have taken the treasures by which they were surrounded for granted.

In fact during the sixties life at Hagley must have been something of a bear-garden. One of its most curious features was the napkin fights. These were started by "the Peer", as his children called George Lyttelton, uttering a loud roar and flinging his napkin in the face of his nearest son. The younger boys had been for some time rolling their napkins into balls hoping for the outbreak of the fray. When the signal came there was, wrote Edward, "an instantaneous bellow from all our throats, and the whole party ran stamping round the room shouting while some six or seven cricketers, all powerful throwers, were ranged in a sadly unequal combat against their father and uncle.* These were always the sides, but I have no idea how the first fight began." On one occasion a nervous guest was so upset that he clambered for safety on to the sideboard.

* Uncle Billy, the Rector.

The apogee of this period of Hagley life was the annual cricket match against the Bromsgrove Boys' School. (Sarah characteristically referred to it as this *"mad* family match plan.") George Lyttelton himself was the eldest player, Alfred, aged ten, the youngest. Uncle Spencer, wearing a magenta suit wandered about the deep field sometimes taking his leisure under an umbrella. Uncle Billy looking "rather manqué", fielded in his braces. As Lavinia said in her reminiscences: "It was a Red Letter Day." After the annual cricket match the family "the old dozen"* as Lucy called them, were always photographed. One of these photographs, probably that of 1864, was considered so good it was sent to Queen Victoria and may be found in the Royal Album. There they all stand, posed in front of a box camera balanced on a tripod, and behind it a man with a black cloth over his head, probably adjuring them not to move, to moisten the lips and to smile.

If the last direction were given they ignored it. They stand or sit beneath the balustrade which surrounds the perron at Hagley with set serious faces, staring in front of them, caught for one moment on a summer day over a hundred years ago.

In the middle is Meriel, matronly in her married dignity of black velvet, her lethargic placidity hiding a nervousness and diffidence which so much resembled that of her grandmother, Sarah Lyttelton. On the left of the picture is Lucy and, typically, she is the only one who has moved so that one cannot make out her features. Lucy, brimming with vitality, enthusiasm and excitement could not bear to keep still a moment, and in her overflowing tenderness, she finds it necessary to bend over the youngest of her adored brothers.

Behind Meriel is Charles, every inch the heir apparent. Tall, erect with auburn hair and fine dark eyes; a slight expression of self-satisfaction overspreading his beautiful countenance. He is everything a Crown Prince in Victorian England should be, a crack shot, a superb games player, yet dutiful enough to give up his all-engrossing cricket to work for the Newcastle scholarship. It is easy to pick out Albert with his unusual mediaeval saint-like countenance. Albert was the eccentric of the family, a sort of Prince Myshkin or holy fool. The Lytteltons are full

---

* She had a habit of using "old" as a term of endearment. Her brothers are frequently referred to as "old Nevy" or "old Charles" while Meriel is nearly always "my old darling".

of stories of "Uncle Albert" with his threadbare clerical clothing and strange jerky way of speaking. It is recalled that he broke the death of one of their relations to other members of the family by exclaiming: "Who's dead? Who's dead? Guess! Guess!" and he used, he said, to admonish his female parishioners who deceived their husbands by telling them to "think of Mrs. Micawber — so faithful." On Charles' right stands Neville who is to go into the Army and is, if not less religious, less Church-ridden than the rest of the family; and on his other side Spencer, who is musical with a fine singing voice. He was afflicted with a slight stammer which may have made him shy, for both he and Albert, unlike their father, were totally averse from any form of sex. It is a family anecdote that his mother asked Spencer if he had ever kissed a woman and he replied: "Once, on the brow," but this is demonstrably untrue as his mother died when he was ten. However, it is illustrative of his character. Owing to his Uncle Fritz's generosity Spencer was the only one of the brothers who enjoyed an independent income and except for a short period as Gladstone's unpaid private secretary, he was free to do nothing throughout the course of his life.

Then come the two younger girls. Lavinia at fifteen or sixteen looking like a woman of thirty. Perched demurely in her chair she might already be in charge of Keble College. Her dress and hair style are extraordinarily unbecoming, but the photograph just shows that the features are uncommonly pretty. May on the other hand standing beside Charles, shows no signs of the blazingly-attractive girl into which she was to develop. The next three little boys with their hands in their pockets stand in front of their elder brothers. Arthur, the only son to inherit anything of his father's scholarship, but a difficult often "fratchy"* character; Bob, the stupidest of the brothers, generally in some sort of minor trouble, falling off his pony, cheating over his sums or catching ringworm. Edward, "the tiny 11th", puny but self-reliant and even now no mean cricketer; and, finally, lounging back in a chair, the only male to be seated, his legs crossed, golden-haired, large-framed, "King" Alfred, the adored of the family, the child who had cost his mother her life.

---

* "Fratchy": not Glynnese but a word much in use among the younger Lytteltons. Lewis Carroll might have described it as an amalgam of fretful and scratchy.

6*

inclined to draw the reins too tight. Her brothers rather objected to having high tea in the Easter holidays in order to fit in with the services and showed their displeasure by sending down for relay after relay of eggs. How much was expected of them is shown by a letter of Lucy's to Meriel dated Easter Eve 1862. "You were right and so was I in supposing they would naturally go to Church everyday; that is Spencer did not on Monday; though the others did; but every other day has done like the rest. Of course it was a blow that (except Albert) they only went on the evenings of Wedy and Thursday but on the whole they have been very good." The "boys" were at this time aged between sixteen and twenty.

Lucy's rule was sometimes resented by her younger sisters and perhaps her greatest success was with the little boys whom she adored and who readily responded to her religious training; but she was so sincere, so loving and so idealistic that her family forgave her even when she pushed them hard.

She took her responsibilities very seriously and when in 1863 she, to her great excitement, was appointed one of the Maids of Honour to Queen Victoria, she wrote that she thought it would be "pleasant and comfortable ... to think of being ordered about and relieved of responsibility; with nothing to settle for myself. I have had enough of my own way, and all the cares it entails, to make this sort of dependence one of the things I most look forward to."

Although at first she felt desperately shy and strange and declared that she would ever afterwards sympathize with "poor peggies* launched at their first place" Lucy was on the whole very happy in her short tenure of office. Her account of the Queen contrasts amusingly with her grandmother's more down-to-earth description. "I can't tell exactly what it is in her face which is altered," wrote Lucy, making no mention of its having become 'so *very fat*', "but she has gained an expression which used not to be there; her grief has set its stamp there, but so as to refine and ennoble it. Her sweet and kindly smile went to my heart."

In spite of her royalist enthusiasm it was not Lucy's fate to remain long at Court. In December 1863 her father took her to stay at Chatsworth where, she wrote in her diary, "at dinner I

* Maidservants. I do not know if this was a general Victorian term or peculiar to the Lytteltons.

got into an argument with Ld. Frederic Cavendish* on the
Church, which excited and interested me. I don't think I was
wrong, as I did not introduce the topic on purpose; but I wish
I had been somebody who cd. have convinced him!" It does not
sound a very promising conversation for Lucy was fanatical
about the Church of England. She was not only deeply and
sincerely religious but as far as ecclesiology went she might
almost have rivalled her Uncle Stephen. "Church is Lucy's
public house" said her sister-in-law Mrs. Neville Lyttelton,
"and the worst of it is one cannot get her out of it." On one
Sunday she was delighted to hear no less than four sermons and
the entry most joyfully recorded in large capitals in her early
diary is, "The Vestry CONSENTED UNANIMOUSLY AND JOY-
FULLY TO THE CHOIR SURPLICES!!!" For it was not only
the Church but specifically the Tractarian Church which roused
her enthusiasm. Surplices, chanting, vestments, open pews, the
Eastward position, were all necessary to gain her approval, and
on a previous visit to Chatsworth she had been horrified as she
wrote to Meriel: "But oh my dear, the Church! The *whole* of
the E. wall is occupied by a gigantic and purely heathen monu-
ment to the 1st Earl of Devonshire." And she amplifies this in
her diary by adding: "Oh dear! How can people go Sunday
after Sunday to such a place, and think they are worshipping
God in the beauty of holiness?" Lord Frederick, who was not
particularly High Church, might have been put off by such
criticism but he probably was more impressed by her sincerity,
her vitality and her charming, lively, mobile face. Certain it is
that when two weeks after the Church discussion at Chatsworth he came to stay at Hawarden his attentions became what
in Victorian days was known as "marked". He had been
invited with some idea that he might do for Agnes Gladstone
but it was not towards Agnes that he turned. "Well my dear,"
Lucy wrote to Meriel, "on Friday I was doing my crochet in the
library among the others (when) Auntie P. called Ld. F. to buy
some photographs for a charity. He chose some of her and Uncle
and William and Agnes; and then, shooting† one of me (in

* The second son of the Duke of Devonshire.
† *Glynnese.* "To shoot. This is of course either a sporting or a military
metaphor . . . It means, rapidly and suddenly to discover or hit upon,
especially perhaps something at a little distance; from which definition a
remote clue to its derivation may no doubt be gathered by the perspicacious

her book, *not* among those she gave him), he said 'May I have that?' and when she gave it him he took her hand and squeezed it."

The enthusiastic Auntie Pussy opined from this (quite rightly as it turned out) that Lord Frederick was "committed and decided", but the Lytteltons felt that this was premature and "sadly unwise". "Your father called it 'Catherine's blundering again'," wrote Sarah to Meriel, but she added, "Your father is *much* pleased — *very anxious for it*." Then there was another scare started by Mrs. Talbot. She had heard that Lord Frederick had read *Essays and Reviews* and approved of its shocking principles. George Lyttelton wrote to his sister-in-law to enquire about this, saying that "though I do not myself judge severely of all those who are supposed to be in that way it would certainly be very unpleasant to those who have been brought up as Lucy has." He added a post-script, perhaps occasioned by a twingle of conscience over his animadversions on "Catherine's blundering", saying "It is very, *very* kind of you to be so hearty in this matter."

Sarah Lyttelton was even more deeply worried than her son over Lord Frederick's possible Erastianism. "People do slide downhill so awfully when they have begun to doubt or cavil," she wrote. "Certainly before *Essays and Reviews* appeared one would not have minded a degree of liberalism." It all seems rather a storm in a teacup nowadays; it is hard to visualize the state of mind that would regard the very mild degree of religious open-mindedness expressed in *Essays and Reviews* as an insuperable obstacle, but perhaps it is a more worthy state of mind than that of the eighteenth century and of Sarah's grand-parents, who married their fifteen-year-old-daughter to a man she had never seen and who was quite unsuited to her, simply because he was a Duke and had great possessions.

Lucy's marriage, if not so spectacular as that of her great-great-aunt Georgiana, was nevertheless from the worldly point of view a great catch. The Cavendishes were no better born than the Lytteltons and were of course closely related to the Spencers, but for generations they had wielded the power of aristocracy allied to great riches. They were the leading Whig family in

---

reader. Example given by the Dean of Windsor, 'Last night I shot the Bishop of London in a corner at the Queen's party.' "

England. They possessed an enormous amount of property; great estates, Chatsworth, Hardwick, Bolton Abbey, Holker, as well as a sizeable portion of London. Moreover the eldest son of the Duke, Lord Hartington, seemed unlikely to marry. He had begun his *"vie d'amour"* with a liaison with the notorious Skittles, a lady of the town, and was now enmeshed in an affair with the German-born Duchess of Manchester. It appeared likely that Lucy might become one of the most important Duchesses in England or might, in any case, mother a future Duke. For all this the Lytteltons cared very little and Lucy not at all; she would have been just as happy married to a hard-working curate, provided of course that he was sufficiently High Church!

She did naturally have a healthy normal girl's pleasure in setting up her new home and indulging in such a luxury as a carriage and horse of her own. To clothes and jewels she was more or less indifferent. She was happy because she loved and admired her Freddy and because her new position enabled her to do things for her relations, particularly her younger sisters.

The marriage proved a remarkably successful one, but there were a few drawbacks. The major one was that it was childless. It must have been a strain on even Lucy's conception of an all-wise Providence to see Meriel, who had never much wished for children, punctually replenishing the Talbot nursery year after year, while Lucy who so yearned for a child remained barren. In Lavinia's opinion it was the deepest and most poignant sorrow of her married life, even more deeply felt than its tragic ending.*

The minor unpleasantnesses were concerned with her relations with her new in-laws. The Duke who had been an early widower was a formidable and silent man. All the Cavendishes were intensely reserved and talked little, commenting only on the weather and the day's bag. Lucy, accustomed to the continual exchange of opinions and ideas at Hagley was oppressed by this, tried to lighten the atmosphere, and ended by talking too much and telling too many anecdotes about her brothers. Two years after the marriage Lavinia records that: "Lucy is still rather on pins and needles with the Duke."

But if Chatsworth was constrained Hagley made up for it!

* Lord Frederick was assassinated by Fenians in Phoenix Park, Dublin on May 6th 1882.

"I wonder if I could at all convey," wrote Lavinia, "what those Hagley times were when we were all so thick on the ground ... Lucy as the happiest of wives falling in with the whole thing in her own special and brilliant way, and the 8 brothers and the singing and the fun and endless jokes — the deafening talk at the meals, with Uncle Billy so often there, undergoing the chaff from the Etonians over his Winchester school ... it is all unforgettable, the noise and merriment suddenly ending perhaps in a return to books or to a lot of part singing, and to Spencer's beautiful voice singing song after song to Albert's, and often May's accompaniments. And Granny in her chair opposite Papa amused and happy if a bit deafened."

Lavinia was now the head of the household at Hagley and it seems strange that so much authority was vested in a girl of fifteen. "I recall," she wrote, "how nervous I was at having to scold or 'have a little talk' with the maid-servants now and again." Mrs. Ellis was a strict disciplinarian and when she disapproved she used to "turn on" Lavinia to check and give advice to "the silly gal". In such circumstances it seemed inevitable that Lavinia and May should be liberated from the thraldom of a resident governess. These poor ladies had always supplied a perpetual problem. Miss Annie Smith had won golden opinions at the beginning of her stay. Mary Lyttelton gave her a brooch as a last bequest, George asked her to contribute her recollections to the Memorial of Mary's death and Lavinia had a dream in which she saw herself, her sisters and Miss Smith beckoned up to heaven by a Mamma surrounded by angels. This dream, the quintessence of Victorian sentimentality, enraptured the family. Lucy made the child write it down and George sent it to Catherine Gladstone who wrote: "Oh that heavenly dream. I cannot get it out of my head," and added: "William was equally touched by it." It is doubtful if Sarah Lyttelton, with the drier outlook of an earlier generation, was equally moved; and in any case she soon perceived that Miss Smith was getting above herself and was inclined to fancy that she might console the widower. She embroidered slippers for him and waylaid him in the park. He was quite oblivious of these attentions but Miss Smith had to go. Sarah summed her up as "the goose of all geese".

The next governess was a Miss Window, and her name drew forth a characteristic example of George Lyttelton's sense of humour. Writing to Billy he begs him to exercise "forbearance and self denial . . . in the name of our common ancestry" and not to make more than two puns a week. He then perpetrates a series of excruciating ones himself, concluding: "I inscribed 'Win and Min'" (the girls' nicknames) "on her with a diamond."

Miss Window was satisfactory in spite of the fact that she had a beard and moustache but she was delicate and she died during the Easter holidays of 1863. Lord Lyttelton, notwithstanding his impecuniosity, bought Miss Window a plot in Highgate cemetery.

The last governess was called Miss Merlet. "Her tone of mind and conversation," Lucy wrote in her diary, "is flippant and sarcastic." This was not at all suitable for the Lyttelton family and Lord Lyttelton had to make a special journey to Worcester in order to dismiss the flippant lady by letter, lacking, one supposes, the courage to do so face to face. On receipt of the letter, Lucy wrote, "Miss M. looks unutterable things, but says nothing." After that there were no more governesses.

In the winter of 1867–68 George Lyttelton went for the first time to New Zealand to visit the settlement that he had done so much to found. Catherine Gladstone, well aware of the rocky state of the Lyttelton finances, was anxious that while the owner was away Hagley should be shut up, most of the servants dismissed, and that the entire family should migrate to Hawarden. For this she received a most delicately administered but unmistakable snub from Sarah Lyttelton. The old lady had been very ill in the autumn but her even, delicate, eighteenth-century handwriting is as strong and legible as ever. "Dearest Catherine," she wrote, "Caroline has just shown me your letter — and as you mention me and my opinion in it, I can't help writing to thank you for this kindness; and for all the affectionate trouble and interest you are taking in laying out our winter plans. As to my opinion about them, I can only feel that whatever might be their advantages, it would not be right to adopt them in George's absence. He wished, I know, to find everything much in its usual state — If you had happened to think of such an arrangement before his departure, and had talked it over with him, and obtained his consent (I own I think it would have hardly been even in *your* power to obtain it!) it would have been different — but I cannot think it would be fit as matters stand. We will be as stingy as we can, at Hagley — but I fear this prospect of much saving is rather visionary."

One can see both sides of the question. It was certainly not Catherine Gladstone's business to interfere in her brother-in-law's affairs; but she loved Mary's children almost as her own and she was deeply worried at seeing their heritage eroded. In the end the matter came to a compromise. Hagley was not shut up but the younger fry were dumped at Hawarden for two months. It probably did not effect much saving but for the adolescents especially for the two younger girls it was a memorable visit, the most exciting aspect of which was the getting to know their Uncle William. "It was the time" wrote Lavinia, "which drew out my deep love for him always mixed with a certain very wholesome awe. I had hardly known him *well* before, & I felt his kindness enthusiastically. There were delightful moments of fun, so captivating in a man like him. Once one evening someone declared after a visit to Chester that the Bp. was the ugliest man he knew. 'No' cried out another, 'the Dean is much uglier.' Upon wh. Uncle William divided us into 2 parties as in the H. of C. with Speaker & all, & made an absurd speech himself dwelling on the marked features & the plain looks in the 2 men with eloquent choice of adjectives. Then there was the placing of the company into 2 parties ready for voting & speeches followed Uncle W's & a taking of votes with shouts of laughter, & the declaration of the result. And I can't remember which side won!" -

The core of Hawarden is an eighteenth-century house. It is almost indistinguishable from outside, being overlaid with the towers, battlements and crockets added on by Catherine's and Mary's father, but inside there is a fine hall and staircase enriched with swags of fruit and flowers and one particularly lovely square room on the ceiling of which two delicate gilded cranes, one just landing, one about to take flight, face each other across an elaborate pattern of roses centred on a golden sunburst and a bas relief of Apollo. The long room leading out of this is less beautiful but still elegant with its coarser early nineteenth-century plaster work and its enormous sashed plate glass windows looking out onto the terrace. It is known as the library though it contains few bookshelves and one of these is a dummy. The sham book titles (*Witchcraft by a Hawarden Lady, Doubts on the Dungeons, Sally Ports at Hawarden Castle, Ways with a Hatchet*) were invented by Gladstone, and the door they cover leads into his private study, known as the Temple of Peace.

Although George Lyttelton remained the central figure in his own household and in his children's lives after Mary's death Sarah naturally occupied a very much more important place at Hagley than she had during the years of George's marriage.

"Granny", as Sarah Lyttelton was now universally called, and "Aunt Coque" came down every holiday to Hagley. Sarah was beloved by all the children though she could be quite severe with them. "She had always the Tapestry Room close to the Dining room," wrote Lavinia—"and I have the happiest recollections of the quiet of the room and a certain sweet perfume of something, and of the tidyness of the writing table with her little old-fashioned pretty things lying about." She used to read aloud to them in the evenings, "spouting" as they rather inelegantly termed it; and if she found it necessary to bowdlerize Shakespeare for her granddaughters her own taste was refreshingly robust. She stigmatized the *Christmas Carol* as "a mawkish & unreadable effusion of Dickens's". She taught all the children French; and Edward recalled that he and Alfred used to be called in from the cricket-pitch about 7 p.m. in the summer by the sight of a *Times* spread out below Granny's window. "The signal" he went on, "odd to relate— was duly obeyed; but Granny gave significance to this trifle by telling us our punctuality gave her real pleasure." Truly she must have had a remarkable influence on her descendants; the authority she had learnt to impose on little Princes and Princesses stood her in good stead.

Aunt Coque was less popular with the rising generation; "she was too fussy and restless—and so *very* constantly sent us on messages! and she scolded us, not without good reason, in public, wh. is so much disliked by children."

Nevertheless in spite of grandmother and aunts the reigning Miss Lyttelton was very definitely the head of the household.

After Meriel's marriage the honour devolved on Lucy, who with her intense devotion to Church services, was perhaps,

It is rather a dingy little room, lined with musty books which are surmounted by plaster busts of statesmen he admired, including rather oddly one of Disraeli. There are two desks, one for work and one for pleasure (by which he meant translations from the classics) and a short rather shabby leather chaise longue. Into this sanctum Gladstone allowed his own family and the Lyttelton cousins to penetrate on the strict understanding they never said a word. "Sometimes however," wrote Lavinia, "he would *begin* a little talk to our great pride and some nervousness," and he encouraged the young people to bring him any difficulties which they found in their Bible reading. He would also hold forth about Romanism, about the capability of appreciating fine scenery, how it did not exist two hundred years ago and had still not penetrated to the poorer classes, and about poetry and music, "extolling the former," although when music was going on in the library he liked to leave the door open and would roll out "In questa tomba", in a fine sonorous bass.

Altogether these weeks gave the girls a glimpse of wide horizons. It is not surprising that when they returned home to a "long sit" at the Rectory with their rather parochial-minded Aunty Emy, they found that "somehow the talk was rather uphill".

It is possible that George Lyttelton may have experienced something of the same flatness when he returned from New Zealand, for he was visited, by one of his fits of deep depression. It may have been partly due to his tangled money affairs since at this time he wrote to Gladstone asking his advice about selling the estate and even seems to have overcome his dread and dislike of office so far as to ask his brother-in-law, now Prime Minister, if anything was possible in that line since Gladstone replied: "As regards office I have no doubt of your fitness for the duties you refer to, indeed of your eminent fitness — if you were not unmanned by your own doubts — but it is ill to get, and slippery to hold."

Shrewd little Lavinia, however, was probably right when she wrote in her diary. "Papa still very low & though the moneyums* may have something to do with it — but [*sic*] I think it is an illness."

---

* *Glynnese*. "The affix *ums* is tagged on to some substantive or adjective, and the ugly compound is then dragged into some sort of meaning by the aid of the auxiliary very *to have*, and the definite article *the*. Thus, '*to have the*

The depression lingered on, for in November we find May writing: "Papa is really better though not quite well, he is generally rather bad in the mornings ... there is no restlessness & he isn't often tender over us, but then he thinks L & I don't know, poor dear Daddy as if he could hide it for a moment."

In the spring of 1869 George Lyttelton took his own measure for combatting his depression; he became engaged to Sybella Mildmay, née Clive, the daughter of a neighbouring Worcestershire landowner.

"She is not in the least pretty," wrote Lucy in her diary, "and looks some years older than she is (33), but she has a dear good face, and nice, steadfast-looking kind eyes; a very sweet voice and a manner at once dignified and gentle."

Sybella had not had a happy life. She married in 1860 Humphrey Mildmay, who was mentally unstable and went completely off his head during their honeymoon. She refused, however, to have him put away saying that she had taken him "for better for worse" and that this was the worse and she kept him by her till he died in 1866. She was left well off and her family were of course opposed to her marrying Lyttelton, an impoverished man with twelve children, but she told her father that she had married the first time to please him and the second time she meant to please herself. She was in fact devoted to George and revered him greatly. She told Lucy after his death that though he never taught her by precept "yet by degrees, as she learnt more and more of his character and its motive power, she grew into sympathy with his religion, and that learning to feel with him 'doubled and trebled' her love for him".

Nevertheless she might well have been daunted by the task she had taken on. Her new family was on the whole co-operative but she met with some criticism.

Lavinia felt that her step-mother was far too much of a worrier, occupied continually with small domestic details and "trolling" away for hours about "small arrangements hows and wherefors, buying & selling". She contrasted this sort of

---

churchums' (a phrase signally and almost exclusively applicable to Sir S. Glynne) means to be much occupied in, and specially to devote much of one's conversation to, the subject of churches. *To have the deadums* would be similarly applied to an undertaker, or to anyone who happens to have been much concerns about such scenes, and is inclined to talk about them."

conversation with the tabletalk they had been accustomed to hear from Granny and Aunt Coque.

Aunt Emy, who quite plainly disliked her new sister-in-law, found that she "had not great depths or religious aspirations" and complained that "my little efforts at remarks are often quite unheeded".

Among the boys Charles held out the longest. He, the eldest, had the strongest recollections of his own mother and he would not have been human if he had not considered the effect that a jointure and a possible second family* might have on his already much impoverished prospects. He was, however, soon won over by Sybella's tact and became her ally in her attempts to civilise the somewhat unruly bear-garden Hagley had become since Mary's death. Family tradition has it that she said to him: "Charles! This house will someday be yours, but there will be little of it if the boys are allowed to continue playing cricket in the Long Gallery."

On the whole therefore the family was prepared to welcome the newcomer. "We can all feel thankful that it has been brought to pass," wrote Lucy. "There has been no managing or interference; it has come about quite rightly and naturally, and so one can rest in the certainty that it is God's hand that had led dear Papa to this 'evening-time light'. "

Sarah Lyttelton in all her letters also emphasizes the fact that the engagement had come about without any influence or management; so much so that one wonders if the previous attempt on Lady Waterford had been inspired by her advice. It would have been unlike her usual good sense but she must have been at that time so deeply anxious for George that perhaps she clutched at straws. She was, however, more than prepared to welcome Sybella. "She has so many excellent qualities that she is already endeared to his daughters and to me," she wrote in one letter and in another she praises Sybella's charming kindness and uncommon tact.

It seemed at first that Sybella's cares and worries might be considerably reduced when her two unmarried step-daughters both became engaged.

---

* Sybella had three daughters by George Lyttelton. Their half-brother Neville, who must have rivalled his father in tactlessness, is said to have remarked to one of them, Mrs. Alington, "and then there were those three little girls, nobody wanted *them*."

For a time all was excitement and bustle. Even the Queen was aware of it and she said graciously to Lavinia at a summer garden party: "I hear you are both going to marry two Edwards!"

George Lyttelton who thoroughly enjoyed his daughters' love affairs and thought it very dull when no "Herr Liebster" (as Sarah termed them) was on the horizon wrote to his brother Billy in high glee. "Tennyson says that in these days Cupid is a Lawyer's desk & there is a general idea that love-matches are going out. Far from the fact my reverend friend. E. Talbot the *night before* Win accepted him was told by Lucy not to make too certain. Whereupon what does he do? He goes into Meriel's* dressing-room before she went to bed, makes her sit down to talk to him and comfort him, & *lay on the floor with his head on her lap*, (like Samson & Delilah) moaning and groaning. At last the infuriated John rushed out, about 4 *a.m.* and asked Meriel if she was coming to bed. This from a grown Oxford Don & Head designate of Keble College. The other case is at present as matter of fact. Poor E. Denison wrote me a letter which since the days of Ovid has never been exceeded; & today I have seen him. I should think it is the most virulent case on record: he could hardly hold up his head or say a word."

Lavinia had been somewhat doubtful about accepting Edward Talbot. She was both to give up her butterfly life (she and May had had two very successful London seasons under Lucy Cavendish's aegis) and settle down as the wife of a clergyman and an academic. She had grown up side by side with Edward and had been more or less aware of his feelings for her since he had been in love with her since she was fifteen. He was a tall lanky young man who had had to leave Charterhouse owing to an attack of periostitis which condemned him to three years of a semi-invalid life. However, at Oxford he carried all before him, became a tutor at Christ Church and in 1869 at the age of twenty-five was offered the Headship of the new Tractarian College which was to be called after John Keble. It was then that he proposed to Lavinia in a scene that is strangely reminiscent of her parents' courtship. Like Mary, Lavinia was unsure of her own heart; her relations, again like Mary's, thought they knew better, and the young couple were

---

* Meriel was of course not only the sister of his love, but his sister-in-law, having married his brother John.

left alone in the drawing-room of a London house "opposite each other at a round blue velvet table", much as Mary and George had been thirty years earlier. The outcome was the same and the marriage was equally successful.

But May was never to be as lucky as her sister. Edward Denison was some ten years older than her, an intellectual, idealistic young man, already member for Newark and with strong ideas about improving the lot of his fellow creatures. Anticipating Arnold Toynbee he had for two years made his home in the East End of London feeling that this was the only way to gauge the problem of poverty and his privately printed letters (unfortunately all personal allusions have been cut out) show how deeply he was exercised and how sensible his conclusions were. He was also very acceptable socially; he was the son of a Bishop of Salisbury and the nephew and heir of the Speaker, John Evelyn Denison, who had a large landed estate at Ossington in Nottinghamshire and was an old friend of Lord Lyttelton's.

Unfortunately it was this wealthy uncle who put a spoke in the wheel. He refused to countenance the marriage. Why, it is not quite clear. He may have objected to May's lack of fortune, the Lytteltons thought he wanted Edward to marry another young lady; or he may have felt that his nephew was not healthy enough to marry. If this was so he was quite right. Doctor Clarke examined Edward in October and declared that his lungs were in a dangerous state. Lord Lyttelton thereupon decreed that any idea of marriage must be given up. The young man was sent abroad for a long sea voyage and died at Melbourne on January 30th.

The Speaker's veto on her engagement was naturally a great blow to May and her family were deeply sympathetic. The only exception was Aunt Emy who wrote that: "May rather disappoints me by being quite unaltered in the way of loudness and brazenness. I wonder if Mr. Denison has the slightest idea what she is really like." But Sarah Lyttelton, even in her last illness was much moved by the young girl's disappointment and kept murmuring: "Poor May! poor brave May!" They were almost her last words, for Sarah's long life was drawing to a close.

She was now eighty-two and had on the whole enjoyed remarkably good health except for a cataract which had caused

her to lose the sight of one eye. At the beginning of 1869 she
was still taking a great interest in life and was able to toddle out
to visit another old friend. "Well & I went to the Queen
yesterday," she wrote to George on March 13th, "and found
H.M. very fat and rather red, but by no means disagreeable to
look at—and quite as charming as ever in manner & kindness.
We had a long, long talk, not notable of course—but about
everybody she could think of belonging to me—Praised Ld.
Spencer* & his wife—said *you* are grown fat—(a mistake)—
asked me suddenly with a comical little face 'What is *your*
opinion of the Irish Church?'—Of course I answered the truth,
that my opinion changed so as to agree always with the last
person I had heard speak of it—which amused H.M. I added
however very earnestly that one opinion I had never changed;
which was that Mr. Gladstone was sincere & honest & well
intentioned to the bone and all through.—She gave a quiet but
serious assent—I asked if it was true that a man had tumbled
down before her at the Levee? she said; 'Oh several have done
it—but *one* man, the last levee, fell full length and *rolled* away,
having seized & kept hold of my hand to pull himself up!' I
said 'did he drag Y.M. *along with him*?' 'He did,' she said most
positively—but only for a little way'—and she laughed
immoderately."

The picture of the two dear old ladies, laughing together,
talking of their ailments and their grandchildren, is charming;
but it was the last time that they were to meet. In October while
she was staying at Hagley Sarah Lyttelton was taken ill. It is
not clear what ailed her but of course the basic trouble was old
age. She had to decide when she got a little better whether she
would return to her house in Stratton Street or remain at
Hagley for ever. The old family doctor, Mr. Giles, would, she
told Mrs. Talbot, sanction one journey but it should be the
"last long one while I live". She wavered for a while but finally
came down in favour of Hagley the home of her married life,
the centre of the Lyttelton family. The last few months of her
life seem to have been peculiarly blessed.

"I should like to speak to you rather than write of the dear
Granny," Edward Talbot her grandson-in-law-to-be wrote.
"I can hardly convey to you the sunny impression of bright

* 5th Earl Spencer, Sarah's nephew, m. 1858 Charlotte Seymour who
was so lovely she was known as "Spencer's Fairy Queen."

calm cheerfulness wh. my visit to her left with me. Her talk was all placid content & thankfulness; her interest keen and her manner bright as usual or even more so; with more of gentleness & loving affection—& her face is—I think not at all—certainly as little as possible altered. Maybe a shade paler—no change of expression." Lavinia at Christmas had the same tale to tell. Granny, she wrote, "has sent away her wheel chair & ... has almost entirely got back to her former ways; it's nice to find how little oppressed she is by our size & noisiness, even when Uncle B. dines. It is a great mercy, & what a difference it has made this Xmastide!"

By February, however, Sarah had weakened considerably and she was also suffering from "a horrid rheumatism". This, Aunt Emy, always the most realistic and the most disagreeable among the Lytteltons, described as making her "very irritable ... when At. Coque is there it is very distressing from her want of patience with her & when she is away as at present poor Granny vents it all on dear At. Kitty who never for a moment loses her patience and wonderful gentleness."

Sarah lived on for another two months. At moments she was quite her old self. She would recognize her grandsons, Charles and Neville, "her whole face beaming with delight." She looked out her carbuncle bracelet to give as a wedding present to Lavinia; "she heard and followed Uncle Billy's prayers—her face with a heavenly expression." But she suffered a great deal and was very often lost in drowsiness or what was worse in delirium or moaning unconsciousness. It was a relief when on April 13th 1870 the end came. She died very peacefully with all her children around her, George leaning over the bed and holding her right hand, Caroline on the left holding the other, poor scapegrace Spencer at the foot of the bed, and Billy kneeling to read the Blessing and the Commendatory Prayer. It must have been a comfort to them all except Sarah herself who had gone beyond prayers and forms. She slept so quietly that they could scarcely hear her soft breathing and were not quite sure when it was stilled.

A few weeks later "old Elly", the housekeeper who had come to Hagley fifty years earlier and had been there to welcome Sarah and William Henry in 1826 followed her mistress to the grave.

ALL the Lyttelton girls kept diaries but the first volume of May Lyttelton's which has survived only begins three days after her grandmother's death and this in some way seems more than a coincidence. For if with Sarah Spencer we enter into the intensely strong almost claustrophobic atmosphere compounded of family and religion which characterizes the upper classes during the era we loosely classify as Victorian, with May Lyttelton we begin to leave it. Her diaries exude a different atmosphere from those of Lucy or Lavinia. She is restless and discontented, an incipient rebel. She wants something different, she longs to be a man, she writes that she "hates everything" but "myself most".

She remained as religious as the rest of her family but two of the men she loved were sceptics, and she would write in her diary: "Bliss not going to church," an entry which it would be impossible to parallel in any other Lyttelton diary of the period.

She and Lavinia were only fifteen months apart in age and they were "a pair" as Catherine and Mary Glynne and as Meriel and Lucy Lyttelton had been. Nevertheless it is obvious from diaries and letters that May was fonder of Lavinia than Lavinia was of her. "Wish more feeling for religion," Lavinia wrote in her diary on the occasion of May's twelfth birthday, "I should love her a great deal more."

Lavinia was in fact a little prig. She had always grown up on the sunny side of the wall. She was welcome to her mother as an unusually tiny baby and among a tall family she retained this fairy-like smallness which coupled with the fact that she was extremely pretty made her something of a family pet.

May, however, was carried by her mother when the latter was intensely worried over the death of Jessy Gladstone. "This day month," she wrote in a thoroughly depressed mood, "I expect my poor little baby." And May, when she did arrive, turned out a thoroughly plain child. She grew no prettier as the years went by. "May, I think, is a degree less ugly," Lucy wrote temperately in her diary and her grandmother referred to her at the age of fifteen as "the poor giant girl."

Quite suddenly, however, the Lytteltons' ugly duckling turned into a swan. By the time she was eighteen she had become a charmer. She was never regularly pretty but she was tall and well developed with a mane of shining dark auburn hair and wide-apart brown eyes. Moreover, she exuded a charm and a radiance which were instantly compelling. She did not enjoy the robust good health of the rest of the family; May's entries in her diary end "tired", "horribly tired", "very bad headache" and so on; nevertheless like many sufferers from nervous troubles such as migraine she would, when she was amused, blaze up into a fire of vitality, and do much more than was good for her. She had a great appetite for admiration, probably the result of her ugly childhood and adolescence, and was a tremendous flirt. The Lytteltons frequently disapproved of her. They had hoped that her sad experience with Edward Denison would have, as Lavinia put it in a letter to Meriel, "permanently have quieted & settled her, disinclining her to jump down any stray Captain's throat, or seem to be so desperately anxious to be singled out".

This was unkind of Lavinia, whose natural tendency to priggishness was increased by matrimony and becoming wife to the Head of an Oxford college. (Lucy used jokingly to call her Mother Keble.) It seems all the more unkind when we read May's diaries and her misery when she was left alone after Lavinia's marriage. "Anything like the desolation of this aft. and evening I have never felt," she wrote after the wedding and her attachment to Lavinia remained in many ways the central emotional prop of her life.

However, she did of course recover both from Edward Denison's death and Lavinia's marriage, and proceeded to enjoy a social life gayer and more varied than anything her sisters had known. Meriel and Lucy had been very strictly brought up, they were almost the last girls in London not allowed to waltz and they were taken out of the theatre before the ballet began. Lavinia and May had had much more freedom and now May, under the care of an indulgent step-mother much burdened by pregnancies and babies, was almost entirely left to the chaperonage of her brothers. Charles took her to smart house-parties at Ashridge and Belton which she enjoyed very much but her real friends were the little group which formed round her, her brother Spencer, and her cousin Mary Gladstone. This set consisted of the Palmers, the daughters of Sir Roundell and Lady Laura Palmer; Frances and Amy Graham, the daughters of William Graham, a rich Scottish merchant, the art collector and patron of the Pre-Raphaelites; and Spencer's college friends, Hubert Parry, the composer, J. W. Strutt, afterwards Lord Rayleigh, the eminent scientist, and Arthur James Balfour. Their linking interest was music. Mary Gladstone and May were both pianists, Spencer sang and Balfour played the concertina. They made music among themselves, they got up professional concerts (Mary as the Prime Minister's daughter had no difficulty in persuading such figures as Joachim and Neruda to perform for them), they religiously attended the "Monday Pops" and they went wild with enthusiasm over the Handel Festival.

There were of course some emotional cross currents. Mary Gladstone was in love with Arthur Balfour, a match much favoured by her parents, and Arthur Balfour was in love with May. The early progress of this affair was amusingly chronicled by Lavinia in a letter to Meriel dated January 9th 1871 describing a visit to Hagley. "I ought to be too tired of the name of Mr. Balfour to write you anything about him but yet I must I think. To be sure how glad I was when 8.30 came last night & the eratic [sic] youth thought fit to go off to Scotland to travel all through the night to his home. He is at bottom I have no doubt very clever & good, & starts in life with an attractive dreamy sometimes amusing manner, & he is most highly spoken of by angels like Mr. Strutt (sen. Wrang). But he is a bit spoilt by a round of visits lasting 4 months, & is to my mind conscious of his impulsiveness & attractions, as well as of the fact that all the young ladies during his 4 months visit have been at his feet. You know we were quite agog over Mary G. and he, hoping something could or might happen some day, & May began by promoting this, & tried to get them together etc. It was certainly not needed for Mary has hovered over & round him all the 3 days wh. hovering reached a climax last night when he & she remained in Ch., long after everyone had gone, to listen to the Handel voluntary. But I don't want to be hard on her, I believe she really likes him a bit, & till yesterday there was nothing very outrageous, tho' I hate the whole style &

evident way of perpetually seeking out people before you are sought first. He don't appear to care for her more than anyone else, but that may come some day. You see May was not in active prominence this time, tho' *when* not with Mary, May claimed his attention & conversation & was perhaps at times to blame in too loud talking across the table at him & in her wonderful absence of shyness. But she most conscientiously tries hard, & now fails not so much in act as in manner."

It was at the end of this visit that Neville was heard to remark sourly: "I don't think much of Spencer's friend, he was always hanging around the girls."

During the London season of 1871 he hung around still more conspicuously. May's diary records that she met him somewhere or other almost every single day during May and June. They rode in the Row together, they attended the Handel Festival and there were delicious teas and dinners in Arlington Street, Balfour's home, where she found it "pleasant seeing them all together a happy family party," and where they "laughed till [*their*] sides ached" over the misfortune of a caterpillar in the salad.

It is generally assumed by Balfour's biographers that the long hitch in his attachment to May Lyttelton was caused by his unwillingness to commit himself. It is probable that they do him an injustice. Hitherto all they have had to go on are the extracts from May's diary concerning himself which were copied out for him after May's death by Lavinia. When one approaches the full text, however, one sees that at the height of her involvement with Balfour May met and fell in love with somebody else.

She was riding in the Row with Frances and Amy Graham* when it came on to rain. She took shelter at their house in Grosvenor Place where she "made acquaintance with their brother an attractive youth". It appears to have been a case of love almost at first sight.

As was only to be expected her family disapproved. Rutherford Graham was described by his sister (afterwards Lady Horner) as "brilliant and adored," he was moreover the eldest son of a very rich man. This, however, carried no weight with the Lytteltons. The fact that William Graham was a self-made

---

* Afterwards Lady Horner and Mrs. Muir Mackenzie respectively.

man, in trade and outside the closely-knit circle of London society (his daughters were never asked to fashionable London balls) may not have weighed with them unduly, but that he was a Presbyterian would surely have been regarded as a grave objection. Worse still, however, was the fact that Rutherford's own moral character did not stand up to their close scrutiny. Lavinia described him as "slippery" and believed that he had played fast and loose with other young ladies. Sybella Lyttelton heard very bad accounts of him from her brother Archer Clive, who was himself in love with May, and was frantically against the match. Lord Lyttelton went down to Oxford (Rutherford was still at Balliol) to make enquiries about the young man and when he came back categorically forbade any further involvement. May bowed to family pressure and twice refused her suitor, once in the autumn of 1871 and again in the spring of the following year. It was clear, however, that her heart was differently inclined. Although she was forbidden to go to balls where she might meet him, she saw him at musical lectures and Monday Pops. She records one of the latter where she "watched ∼ all the time". On one occasion he came up to her and said: "Won't you shake hands?" The diary at this point is full of erasures, blanks and entries in illegible German script in which one can just make out the one word "Photografie".

It was obvious that in the long run May was determined to have her own way. Her diary is not explicit enough for us to follow the exact sequence of events but we read that on May 25th 1872 she went down to Oxford and wrote: "Things settled as I wished, & great comfort in consequence.", and we learn from Lady Horner that she obtained from Rutherford the promise that he would not go into the 10th Hussars on which his heart was set, but would instead enter his father's business. After a year's probation she hoped her family would relent. It is almost certain they would have done so. Lord Lyttelton, as we have seen, was very soft-hearted about love affairs and was no match for May's determination, but Fate stepped in. Rutherford Graham died quite suddenly of diphtheria at Liverpool on his way to America.

May was heart-broken. Her family was on the whole sympathetic, "her feeling was *very* real," wrote Lucy, "& had only deepened since the refusal". Aunt Pussy opened her arms to the poor girl. "There is no-one like darling Auntie when one is in trouble," May wrote gratefully. Aunt Emy on the other hand was as usual critical. "She seems to have given way to weak self-indulgence & nobody to have hindered her."

It was a long time before May recovered. Rutherford Graham died in January 1872 and in the summer of 1873 the entries in her diary are still very lugubrious. She rides in the Row but "hates the sun & the horrid smirking people," she is so tired of her own thoughts and find a "dreary monotony in never caring to go to one place more than another." Another entry runs "Haunted. Do mind everything so impossibly."

By the autumn, however, she was beginning to recover a little and Arthur Balfour came sauntering back into her life.

He came to stay at Hagley and participated in one of those gigantic yearly expeditions which the Lytteltons always made to some beauty spot in the neighbourhood. This year it was the Wrekin and the party of assorted Talbots, Lytteltons, Pole-Carews and Gladstones numbered twenty-two. They picnicked in a "lovely rocky crevicy place where the view was perfect" and sang part songs. Would that some Victorian genre painter such as Augustus Egg or Frith had commemorated the scene!

Arthur Balfour's charm is plainly shown in the delightful picture May, in a letter to Meriel, gives of him lying full-length on the sofa and having a historical discussion with Mary Talbot aged ten. She "kneeling at his feet with dilating eyes and red cheeks, he with his usual nonchalant manner but not talking a bit less cleverly than he would to Lord Salisbury".

Balfour makes frequent appearances after this but there is nothing significant till, over a year later, in December 1874 he and May and Spencer Lyttelton travelled down together to spend a week-end at Latimer, an ugly red-brick house in Buckinghamshire, belonging to Lord Chesham. Although it was December and a hard frost they played lawn tennis, and on Monday May records "Mr. Balfour and I not very good;" and on Tuesday that the tennis was "something of a failure as neither he nor I could play." Mr. Balfour travelled back with her and Spencer, "funny journey" she comments. He came to tea and also to dinner. She was alone with him and her two brothers Spencer and Charles. She "played a little, gt. failure."

It is impossible to know what exactly occurred. Arthur Balfour always insisted that he had proposed to her during that week-end and that she had accepted him. Yet it is non-proven;

although probably slightly agitated, May makes no explicit statement of any kind nor are there any erased passages or sentences in German code. The only further mention of "Mr. Balfour" is a week later, December 23rd, when he "came in for a minute" and Sarah (the little half-sister) "knew him quite well."

Three days later another little half-sister was born (George Lyttelton true to form gave Sybella three babies in four years), and May returned from a brief visit to Meriel to find a state of affairs which as she rightly said were enough to drive her step-mother mad. "I should have thought Papa's experience might have taught him better," she told Lucy, "but no! The nurse says 'His Lordship is quite unmanageable' on Sunday the day after" (the birth) "having both children scouring the room, and Papa tossing Sybil till Sybella started with terror . . . I am happy to say I lost my temper and lectured right and left with such energy that everything since then has been beautifully quiet like a lamb!"

The diary only continues for twelve more days. On January 12th 1875 it ceases for good.

May had gone down to Hagley to collect her things for a country house visit. The roof of the Hall was undergoing repairs so she stayed at the Rectory. There she was taken ill with what afterwards proved to be typhoid fever.

She was ill for ten weeks and for a long time the fever was not diagnosed. Indeed it was not till Aunt Emy caught it that they took precautions about infection. It was nearly ten years after Mary's death and by this time it was possible to obtain good professional nurses, and Newmanny the old nursery nurse was at hand to share the burden. (Her name had all along been oftenest on May's lips and it was her last word.) Auntie Pussy also came down to help with the nursing.* Nevertheless it must have been a chaotic time. At one moment May, Aunt Emy and

---

* This is often regarded as a great act of self-sacrifice on Catherine Gladstone's part (which indeed it was for Gladstone was on the point of retiring which involved heavy domestic problems), but it seems to me to show a lack of judgement. There was no clear over-riding necessity as there had been at the time of Mary's death. No anguished cry of "Pussy" from a child who would not be abandoned. The Rectory was tiny and over-burdened. Indeed Aunt Emy wrote that "I do very much hope it won't be thought necessary for Aty. Pussy to stay beyond Monday . . . the poor little house is quite bursting — and it will be a long, long business."

Aunt Pussy (who developed erysipelas) were all in bed in the tiny Rectory. Sybella and George were at the Hall. Sybella had only just had her baby and it must have been a relief to everyone that George was hardly allowed near the sick-room. Moreover Lavinia, perhaps the person most closely concerned, discovered during these weeks that, after four years married life, she was for the first time with child.* May's strength fluctuated and she went up and down during the long weary weeks; the watchers alternating between hope and despair. She was often delirious but neither in her conscious or her unconscious moments did she mention the names of any of her loves— Edward Denison, Rutherford Graham or Arthur Balfour. Once she said to Newmanny: "You know it is not true that Granny died."

On March 21st Palm Sunday she herself died peacefully and quietly without a sound or a pang. It was four years since she had written in her diary. "Very hot night, all sat out on the perron the whole evening, looking at falling stars, wh. always gave me a sense of sadness; so bright & living & then quenched in such complete darkness."

Arthur Balfour came down to the funeral. He gave Edward Lyttelton an emerald ring which had belonged to his mother and which he asked him to have placed in the coffin since May was his affianced wife. He did not have the courage to go to the church but sat under a sycamore tree in the Park, weeping.

* There is a legend among Meriel Talbot's grandchildren that after four years Meriel questioned her younger sister about the non-appearance of a baby. To which Lavinia replied: "Well you see God hasn't yet sent one down in a little basket" (short a). Meriel then got her husband to instruct Edward Talbot in the mechanics of reproduction. I regret I am unable to believe this story.

Arthur Balfour was not the only one to mourn May. Lavinia, although consoled by the arrival of her baby, another Mary Catherine, in October 1875, nevertheless felt continually bereft by the day-to-day loss of her companion sister. Her diary frequently included the entry: "Longed to tell May." May's brothers too felt her loss very deeply. She had been the only unmarried sister amongst them for four years and as such had held a special position. Charles was proud of her and liked taking her about; she was even more closely woven into Spencer's life with their musical tastes and many friends in common; she had read side by side with Arthur when he was studying for his First, and she was the confidante and sympathizer to the two younger boys, Edward and Alfred. Last but not least there was her father. "The intense feeling of *longing* to see her again cannot be described," he wrote to his old tutor Blakesley, now Dean of Lincoln.

The shadows were beginning to close around poor George Lyttelton. For many, many years he had been subject to fits of depression. They came on, lasted for two or three days and then the clouds rolled away as if they had never gathered. His family was completely accustomed to them. Lavinia's and May's diaries frequently contain the entries: "Papa grubous," or "Papa bluish". They were inclined to think his new wife worried too much about him and fussed him by so doing; but as the seventies wore on it was plain that the situation was becoming worse. Lucy in November 1872 could still write light-heartedly, "darling dad came in from a club dinner in gt. force; having just recovered, by means of a black dose, from a fit of the blues;" but in the following year her tone was much graver. "Poor Papa had a bad fit of the blues, and looks so worn & thin & languid as to go to one's heart."

Little is known about the cause of melancholia even today, though treatment can sometimes be successful. A century ago there was no treatment and the causes were put down to

183

7

"suppressed gout" or "bilious derangement". Lord Lyttelton exhibited all the classic symptoms, insomnia, loss of weight and an ever increasing sadness and apathy. Although his second marriage seemed to be a very happy one it was unable to dispel the clouds which hung about him. As early as 1869 Aunt Emy had written: "I confess to a disappointment about your father; he seems to me not brighter in the way one hoped: of course he is really & one knows she is the greatest comfort to him, but there seems to be a want of élan about him. But I think that is probably a good deal due to the Commission which sits upon him rather."

The Commission was certainly by no means a helpful factor. It was the Commission for Endowed Schools set up by the Gladstone Government in 1869. The recommendations of the Taunton Report had been too radical and far reaching and, its only result was this Commission of three members with limited powers to redistribute existing endowments and to draw up schemes for reform for the schools receiving them.

Lord Lyttelton did not want to accept the chairmanship. He felt that he had been soaked in educational work since 1861, (he had been a member of the Clarendon Commission on Public Schools before the Taunton Commission); that his views were too well known, and that he had already made a good many enemies. Gladstone, however, insisted. One cannot help wondering if the £1,500 which went with the chairmanship was a factor in his thinking. The Lyttelton finances were in a perilous state; George had, in spite of his strong disinclination for office, already sounded out his brother-in-law to see if this was a possibility. Gladstone was the very last man on whom a suspicion of nepotism could rest and quite plainly he felt George unsuited for a Parliamentary career but the Commission seemed to him the very roundest possible hole for a circular peg. George was an authority on education and only needed what Gladstone called a "manful effort to fulfil the law of duty" for him to succeed. Against his better judgement George yielded.

The next three years were a penance. Although the Commission did much valuable work (it had 235 schemes for educational reform approved by the Education Department and only ten rejected) it gained little sympathy either among the schools, the local authorities or the general public. It was violently attacked, and Lyttelton bore the brunt of these attacks, in particular those mounted by the Church over the Conscience Clause,* and it was flouted by Edward Thring the powerful headmaster of Uppingham, who had been an embittered enemy of the Taunton Report.

In 1874 the Gladstone Government fell and Lord Lyttelton received the following letter from the new Privy Seal, the Duke of Richmond.

> Dear Lyttelton,
>
> The Cabinet have decided to bring in a Bill to amend the Endowed Schools Act.
>
> It is proposed to transfer the powers of the Endowed Schools Commissioners to the Charity Commission, three new Commissioners to be added to the existing Charity Commissioners.
>
> I am sorry to say that this arrangement will if carried out bring your Commission to a close.
>
> Under these circumstances I feel it is best just to give you the intimation before the Bill is introduced.
>
> The Bill is not quite complete or I would send you a copy.
>
>   Yours truly,
>   Richmond

Not one word of appreciation or thanks was added to this icy letter.

It is of course as ridiculous to say that George Lyttelton's depression were brought on or even augmented by this experience as to say that Keats was killed by the *Quarterly Review*. But in both cases lack of appreciation, a feeling every effort put forward had achieved little or nothing, the coldness of the outside world, acting on an unusually sensitive nature can have done nothing to check the ravages of an already established malady whether tuberculosis or melancholia.

By 1876 George Lyttelton's melancholia was so bad that it was decided to see what a change of air would do and he and Sybella and a varying bodyguard of sons set off for Italy. From Naples he wrote a pathetic letter to his brother Billy. George's handwriting was always fairly illegible but now it had deteriorated alarmingly, and it was obvious that he was aware of his condition. "I (word illegible) sometimes fancy (as I

---

* The clause by which non-conformist or agnostic parents could allow their children to opt out of classes on religious subjects.

think you do sometimes) that I am getting muddled, & that this last little arrow of mine (which S.P.C.K. will publish) will be my last shot." (The "arrow" was a pamphlet addressed to young men written in the previous year.) The journey did no good. They arrived home on March 15th. "Poor Papa" wrote Lucy, "sadly thin and dismal, his nights have been miserable & it makes one's heart ache: Syb. wonderfully well and bright, considering not only all she has gone through, but alack: alack; most undesirable prospects* for October."

The house in Portland Place had been sold and on April 7th the Lytteltons moved into a house taken for the season, 18 Park Crescent. The family anxiety mounted. The "Keble couple", as they were always called, came to stay, along with Aunt Coque, Spencer, Alfred and Bob.

Poor George became worse and worse. He was very distressed because he felt he could not carry out his county work properly (his miseries seem frequently to have centred on a sense of inadequacy in public affairs) and he wrote, though he subsequently tore it up, a letter resigning his Lord Lieutenancy. He was able to ride with his family and to go to church, but he was invaded by a settled gloom. Aunt Coque wrote to Lucy that "he has entered upon a different and darker stage: utter lassitude and hopeless distress with occasional paroxysms of misery. Never any delusion or altered feelings towards any of us, but *true* perplexities all exaggerated."

The Victorians were not after all invulnerable. They had come to terms with death, partly by refusing to accept its finality, partly by building up a complicated ceremonial round it: but melancholia could not be accommodated among the optimistic beliefs which they held so courageously. George, who as a small boy, had had such radiant confidence in the future that he ran about the house shouting: "Demain, joli demain," now felt that he could hardly face another morrow.

On Easter Sunday he was so ill that Lavinia asked him if he felt up to staying for the whole service. He replied: "I could not stay away on Easter Day." She sat beside him and "he was fidgetty and scared looking and fancied he had not repented

---

* These "prospects" proved delusory. It was difficult to convince Sybella that she was not going to have a baby but by June it was obvious that she was not suffering from pregnancy but from "time of life". However, the fact that she thought so indicates that George had not lost his sexual potency.

eno' afterwards." The next day was Easter Monday and at night Lavinia watched him "creeping upstairs, taking I shd think 10 minutes going up — talking to himself. Did not like it."

On Easter Tuesday his male nurse attendant, Thomas Barnes, was as usual preparing to shave him when Lord Lyttelton suddenly asked if Barnes could let him have the razor. Barnes replied: "No my Lord, I cannot." After that the shaving proceeded but when one side of the face was done Lyttelton asked Barnes to stop while he walked about a little. He paced the room twice then suddenly darted to the door closing it behind him. Barnes rushed after him and was just in time to see him take two or three steps down the staircase, put his hands on the baluster and heave himself over, falling into the well of the stairs. The Coroner asked if it was an accident and Barnes replied: "No, he threw himself over. He had repeatedly told me that he was tired of life and wished to die."

He was quite insensible when he was picked up and never regained consciousness though he lingered till very early on Wednesday morning. The doctors diagnosed severe fracture of the pelvis, but said that the immediate cause of death was fainting of the heart due to shock.

The verdict brought in was one of "Suicide while of unsound mind."

His family was shattered. "Oh God!" wrote Lucy "what can we all be without him!" "I feel acutely what you said," Alfred wrote to his step-mother several months later, "about the constant expectation of seeing Papa come in and poke about the books in some top shelf, put the one you are reading back in its place, hit the bass of the pianoforte, if you were playing, with the palm of his hand, or perform some act of fun or spirits which seem to have gone out with him from all of us."

A careful little bouquet of tributes was collected, mostly from the family and from eminent churchmen. William Gladstone wrote that he had never known a "cleaner brighter soul, or one that will pass into the rest of the redeemed with fewer of the sad marks of mortality on him". But by far the best summing up of George Lyttelton came from a comparatively unknown clergyman who had once been Billy Lyttelton's curate. "Never surely was there one who put such a high standard before himself and yet was so gentle in his judgment of others — who could be so full of fun and humour and yet be so free from any

tinge of ill nature, whose piety and goodness were so un-
doubted, and yet so unobtrusive and so unmixed with anything
approaching to cant or unreality, and whose great intellectual
gifts made smaller people feel their inferiority so little."

ABBREVIATIONS

R.A.   Royal Archives

H.P.   Hagley Papers

Haw.P.   Hawarden Papers

T.P.   Talbot Papers

P.C.   Private Correspondence of Sarah Lady Lyttelton

C.   Correspondence of Sarah Lady Lyttelton

G.L.   George 4th Baron Lyttelton

M.L.   Mary Lady Lyttelton

S.L.   Sarah Lady Lyttelton

W.L.   William 3rd Baron Lyttelton

W.H.L.   The Rev. William Henry (Billy) Lyttelton

Mrs. W.H.L.   Mrs. William Henry (Emy) Lyttelton (née Pepys)

Meriel   Meriel Lyttelton, afterwards Mrs. John Talbot

Lucy   Lucy Lyttelton, afterwards Lady Frederick Cavendish

Lavinia   Lavinia Lyttelton, afterwards Mrs. Edward Talbot

May   Mary Catherine Lyttelton

Rem.   Reminiscences. (In addition to their diaries Meriel, Lucy and Lavinia all left accounts of their childhoods. Lucy's was published as an Introduction to her Diaries, but Meriel's and Lavinia's remain in the exercise books in which they were written among the Hagley and Talbot Papers.)

R.S.   The Hon. Robert Spencer

REFERENCES

CHAPTER 1

All the quotations in this chapter unless otherwise indicated come from letters written by Lady Sarah Spencer to her brother the Hon. Robert Spencer between the years of 1808 and 1813. The originals of these letters are among the Hagley Papers, but parts of them have been published in the *Private Correspondence of Sarah Lady Lyttelton*, privately printed 1873, and/or in the *Correspondence of Sarah Lady Lyttelton*, published 1912.

page line
2   20   "'I get a good deal from Boo' etc." Lady Caroline Stuart-Wortley to Lady Erne 11.9.20 quoted *The First Lady Wharncliffe & her Family*
3   34   "'Are you not mistaken' etc." S.L. to Countess of Pembroke 1838 C.
4   19   "'Delightful and intensely English' etc." Lady Fredk. Cavendish's Diary 13.5.73 Unpub. Chatsworth
8   11   "'laughing at poor Lord Althorp' etc." *Hary-O* page 21
8   35   "'She has the strongest feelings' etc." Ibid page 189
9   30   "'One minute on a Pillion' etc." Ibid page 327

CHAPTER 2

All the quotations in this chapter unless otherwise indicated come from Lady Sarah Lyttelton's letters to her parents and her sister Georgiana, and from her travel diaries. The originals are among the Hagley Papers, but they have been extensively quoted in *Private Correspondence* and *Correspondence*.

page line
13   16   "'I have now to announce' etc." S.S. to R.S. 8.5.12 H.P.
14   17   "'In a London ball-room' etc." Ibid 7.7.12. H.P.
14   33   "'A bon-mot of your friend' etc." *The Letter Bag of Lady Elizabeth Spencer-Stanhope* Chap. 1
15   14   "'He disappointed in public life' etc." Bishop of Llandaff to Sir T. Phillips 6.1.42 P.C.
15   24   "'His gaiety so irresistible' etc." S.S. to her grandmother Dow. Lady Spencer 6.1.13 P.C.
16   7   "'I must write to you' etc." S.L. to Caroline Estcourt 14.7.55 P.C.
16   24   "'he is a younger brother' etc." S.S. to R.S. 13.1.13. H.P.

page line

16 38 "'I can collect my scattered thoughts to pray' etc." S.S. to Dow. Lady Spencer 2.1.13 P.C.

17 2 "'You never did see such delicacy of feeling' etc." Lady Spencer to Lord Spencer 31.1.13 Althorp Papers

17 8 "'I rather wish for their departure' etc." Lady Spencer to Lord Spencer May 1813 Althorp Papers

17 24 "'he rolled about the floor' etc." Ibid January 1813

17 31 "'What happiness is mine' etc." S.S. to R.S. 10.2.13 H.P.

18 14 "'When she hears the carriage' etc." The Hon. Mrs. Pole-Carew to a Friend 5.3.13 P.C. and C.

18 32 "'The navigation was it must be owned' etc." W. Lyttelton to Lady Spencer 15.1.13 C.

19 10 "'Don't you remember' etc." S.L. to Mrs. Pole-Carew 17.8.13 P.C.

19 35 "Farewell to Sweden" H.P.

23 26 "'a vulgar person and a spoilt child' etc." S.L. to her nephew the 5th Earl Spencer Althorp Papers

CHAPTER 3

The conversations with Bonaparte cited in this chapter were recorded by William 3rd Lord Lyttelton and published in a privately printed edition of fifty copies. I have been unable to trace a copy, but the British Library provided a French translation by Henri Borjane published in Paris in 1936. The sequence of events is therefore as follows; the conversations presumably took place in French, Lord Lyttelton translated them into English, M. Borjane put them back into French and I have re-translated them into English. One hopes that the final result is not too far from the original!

page line

25 18 "'Mr. L. is here' etc." S.L. to Mrs. Pole-Carew 29.5.15 P.C.

25 24 "'opposite a bleak, bare, dazzling sea' etc." Ibid 17.6.15 H.P.

26 1 "'He does not now admit' etc." Ibid 14.6.15 H.P.

26 10 "To my dearest Sally" Undated H.P.

26 22 "'Lyttelton annoys me' etc." Lady Spencer to Lord Spencer 25.1.16 Althorp Papers

31 5 "'Your brother is quite altered' etc." S.L. to Mrs. Pole-Carew 8.2.17 P.C.

31 11 "'I daresay you are' etc." S.L. to Meriel Talbot 6.11.60 T.P.

31 18 "'I shall be sure to affront' etc." S.L. to Mrs. Pole-Carew 8.2.17 P.C.

31 29 "'Mr. Lyttelton is going to town' etc." Ibid 5.6.17 P.C.

32 1 "'The usual baby anecdotes.'" S.L. to Mrs. Pole-Carew 26.10.17 & 9.5.21 P.C.

page line

33 17 "'The said book-room' etc." Ibid 5.7.26 P.C.

33 26 "'But as if to show' etc." S.L. to the Hon. George Spencer 30.7.26 P.C.

33 40 "It was after the move to Hagley that William Lyttelton began keeping a diary." All further quotations in this chapter unless otherwise specified come from the 3rd Lord Lyttelton's diaries which are among the Hagley Papers.

35 30 "'All day I was upstairs' etc." Lady Georgiana Quin to S.L. 21.11.19 C.

36 1 "'I believe' Sarah wrote etc." S.L. to Mrs. Pole-Carew 2.10.21 P.C. & C.

40 40 "'And great pleasure it did give me' etc." W.L. to S.L. 8.11.25 H.P.

41 17 "'To find thee and all the house' etc." Ibid 15.9.31 H.P.

41 34 "'I was all holiday to him' etc." Ibid 18.9.27 H.P.

42 9 "'I was much overcome' etc." Ibid 12.4.31 H.P.

42 39 "Caroline Lyttelton reminiscing etc." Caroline Lyttelton to Maud Wyndham H.P.

43 14 "'Ld. L. has *no preference*' etc." S.L. to Mrs. Pole-Carew 11.1.35 H.P.

CHAPTER 4

page line

44 16 "'For some years Caroline' etc." 4th Earl Spencer to G.L. 3.6.42 H.P.

44 20 "'not very judicious daughter' etc." Queen Victoria to Sir Theodore Martin 3.11.75 R.A. Y/170/89

44 22 "'Till Caroline comes back' etc." S.L. to Lavinia Glynne 5.9.44 P.C.

45 8 "'Caroline and I are *gone out*' etc." S.L. to Mrs. Pole-Carew 1833 P.C.

45 15 "She fell in love once." Caroline Lyttelton to Maud Wyndham H.P.

46 8 "'I don't wonder' etc." S.L. to Caroline Estcourt 9.10.47 H.P.

46 29 "Aunt Coque herself could remember." Caroline Lyttelton to Maud Wyndham H.P.

47 10 "'grown as handsome as red hair' etc." S.L. to Mrs. Pole-Carew 4.5.21 P.C.

48 37 "'Absurd little monkeys'" Lady Fredk. Cavendish's Diary Introduction

49 7 "'This last quality' etc." S.L. to Mrs. Pole-Carew 17.8.29 H.P.

50 4 "'There is nothing to pump out' etc." G.L. to Brookfield 18.6.36 H.P.

50 17 "'a mere machine for Greek and Latin' etc." G.L. to Brookfield 6.11.38 H.P.

50 32 "'Mary Lyttelton observed' etc." M.L. to Catherine Gladstone Undated H.P.

page line

51   31   "a sort of reciprocal hero worship"   Life of Lord John Manners
          by Whibley p. 68
51   34   "'it is quite obvious' etc."   Blakesley to G.L. 10.12.38 H.P.
52   f.   "'The Smythes go tomorrow' etc."   M.L. to Catherine Glad-
          stone Undated probably 1847 H.P.
52   13   "'He was the sun' etc."   Lord John Manners to G.L. 26.11.57
          H.P.
52   25   "'The sort of statesman' etc."   Blakesley to G.L. 10.1.39 H.P.
53   32   "A more earthy compliment etc."   T. Phinn to G.L. 1838 H.P.
54   13   "'your father's never assuming a feeling' etc."   W.L. to S.L.
          25.9.31 H.P.
54   19   "he wrote to his brother Billy etc."   G.L. to W.H.L. 21.11.38 H.P.
54   23   "'If Lord Lyttelton were more aware' etc."   Correspondence of
          Countess Granville 13.12.38
55   3   "'I think George behaved *very* well'"   W.L. to S.L. 16.10.34 H.P.
57   17   "'You funny creature' etc."   M.L. to Henry Glynne 3.6.39
          Haw.P.
57   28   "'Nothing could be sweeter' etc."   Catherine to Henry Glynne
          3.6.39 Haw.P.
58   19   "'My nights are wretched' etc."   Lady Glynne to Catherine
          Glynne 10.8.39 Haw.P.
58   21   "'I poor wretch' etc."   Ibid ?.10.39 Haw.P.
58   28   "Three local bands etc."   Chester Chronicle 26.7.39

CHAPTER 5
page line

59   5   "Mrs. Ellis . . . 'pale and fussy'"   S.L. to W.H.L. 7.8.39 H.P.
60   7   "'My Sweetest' etc."   M.L. to Catherine Gladstone 1839 H.P.
60   32   "'I have just written to Ly. Lyttelton' etc."   Ibid 22.10.39
          Haw.P.
61   1   "'I am sorry to hear' etc."   W. E. Gladstone to G.L. 2.11.39
          Haw.P.
61   10   "'I wish you joy' etc."   S.L. to M.L. 12.12.40 Haw.P.
61   20   "'The darkness only allowed me' etc."   Catherine Gladstone to
          W. E. Gladstone 14.1.40 Haw.P.
61   35   "'Mary seems to do all so nicely' etc."   Ibid
62   3   "'Like old days' etc."   Ibid 17.1.40 Haw.P.
62   6   "'My Pussy resembles a Squirrel' etc."   Ibid 19.1.40 Haw.P.
62   15   "'She says we shall air it' etc."   Ibid 18.1.40 Haw.P.
62   28   "'owing to George's marriage' etc."   S.L. to Caroline Estcourt
          1.12.44 H.P.
63   10   "'If I leave it (my fortune)' etc."   S.L. to G.L. 23.1.40 H.P.
63   25   "'I agree with all your private reasons' etc."   S.L. to 3rd Lord
          Spencer 9.6.37 (but postmarked 27) H.P.
64   2   "'if . . . apartments could *faire le bonheur*' etc."   S.L. to Caroline
          Lyttelton 3.10.38 P.C.

page line

64 23 "'I had sundry things to carry' etc." Ibid P.C. & C.

64 32 "the Maids of Honour . . . 'are very coaxy' etc." Ibid Oct. 1838 P.C. & C.

65 10 "'If H.M. could wear fewer' etc." Ibid Summer 1839 P.C. & C.

65 17 "'No-one could have guessed it' etc." Ibid 28.8.39 P.C. & C.

66 4 "'What do you mean about the Queen' etc." S.L. to G.L. 6.10.39 H.P.

66 9 "'I have not seen Sir James Clark's statement' etc." Ibid 12.10.39 H.P.

66 19 "'Lord Melbourne thinks her a very nice person' etc." Queen Victoria's Journal 20.5.38 R.A.

66 30 "'I shall,' she wrote etc." S.L. to Caroline Lyttelton 25.10.42 C.

66 36 "'Went and played at battledore' etc." R.A. Queen Victoria's Journal 14.9.39

67 4 "'Out I went with Lady L.' etc." Ibid 11.11.39

67 13 "'handsome enough to be the hero' etc." S.L. to G.L. 25.10.39 H.P.

67 17 "'The Queen's look and manner' etc." S.L. to W.H.L. 21.2.40 P.C. & C.

67 29 "'Not a look or a tone of hers' etc." S.L. to Caroline Lyttelton 2.10.40 P.C.

67 32 "'At bedtime the Queen' etc." Ibid Oct. 1840 P.C.

68 1 "'I was pleased to hear the Queen' etc." Ibid 2.10.40 P.C. & C.

68 8 "'The Queen is learning trees' etc." Ibid 14.10.40 P.C. & C.

68 19 "'Many bits of information' etc." Ibid 1842 P.C.

68 33 "'My wishes for the hares' etc." Ibid 18.10.40 C.

69 2 "'It was Prince Albert' etc." Ibid 9.10.40 C.

69 13 "'How strange he is' etc." Ibid 22.7.50 P.C. & C.

69 20 "'There is a transparency in her *truth*' etc." Ibid 1842 P.C.

69 26 "'vein of iron'" Ibid C.

69 27 "'the candour, truth' etc." S.L. to W.H.L. 9.12.50 H.P.

CHAPTER 6

Sarah Lyttelton's chief correspondent during her years at Court was her elder daughter Caroline. All the quotations in this chapter unless otherwise indicated come from this correspondence. Unfortunately I have been unable to trace the original letters; the provenance therefore in every case is either the *Private Correspondence* or the 1912 edition of the *Correspondence*.

page line

70 8 "'a crazy stupid intriguer'" R.A. Add U 2/2

70 15 "'Doctor Clark has mismanaged the child' etc." Prince Albert to Queen Victoria 18.1.42 R.A. Add. U 2/2

70 21 "'The nurses and nurserymaids' etc." R.A. M/129 24.3.42

70 24 "a long rambling letter to the Prince" R.A. M/12/9 13.12.41

page line

71 20 "She ... wrote back suggesting a Miss Brown etc." R.A. M/12/11 2.2.42

71 28 "'Lord Spencer says' etc." R.A. M/12/13 16.2.42

72 2 "'her manner is rough' etc." R.A. M/12/14 16.2.42

72 11 "'a memorandum thirty-two pages long' etc." R.A. M/12/14 6.3.42

73 1 "She applied to Lord Melbourne etc." R.A. M/12/16 24.3.42

73 8 "Lord Melbourne, possibly previously primed etc." R.A. M/12/17 25.3.42

73 12 "'Lord Melbourne is a man of strong, sound sense.'" R.A. M/12/18 28.3.42

73 15 "On April 6th the Queen noted etc." R.A. Queen Victoria's Journal 6.4.42

74 1 "In a long paper etc." R.A. M/12/20 8.5.42

74 10 "she asks permission 'to ask questions'" R.A. M/12/22 11.5.42

74 33 "'dressed in coarse straw hats' etc." S.L. to M.L. 12.7.49

75 6 "'Her daughters are now' etc." R.A. M/12/20 8.5.42

75 11 "Her own proposals were etc." R.A. M/12/24 11.5.42

75 17 "she must be prepared 'to go to the Nursery' etc." R.A. M/12/26

75 21 "Her own words to Stockmar etc." R.A. M/12/19 7.5.42

75 26 "'I have a sort of pride' etc." Caroline Lyttelton to M.L. Undated Haw.P.

75 38 "'The Queen came up to me' etc." Lavinia to Henry Glynne 10.8.42 H.P.

76 3 "'a most gracious bow' etc." Ibid 5.10.42 H.P.

76 16 "'Kind good man' etc." Lavinia to Henry Glynne 7.10.42 H.P.

76 29 "There is a memorandum from Mr. Anson etc." R.A. Z/171 29.6.42.

78 21 "over watched and over doctored" S.L. to M.L. 23.10.41 H.P.

78 23 "'So reasonable and sensible' etc." R.A. Queen Victoria's Journal 17.5.42

78 27 "'Ly L. so agreeable' etc." Ibid 4.10.42

78 31 "'Ly. Lyttelton's kindness' etc." Ibid 25.5.43

79 9 "Her majesty, minuted Anson etc." R.A. Y/55/7

79 13 "'It quite grieved H.M.' etc." R.A. Y/55/16 19.12.43

79 29 "'My dear Lady Lyttelton' etc." R.A. M/12/65 27.12.43

79 39 "'I am sorry to think' etc." Caroline Lyttelton to Caroline Estcourt Undated Haw.P.

80 3 "'Tomorrow is the day of our journey' etc." S.L. to Caroline Estcourt 28.3.43 H.P.

80 7 "'You seem to have been gone' etc." Ibid 12.1.44 H.P.

81 20 "She is *over* sensitive and affectionate." Ibid 3.8.42 H.P., P.C. & C.

82 4 "'Yesterday,' wrote Lady Lyttelton etc." S.L. to Lavinia Glynne 1844 P.C.

page line

82 33 "'Our new governess' etc."   R.A. Y/93/1 2.3.47

83 14 "'He is very intelligent' etc."   S.L. to Caroline Estcourt 3.8.42 H.P.

83 25 "'much improved in size and manliness' etc."   Ibid 9.10.47 H.P.

84 19 "'I was so pleased with what Mr. Birch told me' etc." S.L. to M.L. 11.7.49 H.P.

84 37 "'I send you back at last' etc."   S.L. to G. & M.L. 13.7.49 H.P.

85 22 "'In 1844 Lady Lyttelton' etc."   S.L. to Lavinia Glynne 8.10.44 P.C. & C.

86 1 "'I hear' she wrote 'to my great satisfaction' etc."   S.L. to Lavinia Glynne 1.3.48 P.C.

86 8 "'He is so agreeable' etc."   S.L. to W.H.L. 12.6.50 H.P. & C.

86 13 "'my professional business' etc."   S.L. to Lavinia Glynne 4.10.49 P.C.

86 24 "On March 25th the Queen wrote etc."   R.A. Queen Victoria's Journal 25.3.50

86 32 "The Prince however was loth etc."   R.A. M/14/99 28.5.50

87 5 "'I have a longing' etc."   S.L. to Lord George Quin 5.10.50 H.P.

87 9 "'In many respects it will be a great loss' etc."   R.A. Queen Victoria's Journal 18.11.50

87 12 "'Poor Ly. Lyttelton' etc."   Ibid

87 36 "'Her face is very peculiar' etc."   S.L. to Caroline Lyttelton & Meriel Talbot 12.3.63 T.P.

CHAPTER 7

page line

89 6 "'It is so pretty' etc."   S.L. to Caroline Estcourt 1.12.46 H.P.

89 22 "'Pretty Puss' etc."   M.L. to Catherine Gladstone Undated Haw.P.

90 9 "'It is so silly' etc."   Ibid 27.11.39 T.P.

90 11 "She also tells Pussy etc."   Ibid Undated H.P.

90 16 "'I read the Bible every day' etc."   Ibid Undated H.P.

90 30 "'Pussy always infects me' etc."   M.L. to G.L. 20.4.42 H.P.

90 39 "'I do think it is an insane plan' etc."   Ibid 3.8.49 H.P.

91 7 "'I was so cold in bed' etc."   Ibid 4.3.49 H.P.

91 8 "'To say how I hate solitary bed' etc."   Ibid 5.3.50 H.P.

91 18 "'The Queen, impertinent little creature' etc."   S.L. to G.L. 25.10.39 H.P.

91 24 "'Last night baby was' etc."   M.L. to Catherine Gladstone Undated Haw.P.

91 34 "'Little babie' etc."   M.L. to G.L. 5.8.40 H.P.

92 8 "'My own dearest Pussy' etc."   M.L. to Catherine Gladstone T.P. Undated, probably 1842

92 21 "'I am particularly glad' etc."   Stephen Glynne to G.L. 30.10.42 Haw. P.

page line

92   36   "According to Catherine Gladstone etc." *Mrs. Gladstone* Georgina Battiscombe

93   2   "'I felt very ill' etc." M.L. to Catherine Gladstone 25.5.51 H.P.

93   11   "Lord Stanley of Alderley etc." *The Stanleys of Alderley* Letter 207

93   31   "Sarah in proposing a similar arrangement etc." S.L. to Lavinia Watson 22.11.? H.P.

94   1   "'Get your breakfast butter' etc." M.L. to Catherine Gladstone March 1840 T.P.

94   5   "'How extravagant of Henry' etc." Ibid about 1845 H.P.

94   11   "'I am so afraid' etc." Ibid March 1840 H.P.

94   f.   "Even in 1874 etc." Lady Fredk. Cavendish's Diary 27.5.74 Unpubl. Chatsworth

94   20   "'He spent literally nothing' etc." Rem. Lavinia H.P.

94   31   "'Tom Titten' etc." M.L. to G.L. 5.8.40 H.P.

94   33   "'£50 seems to me' etc." Ibid 12.7.54 H.P.

95   1   "He once wrote to Catherine etc." *Mrs. Gladstone* G. Battiscombe

95   28   "'Servants' wages' etc." S.L. to M.L. 2.10.39 H.P.

95   35   "Mrs. Ellis 'always beautifully dressed' etc." Rem. Meriel T.P.

96   1   "'She nearly cried' etc." M.L. to G.L. 22.10.40 H.P.

96   5   "'I cannot quite endure' etc." S.L. to G.L. 14.10.39 H.P.

96   18   "he gave it as his opinion etc." Rem. Meriel T.P.

96   26   "'It is not Ellis and I who quarrelled' etc." M.L. to G.L. 6.8.40 H.P.

96   31   "which title Sarah wrote' etc." S.L. to M.L. 12.10.39 H.P.

96   41   "the maids slept in attics etc." Rem. Meriel T.P.

97   1   "On Sunday afternoon etc." Rem. Lavinia H.P.

97   10   "The staff dinner etc." Ibid

97   27   "'There was always a baby' etc." Ibid

97   32   "'a large map' etc." Rem. Lucy. Introduction to Lady Fredk. Cavendish's Diary

98   5   "'to respect the rows of little boots' etc." Rem. Lavinia H.P.

98   14   "'Of course', she wrote to her husband etc." M.L. to G.L. 20.5.42 H.P.

98   39   "'she was of course beautiful' etc." Rem. Lavinia H.P.

99   6   "'it was seldom' wrote Lucy etc." Lady Fredk. Cavendish's Diary Introduction

99   14   "'But you can't have everything' etc." S.L. to M.L. 16.9.46 H.P.

99   18   "Lucy records etc." Lady Fredk. Cavendish's Diary Introduction

99   31   "'Now on the subject of Meriel' etc." S.L. to M.L. Early 1842 C.

100   2   "'Meriel has been very naughty' etc." M.L. to G.L. 26.1.43 H.P.

page line

100   8   "The punishment Mamma used etc." Lady Fredk. Cavendish's Diary Introduction

100   17   "'She (Mamma) used to shake her head' etc." Rem. Lavinia H.P.

100   40   "'Miss N's rod of iron' etc." Lady Fredk. Cavendish's Diary Introduction

101   9   "Meriel however etc." Rem. Meriel T.P.

101   15   "Lucy recalled the Christmasses etc." Lady Fredk. Cavendish's Diary Introduction

101   35   "'I do so wish I could look at death' etc." M.L. to G.L. 16.7.50 H.P.

CHAPTER 8

page line

102   6   "I see how rightly etc." S.L. to Caroline Estcourt 1.4. (1843 or 1844) H.P.

102   23   "'But let me ask you must a Ld Lt.' etc." S.L. to G.L. 4.9.39 H.P.

102   30   "'George wrote a capital letter' etc." M.L. to Catherine Gladstone Undated Haw.P.

103   12   "'Women are not like men' etc." Catherine Braybrooke to M.L. 14.7.31 Haw.P.

103   26   "'Cambridge will *disgrace* itself' etc." M.L. to G.L. 27.10.40 H.P.

103   33   "'They think you have taken the shilling.'" Lord John Manners to G.L. 1840 H.P.

104   4   "'I wish you would put "lady"' etc." G.L. to W. E. Gladstone 14.12.38 Gladstone Papers Brit. Mus. Vol. CLIII

104   16   "'Dear Wm.,' George wrote etc." Ibid

104   38   "'I need not waste words' etc." W. E. Gladstone to G.L. 6.1.46 Haw.P.

105   7   "'Butlers were first under-butlers' etc." M.L. to G.L. 8.1.46 H.P.

105   16   "'The attacks,' his mother wrote etc." S.L. to Mrs. W.H.L. 4.7.60 H.P.

105   25   "'Lest I forget it' etc." W. E. Gladstone to G.L. 2.5.46 Haw.P.

106   5   "'Lord John Russell' etc." M.L. to Catherine Gladstone Undated Haw.P.

108   10   "'I am half ashamed' etc." S.L. to M.L. 10.7.52 H.P.

108   15   "'I am grieved at what you say' etc." S.L. to G.L. 20.6.52 H.P.

109   29   "'We had great fun with Lady Lyttelton' etc." R.A. Queen Victoria's Journal 29.1.40

110   1   "he wrote his mother etc." Copied by Caroline Lyttelton in a letter to W.H.L. 1846 H.P.

110   15   "Her letter to the former etc." R.A. Z/129/53

110   25   "'You acted so well' etc." R.A. Z/129/52

110   31   "Mary writes of his 'pecking' etc." M.L. to G.L. 11.9.44 H.P.

page line

111   3 "'As far as I know' etc."   S.L. to 4th Earl Spencer 10.3.46 H.P.

111   10 "she believed he was deeply attached etc."   Ibid

112   2 "'I forgot to answer your question' etc."   R.A. Y/39/8 15.12.48

112   12 "'the wretched couple' etc."   S.L. to W.H.L. 12.10.60 H.P.

112   17 "One hot summer in London etc."   M.L. to W.H.L. Undated
          H.P.

112   27 "she had better write to Henrietta etc."   S.L. to M.L. 6.8.50
          H.P.

113   1 "'an obstinate refusal' etc."   S.L. to M.L. 2.8.50 H.P.

113   18 "'Mrs. Cornewall' etc."   Ibid 24.4.51 H.P.

113   26 "In 1855 Spencer etc."   Spencer Lyttelton to Duke of Devon-
          shire 4.7.55 D. of D. to Spencer Lyttelton 8.7.55 Chatsworth
          MSS.

114   3 "'I only wonder he didn't do it before' etc."   S.L. to Kitty
          Pole-Carew 1869.

114   12 "somewhat shocked her in-laws etc."   Lady Fredk. Cavendish's
          Diary 4.5.70 Unpublished Chatsworth MSS.

114   19 "'the sunshiniest person I know.'"   Blakesley to G.L. 30.12.42.
          H.P.

114   26 "She was 'very sorry' etc."   S.L. to Caroline Estcourt 1.12.44
          H.P.

115   10 "'to a very large extent Dissenters' etc."   G.L. to W.H.L.
          19.10.44 H.P.

115   16 "'I do not at all mean' etc."   Ibid 25.10.45 H.P.

115   31 "she answered with a supremely tactful letter etc."   S.L. to G.L.
          18.1.46 H.P.

117   1 "'Güggenbühl' etc."   G.L. to W.H.L. 9.11.55 H.P.

117   6 "'About dear Billy' etc."   Caroline Lyttelton to M.L. Undated
          Haw.P.

117   23 "'I pumped the Bishop of Birmingham' etc."   M.L. to W.H.L.
          1851 H.P.

117   27 "'As for Miss Pepys' etc."   Ibid 28.10.53 H.P.

117   32 "'What it must be to you' etc."   Ibid 21.8.54 H.P.

118   6 "'she had' wrote her eldest niece etc."   Rem. Meriel T.P.

118   10 "'that the little grey mare' etc."   S.L. to M.L. 5.5.56 H.P.

                        CHAPTER 9
page line

119   13 "'She is peculiar' etc."   S.L. to Caroline Estcourt 1843 H.P.

119   24 "'they flew apart' etc."   S.L. to Caroline Lyttelton Undated
          H.P.

119   f. "'He is much improved' etc."   Lavinia Lyttelton to M.L.
          4.9.42 H.P.

120   8 "'He is always slow' etc."   M.L. to G.L. Undated H.P.

120   17 "'Henry Glynne is not the man' etc."   S.L. to Caroline Estcourt
          28.8.45 H.P.

121   10 "'ever since' wrote her mother etc."   Ibid 31.8.44 H.P.

page line

121 24 "'My dear Catherine' etc." S.L. to Catherine Gladstone Undated H.P.

122 2 "'Pussy is quite out of heart' etc." M.L. to G.L. 10.11.49 H.P.

122 7 "'She admits that these consolations' etc." S.L. to Caroline Estcourt 30.10.50 H.P.

123 1 "'It is better not to talk' etc." M.L. to G.L. 28.3.51 H.P.

123 11 "'Many little and great trials' etc." S.L. to Caroline Estcourt 30.10.50 H.P.

125 10 "'I get sick when there is no letter' etc." M.L. to G.L. 4.4.50 H.P.

125 24 "'She does not much enjoy pictures and churches' etc." M.L. to G.L. 17.7.50 H.P.

125 30 "'I do feel for your disappointment' etc." M.L. to Catherine Gladstone. Undated. H.P.

126 16 "'Missy came in *singing*' etc." Lady Caroline Stuart-Wortley to Lady Erne November 1811

126 23 "'You will let me say us' etc." Mrs. John Talbot to Catherine Gladstone 12.10.57 Haw. P.

127 1 "'Mr. P. full of Gorham' etc." M.L. to Catherine Gladstone Undated H.P.

127 3 "'William's lowness about Gorham' etc." M. to G.L. 10.3.50 H.P.

127 9 "'the terrible prospect of the future' etc." Sir Stephen Glynne to G.L. 1.1.51 H.P.

127 18 "'Henry full of joy' etc." M.L. to W.H.L. 6.10.54 H.P.

127 32 "'the deep regret' etc." S.L. to G.L. 13.6.55 H.P.

127 39 "'I feel more and more moribund' etc." Lady Glynne to Catherine Gladstone Oct 1839 Haw.P.

128 6 "'I was obliged to make Mama' etc." M.L. to Catherine Gladstone 1849 H.P.

128 11 "'I have such a deal of accounts' etc." M.L. to G.L. May 1849 H.P.

128 23 "'I was trying to cry' etc." M.L. to G.L. 1854 H.P.

128 26 "'She was quite herself' etc." Ibid 29.3.54 H.P.

CHAPTER 10

All the quotations in the following chapter unless otherwise indicated come from the Memorial on Mary Lyttelton's death. As will be seen in the text George Lyttelton asked everyone who had been present at his wife's deathbed to write down their recollections of the occasion and these accounts were woven into a continuous narrative. It was never printed but hand-written copies were made and distributed among the family and friends. The copy I worked on was the one given to Mrs. Oxley (once Miss Pearson, the Lyttelton governess, see page 101). After her death it was returned to the family and given by Meriel Talbot to Willy Gladstone, the eldest son of the Prime Minister. It is now among the Hawarden Papers.

page line

129 9 "'I am rather weaker than usual' etc." M.L. to W.H.L. 5.2.52 H.P.

129 15 "'I hope you will not move about too soon' etc." S.L. to M.L. 7.1.53 H.P.

129 22 "'Take in that this last baby' etc." M.L. to W.H.L. 30.1.54 H.P.

129 28 "'the tiny 11th.'" Ibid 23.8.55 H.P.

130 5 "Lord Chandos . . . says in his autobiography etc." *From Peace to War* p. 19

130 21 "'I can't help being still fussy' etc." S.L. to G.L. 6.11.55 H.P.

130 29 "Mrs. Talbot wrote . . . that she hardly dared hope etc." Mrs. Talbot to Catherine Gladstone 31.10.55 Haw.P.

131 2 "'Alas there is a secret at Hagley' etc." *Mrs. Gladstone* by Georgina Battiscombe p. 108

132 15 "'nothing wherein and little whereon' etc." Lady Fredk. Cavendish's Diary 22.12.50

133 2 "'rather horrid for a strong man.'" Ibid 19.7.56

133 5 "'perfectly restored, with encaustic pavement' etc." Ibid 17.18. & 19 56

133 8 "In fact as Sir John Betjeman writes etc." Hymn by John Betjeman, "Mount Zion"

133 17 "'the whole tribe of Gladstones' etc." Lady Fredk. Cavendish's Diary 1.1.57

133 27 "'a gushing overpowering sense' etc." Ibid 7.2.57

134 1 "'What a bit of road' etc." S.L. to G.L. 10.2.57 H.P.

134 7 "'unearthly manners in the sickroom' etc." *Mrs. Gladstone* by Georgina Battiscombe

134 30 "'I know', Lucy wrote etc." Lady Fredk. Cavendish's Diary 4.6.57

136 21 "'I want to hear more' etc." *The Stanleys of Alderley* 21.9.41

137 12 "'He' (Lord Lyttelton) 'was so anxious for it' etc." Mrs. Talbot to Catherine Gladstone Undated Haw.P.

CHAPTER 11

page line

142 5 "'the universal blackness' etc." *The Daisy Chain* by Charlotte M. Yonge

142 6 "Queen Victoria wrote etc." Queen Victoria to the Princess Royal 18.5.60 *Dearest Child* p. 248

142 12 "'How sad it will be' etc." Memorial

142 22 "'the smell of crepe' etc." Rem. Lavinia H.P.

143 9 "'I went in the twilight' etc." Lady Fredk. Cavendish's Diary 29.7.59

143 13 "'quite young children' etc." Rem. Lavinia H.P.

143 25 "'He seems like a child' etc." S.L. to Lavinia Watson 28.6.57 H.P.

page line

143   34   "'Dear George looks very ill' etc."   Ibid 9.7.57 H.P.

144   9   "On her death-bed Mary etc."   Ibid 26.8.57 H.P.

144   20   "'My own precious' etc."   M.L. to G.L. 7.8.40 H.P.

144   21   "'Bless you my precious' etc."   Ibid 14.7.57 H.P.

144   35   "'She was a great companion' etc."   Rem. Lavinia H.P.

145   12   "'so radiant with the new happiness' etc." Lady Fredk. Cavendish's Diary 26.5.60 Unpub. H.P.

145   18   "'he loved Meriel the best' etc."   Rem. Lavinia H.P.

145   22   "'George has been unwell' etc."   S.L. to Mrs. W.H.L. 4.7.60 H.P.

145   33   "'I have still the same complaint' etc."   W.H.L. to Lady Fredk. Cavendish 8.11.78 H.P.

146   8   "Lavinia, then a small girl etc."   Private information

146   15   "'Miss Lyttelton mentioned' etc."   Mrs. Talbot to G.L. T.P.

146   39   "'I feel I dare hardly wish' etc."   Mrs. Talbot to Catherine Gladstone 31.10.55 Haw.P.

147   2   "'You are indeed most certainly' etc."   Ibid 12.10.57 T.P.

147   27   "'I have only told my mother' etc."   G.L. to R. S. Selfe 1.12.57 H.P.

148   8   "'I was glad lately' etc."   G.L. to W.H.L. 22.6.61 H.P.

148   31   "'Ld. Canning told Ly. de T.' etc."   M.L. to G.L. 4.5.42 H.P.

149   7   "'Dear Lady Canning' etc."   G.L. to Viscountess Canning 29.5.61 Harewood Papers

151   6   "'very great kindness' etc."   Ibid 24.8.61

151   24   "'the continual discomforts' etc."   G.L. to W.H.L. 15.10.64 H.P.

151   25   "'the heavy chain' etc."   Ibid 28.5.67 H.P.

151   26   "'being of the earth' etc."   Ibid 4.5.69 H.P.

151   29   "'You may sometimes hear' etc."   *Alfred Lyttelton* by Edith Lyttelton Chap. 2

152   4   "In 1862 he gave a lecture at Hagley etc."   *Ephemeral* by G.L.

152   18   "'Never', he wrote in 1863 etc."   G.L. to W.H.L. H.P.

152   21   "'I heard Papa whistle' etc."   Lady Fredk. Cavendish's Diary 26.11.62

152   33   "'Re Sappho' etc."   William Gladstone to G.L. 24.12.62 H.P.

153   15   "the most determined and unceremonious etc."   *The Age of Equipoise* by W. L. Burn

153   17   "One of the most impressive etc."   *English Philanthropy* 1660–1690 by David Owen

154   39   "'Births' etc."   Undated Paper H.P.

156   15   "Our elder sisters etc."   *Memoir of Alfred Lyttelton* by Edward Lyttelton

156   26   "just out of sight with a pocket classic etc."   Ibid

156   38   "'It is amazing' etc."   S.L. to W.H.L. 12.7.61 H.P.

157   19   "'is as complete and fine' etc."   Lady Wenlock to Catherine Gladstone dated Sunday 1839 quoted *Catherine Gladstone* by Mary Drew

page line

157   34   "an instantaneous bellow etc." *Memoir of Alfred Lyttelton* by
           Edward Lyttelton

159   1   "The Lytteltons are full of stories etc."   Private information

CHAPTER 12

page line

160   8   "She had always the Tapestry Room etc."   Rem. Lavinia

160   17   "'a mawkish and unreadable effusion' etc." S.L. to G.L. 24.
           24.12.50 H.P.

160   21   "'The signal,' he went on etc." *Memoir of Alfred Lyttelton* by
           Edward Lyttelton

160   28   "'she was too fussy and restless' etc."   Rem. Lavinia

161   6   "'You were right and so was I' etc."   Lucy Lyttelton to Meriel
           Talbot Easter Monday 1864 T.P.

161   21   "'pleasant and comfortable' etc."   Lucy to Lavinia St. Peter's
           Day 1863 H.P.

161   31   "'I can't tell exactly' etc."   Lady Fredk. Cavendish's Diary
           10.9.63

162   1   "'at dinner I got into an argument' etc."   Ibid 4.12.63

162   8   "'Church is Lucy's public house' etc."   Ibid Preface

162   13   "'The Vestry CONSENTED' etc."   Ibid 21.5.62

162   19   "'But oh my dear the Church!'"   Lucy to Meriel 25.11.62 T.P.

162   32   "'Well my dear' etc."   Ibid 16.12.62 T.P.

163   7   "'Your father called it' etc."   S.L. to Meriel 13.2.64 T.P.

163   13   "'though I do not myself judge' etc."   G.L. to Catherine
           Gladstone 1864 Haw.P.

163   23   "'Certainly before *Essays & Reviews*' etc."   S.L. to Meriel 2.2.64
           T.P.

164   37   "'Lucy is still rather on pins and needles' etc."   Lavinia's Diary
           9.11.66 H.P.

165   1   "I wonder if I could at all convey etc."   Rem. Lavinia

165   15   "'I recall,' she wrote etc."   Ibid

165   30   "'Oh that heavenly dream' etc."   Catherine Gladstone to G.L.
           29.11.58 H.P.

165   40   "'the goose of all geese'."   S.L. to W.H.L. 12.5.62 H.P.

166   1   "'forbearance and self-denial' etc."   G.L. to W.H.L. 16.2.21
           H.P.

166   10   "'Her tone of mind' etc."   Lady Fredk. Cavendish's Diary
           2.3.64

166   26   "'Dearest Catherine,' she wrote etc."   S.L. to Catherine
           Gladstone 31.12.68 H.P.

167   10   "'It was the time' etc."   Rem. Lavinia

168   20   "a 'long sit' etc."   Lavinia's Diary 9.2.68 H.P.

168   31   "'As regards office' etc."   William Gladstone to G.L. 17.8.68
           Haw.P.

page line

168   36 "'Papa still very low' etc."   Lavinia's Diary 7.5.68 H.P.

169   2 "'Papa is really better' etc."   May to Meriel 8.11.68 T.P.

169   10 "'She is not in the least pretty' etc."   Lady Fredk. Cavendish's Diary 8.5.69

169   25 "'yet by degrees' etc."   Ibid

169   35 "'small arrangements' etc."   Lavinia to Meriel October 1873 H.P.

170   4 "'had not great depths' etc."   Mrs. W.H.L. to Meriel 2.4.69 T.P.

170   19 "'We can all feel thankful' etc."   Lady Fredk. Cavendish's Diary 27.5.69

170   31 "'She has so many excellent qualities' etc."   S.L. to Rev. Girdlestone 21.6.69 H.P.

170   33 "in another she praises etc."   S.L. to Lady Duff Gordon 19.1.70 (not in her own hand either dictated or copied) H.P.

171   3 "'I hear you are going to marry' etc."   Lavinia's Diary 28.6.69 H.P.

171   8 "'Tennyson says' etc."   G.L. to W.H.L. 29.6.69 H.P.

172   32 "'May rather disappoints' etc."   Mrs. W.H.L. to Meriel 10.8.69 T.P.

173   3 "'Well and I went to the Queen' etc."   S.L. to G.L. 13.3.69 H.P.

173   37 "'I should like to speak to you' etc."   Edward Talbot to Meriel 30.11.69 H.P.

174   7 "'has sent away her wheel chair' etc."   Rem. Lavinia H.P.

174   13 "'a horrid rheumatism' (and) 'very irritable'"   Mrs. W.H.L. to Meriel 19.2.70 T.P.

CHAPTER 13

All the entries in this chapter unless otherwise indicated come from May Lyttelton's Diary 1870–4, which is among the Hagley Papers.

page line

175   21 "'Wish more feeling for religion' etc."   Lavinia's Diary 26.5.62 H.P.

175   30 "'This day month' etc."   M.L. to G.L. 17.4.50 H.P.

175   34 "'May, I think' etc."   Lady Fredk. Cavendish's Diary 29.7.59

176   2 "'poor giant girl' etc."   S.L. to G.L. 24.1.65 H.P.

176   19 "'permanently have quieted' etc."   Lavinia to Meriel 10.1.70 H.P.

177   22 "'I ought to be too tired' etc."   Ibid 9.1.71 T.P.

178   37 "'brilliant and adored'"   Time Remembered by Lady Horner

179   39 "'her feeling was very real' etc."   Lucy to Meriel 4.11.72 T.P.

179   41 "'There is no-one like darling Auntie' etc."   May to Meriel 7.11.72 T.P.

page line
180   2 "'She seems to have given way' etc."   Mrs. W.H.L. to Meriel
          15.11.72 T.P.
180   24 "'kneeling at his feet' etc."   May to Meriel 10.9.73 T.P.
181   11 "'I should have thought' etc."   May to Lucy 1.1.74 H.P.
181   f. "'I do very much hope' etc."   Mrs. W.H.L. to Meriel 12.2.75
          T.P.

CHAPTER 14
page line
183   14 "'The intense feeling of *longing*' etc."   G.L. to Blakesley 22.3.75
          H.P.
183   27 "'darling dad' etc."   Lady Fredk. Cavendish's Diary 14.11.72
          Unpub. Chatsworth
183   30 "'Poor Papa' etc."   Ibid 22.6.73
184   6 "'I confess to a disappointment' etc."   Mrs. W.H.L. to Meriel
          10.8.69 H.P.
185   9 "'Dear Lyttelton' etc."   Duke of Richmond to G.L. 16.6.74
          H.P.
185   38 "'I (word illegible) sometimes fancy' etc."   G.L. to W.H.L.
          6.3.76 H.P.
186   32 "'he had entered' etc."   Caroline Lyttelton to Lucy. Lady
          Fredk. Cavendish's Diary
186   42 "'Demain, joli demain'"   Rem. Caroline Lyttelton H.P.
186   44 "On Easter Sunday etc."   Rem. Lavinia H.P.
187   4 "On Easter Tuesday etc."   *Times* 21.5.76

MANUSCRIPT SOURCES

Althorp Papers   In the possession of Earl Spencer
Gladstone Papers   British Museum
Hagley Papers   In the possession of Viscount Cobham
Harewood Papers   County Archives, Leeds
Hawarden Papers   County Archives, Hawarden
Talbot Papers   County Archives, Maidstone
Diary of Lady Frederick Cavendish   Chatsworth

BIBLIOGRAPHY

Anon. (edit.)   *Private Correspondence of Sarah Lady Lyttelton*. Privately printed, 1873

Bailey, John (edit.)   *Diary of Lady Frederick Cavendish*. John Murray, 1927 (2 vols.)

Battiscombe, Georgina   *Mrs. Gladstone, Portrait of a Marriage*. Constable, 1956

Burn, W. L.   *The Age of Equipoise*. Allen & Unwin, 1964

Carrington, C. E.   *John Robert Godley of Canterbury*. C.U.P., 1950

Cavendish, Lady Frederick & Wyndham, Maud (edit.)   *Correspondence of Sarah Lady Lyttelton*. John Murray, 1912

Chandos, Lord   *From Peace to War*. The Bodley Head, 1968

Curtis, S. J. & Boultwood, M. E. A.   *An Introductory History of English Education*. University Tutorial Press, 1960

Drew, Mary   *Catherine Gladstone*. Nisbet & Co. 1919

Grosvenor, Caroline & Stuart of Wortley, Lord   *The First Lady Wharncliffe and her Family*. Heinemann, 1970 (2 vols.)

Horner, Frances   Time Remembered. Heinemann, 1953

Leveson-Gower, Frederick (edit.)   *Letters of Harriet Countess Granville*. Longmans Green & Co. 1894 (2 vols.)

Leveson-Gower, George & Palmer, Iris (edit.)   *Hary-O*. John Murray, 1940

Lyttelton, Edith   *Alfred Lyttelton*. Longmans Green & Co., 1917

Lyttelton, Edward   *Memoir of Alfred Lyttelton*. Privately printed

Lyttelton, George   *Ephemeral*. John Murray, 1865

Lyttelton, George & Gladstone, W. E.   *Translations*. Quaritch, 1861

Kitson-Clark, George   *Churchmen and the Condition of England 1832–85*. Methuen, 1973

Magnus, Philip   *Gladstone*. John Murray, 1954

Owen, David   *English Philanthropy 1660–1960*. O.U.P., 1965

Stirling, A. M. W. (edit.)   *The Letter Bag of Lady Elizabeth Spencer Stanhope*. John Lane, Bodley Head, 1913 (2 vols.)

Whibley, Charles   Lord John Manners & his Friends. Blackwood, 1925

INDEX